The
Penguin
Book
of
Memoir

The Penguin Book of Memoir

selected and introduced by
Camilla Gibb

PENGUIN
CANADA

PENGUIN CANADA

Published by the Penguin Group

Penguin Group (Canada), 90 Eglinton Avenue East, Suite 700, Toronto, Ontario, Canada M4P 2Y3
(a division of Pearson Canada Inc.)

Penguin Group (USA) Inc., 375 Hudson Street, New York, New York 10014, U.S.A.
Penguin Books Ltd, 80 Strand, London WC2R 0RL, England
Penguin Ireland, 25 St Stephen's Green, Dublin 2, Ireland (a division of Penguin Books Ltd)
Penguin Group (Australia), 250 Camberwell Road, Camberwell, Victoria 3124, Australia
(a division of Pearson Australia Group Pty Ltd)
Penguin Books India Pvt Ltd, 11 Community Centre, Panchsheel Park, New Delhi – 110 017, India
Penguin Group (NZ), 67 Apollo Drive, Rosedale, North Shore 0745, Auckland, New Zealand
(a division of Pearson New Zealand Ltd)
Penguin Books (South Africa) (Pty) Ltd, 24 Sturdee Avenue, Rosebank, Johannesburg 2196,
South Africa

Penguin Books Ltd, Registered Offices: 80 Strand, London WC2R 0RL, England

First published 2011

1 2 3 4 5 6 7 8 9 10 (RRD)

Introduction and selection copyright © Camilla Gibb, 2011

The copyright acknowledgments on page 263 constitute an extension of this copyright page.

Manufactured in the U.S.A.

LIBRARY AND ARCHIVES CANADA CATALOGUING IN PUBLICATION

The Penguin book of memoir / edited by Camilla Gibb.

ISBN 978-0-670-06678-0

1. Authors, Canadian (English)--Biography. I. Gibb, Camilla, 1968-

PS8083.P45 2011   C810.9   C2010-907696-6

Visit the Penguin Group (Canada) website at **www.penguin.ca**

Special and corporate bulk purchase rates available; please see
www.penguin.ca/corporatesales or call 1-800-810-3104, ext. 2477 or 2474

The
Penguin
Book
of
Memoir

Contents

Introduction

by

CAMILLA GIBB

UNTIL FAIRLY RECENTLY, memoir, or more broadly, autobiography, was seen to be the preserve of the long-lived and distinguished, resulting in the privileging of certain narratives over others. Sometime in the 1970s that began to change. The personal is political, we were told, and the value of the ordinary life, the worthiness of its examination, came into focus.

Although there are exceptions and some very early examples of Canadian memoir, such as Susanna Moodie's *Roughing It in the Bush,* on the whole we've been rather slow to warm up to the idea. Perhaps we feared taking a particularly Canadian risk: in setting ourselves apart, we might be mistaken for setting ourselves above. But as all the excerpts in this collection demonstrate, an individual life is virtually never set apart: it unfolds in the context of family and community and is shaped by the social and political forces of a particular time and place. One person's story, then, can offer us a unique insight into common experience, a perspective on shared history, and a way of understanding ourselves.

In a country as difficult to define or contain as Canada, national mythology can only be the result of an accumulation of diverse stories. Much of Canadian memoir begins elsewhere, and to bring memories of those elsewheres together, as this collection does, is to explore what it is to be *here, now, Canadian,* from a number of different angles. As M.G. Vassanji writes in an essay about being a Canadian writer, "new Canadians bring their stories with them, and these stories then become Canadian stories. Canada's past lies not only in the native stories of the land itself, but also in Europe, and now in Africa and Asia."

Several of the excerpts in this collection begin in, or return to, a place of origin: Ernest Hillen's Indonesia, Michael Ondaatje's Sri Lanka, Michael Ignatieff's Russia, Lorna Goodison's Jamaica. From that place one "encounters" Canada for the first time. For an eleven-year-old Ernest Hillen, the concept is at first imaginary. The announcement that his family will be leaving Indonesia for his mother's native Canada conjures up "the land of Grampa, Gramma, uncles, aunts, cousins, canoes, oranges, cowboys, Indians, and now also honey and milk."

His first impression, though, is of none of these things. It is of white—the "dazzling, blinding white" of a snow-covered Maritime morning, where "the sunlit street was edged with grey ice and piles of snow no one played on; the snow tasted gritty, crunched underfoot, and made fine hard balls."

Weather and landscape remain classic preoccupations because Canadian lives and livelihoods depend on them. Barometric readings dominate Wayne Johnston's childhood in Newfoundland, particularly while his father is away at sea; snow and forest surround Dionne Brand in rural Ontario, where the "people are as cold and forbidding as the landscape."

How one experiences Canada, or being Canadian, even if one is born here, has as much to do with when and where one lives as it does with origins. As a boy growing up in Vancouver's wartime Chinatown, Wayson Choy remembers hearing the voices of elders in the streets calling to him: "You never forget you Chinese!" And how could he forget? Surrounding him was a vivid and animated world, a community of extended families, neighbours, mah-jong friends, and ghosts, a busy world of family celebrations, Chinese festivals, and opera at the Chinese theatre.

Beyond those streets, furthermore, was a city where merchants freely advertised "we hire white labour only," a province offering one-way passage home on the condition that those who leave never return to Canada, a country with a Chinese head tax, a government that issued an Exclusion Act in 1923 that prevented more Chinese from immigrating to Canada, and a lack of right to citizenship even to those born in Canada until well after World War II.

Elsewheres and foreignness are relative, of course. Sharon Butala, who gives up an urban life in Saskatoon for ranch life in southern Saskatchewan, writes of a "strange new world which unexpectedly was, at least, on a day-to-day level, as alien to me as if I'd married an Arab or an Inuit and gone to live in his culture."

Dionne Brand, who leaves a multicultural Toronto for a new life in rural Ontario, writes, "Here I do not share the same consciousness. There is some other rhythm these people grew up in, speech and gait and probably sensibility."

Isabel Huggan, who was born and raised in Canada, chooses to live permanently in France as an adult, "making a home in a country and a language not [her] own." Why? she asks. Why beyond circumstance? "There are places on the planet we belong and they are not necessarily where we are born. If we are lucky ... we find them."

Fortune is certainly a big part of it. As Huggan acknowledges, relocation is not always voluntary. To be displaced or made a refugee, to never have the choice of returning home, is the reality for millions in the world.

A sense of alienation or exile, however, needn't always be the result of dis- or relocation. Borders are redrawn by politics. Wayne Johnston's family history, for instance, reflects ongoing societal tensions in Newfoundland that hinged on Confederation in 1949. For the anti-Confederates Canada remains a foreign country, migration a form of betrayal, and Johnston's own trajectory and relationship to his family cannot stand apart from this history.

When Warren Cariou returns home to small-town Saskatchewan after living in Toronto for several years, he finds the rules of engagement have shifted—lines between white and native have become blurry in ways that undermine his own sense of identity and history.

Alienation or a sense of exile might also be the result of a dramatic change in one's personal life. Moira Farr writes about the foreign territory she is forced to tread in the aftermath of a lover's suicide. She does extensive research into depression and suicide in the search for some way of navigating through it. Ian Brown likewise seeks to interview the parents of children who share the rare syndrome with which his son has been diagnosed, a syndrome that positions his son in an unknown, and possibly unknowable, land. Marian Botsford Fraser writes eloquently of grief, how it shifts one's perception of things, slows time, renders the hitherto unremarkable significant.

We do not rest comfortably without answers or when confronted by circumstances we cannot change. Both Jonathan Garfinkel and David Layton embark on quests to reconcile some internal conflict. Garfinkel's ambivalence about his own faith motivates a trip to Israel; Layton's distance from the mythical men of his family leads him to seek some connection to them that will never be satis-factorily realized.

We look to the maps of others in the hopes of gaining some understanding of what is alien to us, and memoir has a role to play in this. Lives laid bare offer us all an opportunity for introspection and the reassurance that we, in all our flawed glory, are not alone.

THESE EXCERPTS ARE bound together by themes of encounter with the foreign, the search for some kind of reconciliation or sense of cohesive identity, and the difficulty of calculating the sum of all parts. Michael Ondaatje's memoir, the earliest published in the collection, perhaps best illustrates this complexity, as autobiography, poetry, meditation, and photographs are interspersed to produce an exquisite postmodern portrait of the sources that inform a life. "I am the foreigner," he writes in Sri Lanka. "I am the prodigal son who hates the foreigner." And there is no contradiction between the two.

Hybridity is our particular challenge because we are not generally required to give up being who we once were. We are people of multiple pasts, and thus nothing in this collection risks being deemed "representative." For Michael Ignatieff these pasts are two—Russian and Scottish—and his is a hybridized identity produced by the meeting of the two in Canada. Ernest Hillen is born in colonial Indonesia to a Dutch father and Canadian mother. Wayson Choy, the Canadian-born son of Chinese immigrants, discovers, at the age of fifty-seven, that he was, in fact, adopted. Warren Cariou: Métis, Norwegian, German, French.

For anyone with multiple pasts the question of who we might have been in each country, culture, or tradition, independent of the other, inevitably arises. We privilege certain narratives over others for any number of reasons, from romantic attachment to political agenda.

Cariou's awareness of his Métis heritage comes late; having not been aware of it growing up, he makes no claim to understand Métis experience from the perspective of an insider. But he feels we are "still largely incapable of understanding and accepting hybridity here ... people are encouraged to cover up certain aspects of their lineage to conform to the generally accepted racial identities that are available to them."

For Ignatieff, who is not of mixed race, hybridity is more easily reconciled. His exploration of his father's history instead of his mother's is compelled by a sense that something will be lost if he doesn't. His father, born in 1913 and still alive at the time the memoir was published, was of the last generation who could have remembered anything of life before the Russian Revolution.

As Canadians we might have a sense of being, if not in the audience, only in the wings of the great dramas and movements of the world. But as many of these excerpts illustrate, we have in fact been situated in the midst of those dramas. We know war, revolution, racism, exile, internment, the Holocaust, colonialism, communism, and Zionism firsthand. Collectively, we know the world. But ultimately it is our desire to understand the human dramas—birth, death, loss, childhood, parenting, family, community, being, belonging—that play out whatever the backdrop, that make our stories at once highly particular and broadly universal.

Missing pieces of family history haunt and preoccupy us all. Questions are raised that challenge what we take for granted, forcing us to look back, reconstruct, and reassess in the hopes of making sense of our present and past. The discovery of a photograph, a secret revealed, the loss of someone we love, the need to recover something or someone—what compels us to search, what takes us into broader social and political terrain, usually originates from something deeply personal in nature.

IT HAPPENS THAT the excerpts included here were all written by writers. For that I am partly responsible. I've made selections (and omissions), both aesthetic and emotional. I looked for beautiful writing, and I looked to be moved. I am also a writer and an immigrant myself. But I am not wholly responsible. Writers are people who make their profession the writing of lives, so perhaps it is no surprise that some of the best memoirs are by writers. Writers are creators, and as Daniel Mendelsohn notes in a recent *New Yorker* article, there is "a troubling association between creativity and narcissism, an association that is nowhere as intense as when the creation in question is memoir." We are all narcissists to some degree: how else would we dare to create, to strive, to reproduce, to live? The particular gift and burden of the writer is the compulsion to put it all down on the page.

In Canadian memoir, there is another element at work. The question of origins, which cannot be separated from Canadian experience, speaks to why we create art—and why the particular art that we do. Janice Kulyk Keefer writes that as much as Canada is home for those of her generation, "we had that other world as well … That world where all the stories come from, a world of cracked spires and suicides as well as clay stoves and nesting storks."

Michael Ignatieff speaks of emigration and exile being so much the condition of our time that it's "almost impossible to find the right words for rootedness and belonging." The experience of exile lends itself to—perhaps necessitates—the search for those words. As Ignatieff notes, "It was exile that made Nabokov a writer; it was exile that turned the taken-for-granted past into a fabled territory that had to be reclaimed, inch by inch, by the writer's art."

Despite being written by writers, this is not a collection of writers on writing, though most make some reference to being conscious, even self-conscious, of the act in which they are engaged. "Like a good mystery," Wayson Choy writes, "one's life should always be read twice, once for the experience, then once again for astonishment."

Seeing our story on the page allows us the distance for astonishment. Reading it, hearing it, writing it down, sharing it: storytelling is necessary because, as Thomas King says, "the truth about stories is that's all we are."

By extension then, we cease to exist if we don't have ownership or the right to tell our stories. Shani Mootoo has written elsewhere that she finds her "migrant's memory of Trinidad pitted against the authority of those who remained behind." In her essay "Poetry

Lesson," she explains that "memory is an imperative, an urgent truth that, in my case, only fixing it to paper can calm."

Fixing it to paper becomes at once an act of personal and political necessity. It is to say: I exist.

THE MAJORITY OF the excerpts included here are from memoirs published between the mid-1990s and mid-2000s—the decade during which the popularity (and bankability) of the genre soared. David Pelzer's *A Child Called It* (1995) and Frank McCourt's *Angela's Ashes* (1996) sold in the hundreds of thousands, revealing a great public appetite for personal narrative, particularly of the miserable kind.

But as Daniel Mendelsohn describes it, "the 'I' became 'we' … memoirs had to bear an awful burden, standing in for the thousands of memoirs that would never be written." It is inevitable that claims to veracity would arise.

By the early to mid-2000s people were beginning to grow suspicious of sensationalist claims. Disillusionment about Iraq, the sobering awareness that political actions had been justified on the basis of lies, and the complicity of the media in reporting "facts" that were often no more than assertions of government agendas, has called "truth," even that of a very personal nature, into question.

The journalistic investigation into the "truth" of James Frey's bestselling memoir of addiction, *A Million Little Pieces,* resulted in the accusation that he had betrayed millions of people. At first Frey asserted that the memoir reflected the "essential truth" of his life, though later, under further pressure, he confessed to having fabricated significant portions of the book. The fact that *A Million Little Pieces* was initially shopped around as a novel tends to be forgotten, with Frey, since dumped by his publisher, left to beg forever, mea culpa.

Canadian memoir has remained relatively free of scandal, in part because of a lack of a celebrity culture of our own and a somewhat muted appetite for sensationalism. Less individualistic as a culture than the United States, perhaps Canada has also been less swayed by the trend toward confession at all costs. But we do rely on the most fallible of sources—memory—and attempt to impose order that might only exist in narrative form. We reconstruct, adding the glue that holds the disparate pieces together and dispensing with the bits that don't serve narrative purpose in order to craft an intelligible storyline. Sometimes we censor ourselves where we risk hurting others; occasionally we very deliberately name names. We make choices, that is all, about who and how to represent, because once loose, as Thomas King says, a story cannot be called back.

The story is at once fixed and loose: definitive on the page yet open to interpretation—another reason why memoir writing is such risky business. We live with the consequences though, because the telling is so necessary. And remembering is necessary for the telling, but the memories we need are not always easily accessible. Remembering is an act of narrative construction, and there are as many ways of telling as there are possible interpretations of dreams. Where memory is elusive, or the past buried in secrets, we have both imagination and research at our disposal. That research can take any number of forms, and it can be painful and fail to produce answers. "There is so much I do not know, can never know," Moira Farr writes. "I must overcome the fear that if I poke around in the wreckage left by that devastation, I will find smouldering embers that still spark and burn ... this is something I must do."

This collection does not seek to be anything more than a complement of compelling narratives that bravely make that effort. And together they hum.

THOMAS KING

from

The Truth About Stories

A Native Narrative

"YOU'LL NEVER BELIEVE WHAT HAPPENED" IS ALWAYS A GREAT WAY TO START

THE TRUTH ABOUT STORIES IS that that's all we are. The Okanagan storyteller Jeannette Armstrong tells us that "Through my language I understand I am being spoken to, I'm not the one speaking. The words are coming from many tongues and mouths of Okanagan people and the land around them. I am a listener to the language's stories, and when my words form I am merely retelling the same stories in different patterns."

When I was a kid, I was partial to stories about other worlds and interplanetary travel. I used to imagine that I could just gaze off into space and be whisked to another planet, much like John Carter in Edgar Rice Burroughs's Mars series. I'd like to tell you that I was interested in outer space or that the stars fascinated me or that I was curious about the shape and nature of the universe. Fact of the matter was I just wanted to get out of town. Wanted to get as far away from where I was as I could. At fifteen, Pluto looked good. Tiny, cold, lonely. As far from the sun as you could get.

I'm sure part of it was teenage angst, and part of it was being poor in a rich country, and part of it was knowing that white was more than just a colour. And part of it was seeing the world through my mother's eyes.

My mother raised my brother and me by herself, in an era when women were not welcome in the workforce, when their proper place was out of sight in the home. It was supposed to be a luxury granted women by men. But having misplaced her man, or more properly having had him misplace himself, she had no such luxury and was caught between what she was supposed to be—invisible and female—and what circumstances dictated she become—visible and, well, not male. Self-supporting perhaps. That was it. Visible and self-supporting.

As a child and as a young man, I watched her make her way from doing hair in a converted garage to designing tools for the aerospace industry. It was a long, slow journey. At Aerojet in California, she began as a filing clerk. By the end of the first year, she was doing drafting work, though she was still classified and paid as a filing clerk. By the end of the second year, with night school stuffed into the cracks, she was doing numerical-control engineering and was still classified and paid as a filing clerk.

It was, after all, a man's world, and each step she took had to be made as quietly as possible, each movement camouflaged against complaint. For over thirty years, she held to the shadows, stayed in the shade.

I knew the men she worked with. They were our neighbours and our friends. I listened to their stories about work and play, about their dreams and their disappointments. Your mother, they liked to tell me, is just one of the boys. But she wasn't. I knew it. She knew it better.

In 1963, my mother and five of her colleagues were recruited by the Boeing Company to come to Seattle, Washington, as part of a numerical-control team. Everyone was promised equal status, which, for my mother, meant being brought into Boeing as a fully fledged, salaried engineer.

So she went. It was more money, more prestige. And when she got there, she was told that, while everyone else would be salaried and would have engineer status, she would be an hourly employee and would have the same status as the other two women in the department, who were production assistants. So after selling everything in order to make the move, she found herself in a job where she made considerably less than the other members of the team, where she had to punch a time clock, and where she wasn't even eligible for benefits or a pension.

She objected. That wasn't the promise, she told her supervisor. You brought everyone else in as equals, why not me?

She didn't really have to ask that question. She knew the answer. You probably know it, too. The other five members of the team were men. She was the only woman. Don't worry, she was told, if your work is good, you'll get promoted at the end of the first year.

So she waited. There wasn't much she could do about it. And at the end of the first year, when the review of her work came back satisfactory, she was told she would have to wait another year. And when that year was up ...

I told her she was crazy to allow people to treat her like that. But she knew the nature of the world in which she lived, and I did not. And yet she has lived her life with an optimism of the intellect and an optimism of the will. She understands the world as a good place where good deeds should beget good rewards. At eighty-one, she still believes that that world is possible, even though she will now admit she never found it, never even caught a glimpse of it.

MY FATHER IS A different story. I didn't know him. He left when I was three or four. I have one memory of a man who took me to a small café that had wooden booths with high backs and a green parrot that pulled at my hair. I don't think this was my father. But it might have been.

For a long time I told my friends that my father had died, which was easier than explaining that he had left us. Then when I was nine, I think, my mother got a call from him asking if he could come home and start over. My mother said okay. I'll be home in three days, he told her.

And that was the last we ever heard from him.

My mother was sure that something had happened to him. Somewhere between Chicago and California. No one would call to say they were coming home and then not show up, unless they had been injured or killed. So she waited for him. So did I.

And then when I was fifty-six or fifty-seven, my brother called me. Sit down, Christopher said, I've got some news. I was living in Ontario, and I figured that if my brother was calling me all the way from California, telling me to sit down, it had to be bad news, something to do with my mother.

But it wasn't.

You'll never believe what happened, my brother said.

That's always a good way to start a story, you know: you'll never believe what happened.

And he was right.

We found our father. That's exactly what he said. We found our father.

I had dreamed about such an occurrence. Finding my father.

Not as a child, but as a grown man. One of my more persistent fictions was to catch up with him in a bar, sitting on a stool, having a beer. A dark, dank bar, stinking of sorrow, a bar where men who had deserted their families went to drink and die.

He wouldn't recognize me. I'd sit next to him, and after a while the two of us would strike up a conversation.

What do you do for a living? How do you like the new Ford? You believe those Blue Jays?

Guy talk. Short sentences. Lots of nodding.

You married? Any kids?

And then I'd give him a good look at me. A good, long look. And just as he began to remember, just as he began to realize who I might be, I'd leave. *Hasta la vista.* Toodle-oo. See you around. I wouldn't tell him about my life or what I had been able to accomplish, or how many grandchildren he had or how much I had missed not having a father in my life.

Screw him. I had better things to do than sit around with some old bastard and talk about life and responsibility.

So when my brother called to tell me that we had found our father, I ran through the bar scene one more time. So I'd be ready.

Here's what had happened. My father had two sisters. We didn't know them very well, and, when my father disappeared, we lost track of that side of the family. So we had no way of knowing that when my father left us, he vanished from his sisters' lives as well. I suppose they thought he was dead, too. But evidently his oldest sister wasn't sure, and, after she had retired and was getting on in years, she decided to make one last attempt to find out what had happened to him.

She was not a rich woman, but she spotted an advertisement in a local newspaper that offered the services of a detective who would find lost or missing relatives for $75. Flat rate. Satisfaction guaranteed.

My brother took a long time in telling this story, drawing out the details, repeating the good parts, making me wait.

The detective, it turned out, was a retired railroad employee who knew how to use a computer and a phone book. If Robert King was alive and if he hadn't changed his name, he'd have a phone and an address. If he was dead, there should be a death certificate floating around somewhere. The detective's name was Fred or George, I don't remember, and he was a bulldog.

It took him two days. Robert King was alive and well, in Illinois.

Christopher stopped at this point in the story to let me catch my breath. I was already making reservations to fly to Chicago, to rent a car, to find that bar.

That's the good news, my brother told me.

One of the tricks to storytelling is, never to tell everything at once, to make your audience wait, to keep everyone in suspense.

My father had married two more times. Christopher had all the details. Seven other children. Seven brothers and sisters we had never known about. Barbara, Robert, Kelly.

What's the bad news? I wanted to know.

Oh, that, said my brother. The bad news is he's dead.

Evidently, just after the railroad detective found him, my father slipped in a river, hit his head on a rock, and died in a hospital. My aunt, the one who had hired the detective, went to Illinois for the funeral and to meet her brother's other families for the first time.

You're going to like the next part, my brother told me.

I should warn you that my brother has a particular fondness for irony.

When my aunt got to the funeral, the oldest boy, Robert King Jr., evidently began a sentence with "I guess as the oldest boy …" Whereupon my aunt told the family about Christopher and me.

They knew about each other. The two families. Were actually close, but they had never heard about us. My father had never mentioned us. It was as though he had disposed of us somewhere along the way, dropped us in a trash can by the side of the road.

That's my family. These are their stories.

SO WHAT? I've heard worse stories. So have you. Open today's paper and you'll find two or three that make mine sound like a Disney trailer. Starvation. Land mines. Suicide bombings. Sectarian violence. Sexual abuse. Children stacked up like cordwood in refugee camps around the globe. So what makes my mother's sacrifice special? What makes my father's desertion unusual?

Absolutely nothing.

Matter of fact, the only people who have any interest in either of these stories are my brother and me. I tell the stories not to play on your sympathies but to suggest how stories can control our lives, for there is a part of me that has never been able to move past these stories, a part of me that will be chained to these stories as long as I live.

STORIES ARE wondrous things. And they are dangerous. The Native novelist Leslie Silko, in her book *Ceremony*, tells how evil came into the world. It was witch people. Not Whites or Indians or Blacks or Asians or Hispanics. Witch people. Witch people from all over the world, way back when, and they all came together for a witches' conference. In a cave. Having a good time. A contest, actually. To see who could come up with the scariest thing. Some of them brewed up potions in pots. Some of them jumped in and out of animal skins. Some of them thought up charms and spells.

It must have been fun to watch.

Until finally there was only one witch left who hadn't done anything. No one knew where this witch came from or if the witch was male or female. And all this witch had was a story.

Unfortunately the story this witch told was an awful thing full of fear and slaughter, disease and blood. A story of murderous mischief. And when the telling was done, the other witches quickly agreed that this witch had won the prize.

"Okay you win," they said. "[B]ut what you said just now—it isn't so funny. It doesn't sound so good. We are doing okay without it. We can get along without that kind of thing. Take it back. Call that story back."

But, of course, it was too late. For once a story is told, it cannot be called back. Once told, it is loose in the world.

MICHAEL ONDAATJE

from

Running in the Family

ASIA

WHAT BEGAN IT ALL WAS the bright bone of a dream I could hardly hold onto. I was sleeping at a friend's house. I saw my father, chaotic, surrounded by dogs, and all of them were screaming and barking into the tropical landscape. The noises woke me. I sat up on the uncomfortable sofa and I was in a jungle, hot, sweating. Street lights bounced off the snow and into the room through the hanging vines and ferns at my friend's window. A fish tank glowed in the corner. I had been weeping and my shoulders and face were exhausted. I wound the quilt around myself, leaned back against the head of the sofa, and sat there for most of the night. Tense, not wanting to move as the heat gradually left me, as the sweat evaporated and I became conscious again of brittle air outside the windows searing and howling through the streets and over the frozen cars hunched like sheep all the way down towards Lake Ontario. It was a new winter and I was already dreaming of Asia.

Once a friend had told me that it was only when I was drunk that I seemed to know exactly what I wanted. And so, two months later, in the midst of the farewell party in my growing wildness—dancing, balancing a wine glass on my forehead and falling to the floor twisting round and getting up without letting the glass tip, a trick which seemed only possible when drunk and relaxed—I knew I was already running. Outside the continuing snow had made the streets narrow, almost impassable. Guests had arrived on foot, scarved, faces pink and frozen. They leaned against the fireplace and drank.

I had already planned the journey back. During quiet afternoons I spread maps onto the floor and searched out possible routes to Ceylon. But it was only in the midst of this party, among my closest friends, that I realized I would be travelling back to the family I had grown from—those relations from my parents' generation who stood in my memory like frozen opera. I wanted to touch them into words. A perverse and solitary desire. In Jane Austen's *Persuasion* I had come across the lines, "she had been forced into prudence in her youth—she learned romance as she grew older—the natural sequence of an unnatural beginning." In my mid-thirties I realized I had slipped past a childhood I had ignored and not understood.

Asia. The name was a gasp from a dying mouth. An ancient word that had to be whispered, would never be used as a battle cry. The word sprawled. It had none of the clipped sound of Europe, America, Canada. The vowels took over, slept on the map with the S. I was running to Asia and everything would change. It began with that moment when I was dancing and laughing wildly within the comfort and order of my life. Beside the fridge I tried to communicate some of the fragments I knew about my father, my grandmother. "So how *did* your grandmother die?" "Natural causes." "What?" "Floods." And then another wave of the party swirled me away....

———•·•———

THE COURTSHIP

WHEN MY FATHER finished school, his parents decided to send him to university in England. So leaving Ceylon by ship Mervyn Ondaatje arrived at Southampton. He took his entrance exams for Cambridge and, writing home a month later, told his parents the good news that he had been accepted at Queen's College. They sent him the funds for three years of university education. Finally he had made good. He had been causing much trouble at home and now seemed to have pulled himself out of that streak of bad behaviour in the tropics.

It was two and a half years later, after several modest letters about his successful academic career, that his parents discovered he had not even passed the entrance exam and was living off their money in England. He had rented extravagant rooms in Cambridge and simply eliminated the academic element of university, making close friends among the students, reading contemporary novels, boating, and making a name for himself as someone who knew exactly what was valuable and interesting in the Cambridge circles of the 1920s. He had a good time, becoming briefly engaged to a Russian countess, even taking a short trip to Ireland supposedly to fight against the Rebels when the university closed down for its vacation. No one knew about this Irish adventure except an aunt who was sent a photograph of him posing slyly in uniform.

On hearing the distressing news, his parents decided to confront him personally, and so his mother and father and sister

Stephy packed their trunks and left for England by ship. In any case my father had just twenty-four more days of high living at Cambridge before his furious family arrived unannounced at his doors. Sheepishly he invited them in, being able to offer them only champagne at eleven in the morning. This did not impress them as he had hoped, while the great row which my grandfather had looked forward to for weeks and weeks was deflected by my father's useful habit of retreating into almost total silence, of never trying to justify any of his crimes, so that it was difficult to argue with him. Instead he went out at dinnertime for a few hours and came back to announce that he had become engaged to Kaye Roseleap—his sister Stephy's closest English friend. This news stilled most of the fury against him. Stephy moved onto his side and his parents were impressed by the fact that Kaye leapt from the notable Roseleaps of Dorset. On the whole everybody was pleased and the following day they all caught the train to the country to stay with the Roseleaps, taking along my father's cousin Phyllis.

During the week in Dorset my father behaved impeccably. The in-laws planned the wedding, Phyllis was invited to spend the summer with the Roseleaps, and the Ondaatjes (including my father) went back to Ceylon to wait out the four months before the marriage.

Two weeks after he arrived in Ceylon, my father came home one evening to announce that he was engaged to a Doris Gratiaen. The postponed argument at Cambridge now erupted on my grandfather's lawn in Kegalle. My father was calm and unconcerned with the various complications he seemed to have created and did not even plan to write to the Roseleaps. It was Stephy who wrote, setting off a chain reaction in the mails, one letter going to Phyllis whose holiday plans were terminated. My father continued with his technique of trying to solve one problem by creating another. The next day he returned home saying he had joined the Ceylon Light Infantry.

I am not sure how long he had known my mother before the engagement. He must have met her socially now and then before his Cambridge years, for one of his closest friends was Noel Gratiaen, my mother's brother. About this time, Noel returned to Ceylon, sent down from Oxford at the end of his first year for setting fire to his room. This in fact was common behaviour, but he had gone one step further, trying to put out the fire by throwing flaming sofas and armchairs out of the window onto the street and then dragging and hurling them into the river—where they sank three boats belonging to the Oxford rowing team. It was probably while visiting Noel in Colombo that my father first met Doris Gratiaen.

At that time Doris Gratiaen and Dorothy Clementi-Smith would perform radical dances in private, practising daily. Both women were about twenty-two and were greatly influenced by rumours of the dancing of Isadora Duncan. In a year or so they would perform in public. There is a reference to them in Rex Daniel's journals:

A garden party at the Residency Grounds.... Bertha and I sat next to the Governor and Lady Thompson. A show had been organized for them made up of various acts. First on was a ventriloquist from Trincomalee whose act was not vetted as he had arrived late. He was drunk and began to tell insulting jokes about the Governor. The act was stopped and was followed by Doris Gratiaen and Dorothy Clementi-Smith who did an item called "Dancing Brass Figures." They wore swimsuits and had covered themselves in gold metallic paint. It was a very beautiful dance but the gold paint had an allergic effect on the girls and the next day they were covered in a terrible red rash.

My father first saw them dance in the gardens of Deal Place. He would drive down from his parents' home in Kegalle to Colombo, stay at the Ceylon Light Infantry quarters, and spend his days with Noel watching the two girls practise. It is said he was enchanted with *both* girls, but Noel married Dorothy while my father became engaged to Noel's sister. More to keep my father company than anything else, Noel too had joined the Ceylon Light Infantry. This engagement of my father's was not as popular as the Roseleap one. He bought Doris Gratiaen a huge emerald engagement ring which he charged to his father's account. His father refused to pay and my father threatened to shoot himself. Eventually it was paid for by the family.

My father had nothing to do in Kegalle. It was too far away from Colombo and his new friends. His position with the Light Infantry was a casual one, almost a hobby. Often, in the midst of a party in Colombo, he would suddenly remember he was the duty officer that night and with a car full of men and women planning a midnight swim at Mount Lavinia, he would roll into the barracks, step out in his dress suit, inspect the guard, leap back into the car full of laughing and drunken friends and depart. But in Kegalle he was frustrated and lonely. Once he was given the car and asked to go and buy some fish. *Don't* forget the fish! his mother said. Two days later his parents got a telegram from Trincomalee, miles away in the north end of the island, to say he had the fish and would be back soon.

His quiet life in Kegalle was interrupted, however, when Doris Gratiaen wrote to break off the engagement. There were no phones, so it meant a drive to Colombo to discover what was wrong. But my grandfather, furious over the Trincomalee trip, refused him the car. Finally he got a lift with his father's brother Aelian. Aelian was a gracious and genial man and my father was bored and frantic. The combination almost proved disastrous. My father had never driven to Colombo directly in his life. There was a pattern of resthouses to be stopped at and so Aelian was forced to stop every ten miles and have a drink, too polite to refuse his young nephew. By the time they got to Colombo my father was very drunk and Aelian was slightly drunk and it was too late to visit Doris Gratiaen anyway. My father forced his uncle to stay at the CLI mess. After a large meal and more drink my father announced that now he must shoot himself because Doris had broken off the engagement. Aelian, especially as he was quite drunk too, had a terrible time trying to hide every gun in the Ceylon Light Infantry building. The next day the problems were solved and the engagement was established once more. They were married a year later....

———•◦•———

TROPICAL GOSSIP

"Darling, come here quickly. There's trouble behind the tennis court. I think Frieda's fainted. Look—Craig is pulling her up."
"No, darling, leave them alone."

IT SEEMS THAT most of my relatives at some time were attracted to somebody they shouldn't have been. Love affairs rainbowed over marriages and lasted forever—so it often seemed that marriage was the greater infidelity. From the twenties until the war nobody really had to grow up. They remained wild and spoiled. It was only during the second half of my parents' generation that they suddenly turned to the real world. Years later, for instance, my uncle Noel would return to Ceylon as a Q.C. to argue for the lives of friends from his youth who had tried to overthrow the government.

But earlier, during their flaming youth, this energy formed complex relationships, though I still cannot break the code of how "interested in" or "attracted" they were to each other. Truth disappears with history and gossip tells us in the end nothing of personal relationships. There are stories of elopements, unrequited love, family feuds, and exhausting vendettas, which everyone was drawn into, had to be involved with. But nothing is said of the closeness between two people: how they grew in the shade of each other's presence. No one speaks of that exchange of gift and character— the way a person took on and recognized in himself the smile of a lover. Individuals are seen only in the context of these swirling social tides. It was almost impossible for a couple to do anything without rumour leaving their shoulders like a flock of messenger pigeons.

Where is the intimate and truthful in all this? Teenager and Uncle. Husband and lover. A lost father in his solace. And why do I want to know of this privacy? After the cups of tea, coffee, public conversations ... I want to sit down with someone and talk with utter directness, want to talk to all the lost history like that deserving lover.

LORNA GOODISON

from

From Harvey River

A Memoir of My Mother and Her People

MY FATHER DID NOT consider his job as a chauffeur for the English manager of the Black River branch of Barclays Bank as a destination in life. His intention was to open his own garage, and along with Doris to run a fine guest house.

My parents were married in the month of August, but when December came around they realized that my father was going to have to spend his first Christmas away from his new bride, because the bank manager was a bachelor who always spent his Christmas holidays at the Liguanea Club in Kingston. The Liguanea Club was then an exclusive members club which did not admit black people. The only black Jamaicans who set foot on those grounds were the waiters, maids, and gardeners. The club's membership comprised almost exclusively expatriates, mostly Englishmen, who ran the affairs of the country when Jamaica was still a colony of Britain.

With a sad heart, Marcus left his new bride in the care of his grandmother and drove the bank manager into Kingston, depositing him at the Liguanea Club. He found accommodation for himself somewhere in downtown Kingston, and he spent all of that Christmas and New Year in the city driving his employer to various functions, waiting all night out in the car until the manager was sufficiently soused and ready to return to the club. He had celebrated Christmases like this before driving for the bank manager, but as a bachelor himself he had not minded hanging out with the other chauffeurs while their bosses drank and bad-mouthed the natives, who were usually outside bad-mouthing the expatriates. But that year he felt different. He was now a married man, and a married man belonged in his house with his family at Christmas. When he returned from Kingston, he promptly resigned from his job and went into partnership with his cousin Charley. Together, they opened a garage, something my father had always dreamed of doing....

———•◦•———

LIFE WAS GOOD FOR my parents in those early years. Unlike her mother, my mother had no difficulty conceiving, and went on to have nine children in all, one every two years from the time she was in her mid-twenties until she was in her early forties. After a year and a half of marriage, she gave birth to the beautiful and intelligent Barbara; two years later a son was born and named Howard, after her beloved brother; and then came Carmen Rose, whom we called Betty; and then Vaughn, who did not like his name, so he christened himself Bunny. (The five remaining children were born in Kingston, in the following order: the twins Kingsley and

Karl, then Keith, me (Lorna) and Nigel.) Their house in Malvern became filled with children and friends always coming and going. There was plenty of domestic help with raising the children and doing the laundry and keeping the house clean, but my mother maintained strict control over her kitchen because my father always claimed that he could taste the difference in the food that she cooked as opposed to food cooked by anyone else. "I can taste your hand, Doris," he always said.

Christmas was the most wonderful time of all. Everyone wanted their car in top shape for the great season of party-going, and the garage was busy day and night. Even the most hard-pay customers would settle their debts in the season of Peace and Goodwill, so Marcus was always able to buy wonderful presents for Doris and the children. Toy pianos that played real tunes, lovely sleeping dolls and spinning tops and music boxes. Fabulous lengths of silk and soft shoes for Doris and more and more lovely furniture for their house. Their house, which always smelled of delicious food cooking, where the Salvation Army choir would stand outside and sing carols and Doris would invite them in and give them Marcus's famous Christmas eggnog as a thank you for serenading them. The Bible promised seven years of plenty, and that promise was made good during those prosperous years before they moved to Kingston. "In those days, we had the very best," my mother always said. And then war broke out in 1939.

My father had feared his grandmother's wicked tongue too much to tell her when his business began to lose money. "You pass you place, Marcus, to go and want to have garage business. You see me, I know my place, you woulda never catch me a eggs up myself bout me a open business. High seat kill Miss Thomas' puss! Nayga people must know dem place, what a way you bright fi go open garage business, is better you did keep you good, good work with the bank manager, it serve you right. Is that Hanover woman you go married to who encourage you inna that damn foolishness."

As it turned out, Marcus was to lose everything he owned. In the late 1930s, car parts and gasoline became increasingly scarce, and many of my father's customers were forced to convert their cars into horse-drawn carriages by removing the engines. Also, Uncle Charley, who was supposed to look after the bookkeeping side of the garage business, drank and spent money in the same manner in which he ate.

Marcus never told his grandmother when the business closed. When she sent to call him, it was a week after he had had to padlock the gates himself, and pay off the two mechanics who worked with him. Dorcas had summoned my father when people in the village had brought her news of his failed business. He received a message from her that said: "Come and see me, but don't bring your wife." He went to see her and found her sitting up in her rickety old iron bed, her airless bedroom lit by one small, irritable little kerosene lamp. The room reeked of her old lady musk smell, the camphor oil she used to anoint her creaking limbs, and the kerosene oil from the lamp. She spoke these words to my father through the semi-darkness:

"I decide out of the goodness of my heart that since you fall so low, you can come back here and live with your wife and children and help me to plant red peas and cassava. But, you and that Hanover woman and your damn children will have to live under my jurisdiction. Although you are a big married man now, I am still your grandmother and under my roof, my word is law." The old iron bed creaked and groaned as Dorcas threw herself into her homily on the sins of flying past your place. She all but stood up in her bed in order to remind my father how she had never failed at anything in her life, because, "He who is low, fears no fall." She repeated her offer to have my parents come back and live with her, an offer she accompanied by the thumping of her fist on her bony chest to underscore the phrase "My word is law." My father responded by leaping up from the chair in which he was sitting, and as he strode out the door, he said, "Don't worry about me, don't worry about me, my wife, or my children. We will be all right."

"I would prefer to die than to live under her roof again," he had said to my mother of Dorcas's offer. After Marcus's refusal, his grandmother took his name off her will and bequeathed her land to the government. Going to live in Harvey River was out of the question; there was no way to earn a living there. So my parents decided that their only alternative was to move to Kingston.

They had had one last dinner party in their Malvern house. One last big dinner party before the new owners came to take possession, before the truck that would take them into Kingston backed into the yard, drove over one of the flowerbeds, and parked by the front door so that they could load what was left of their house filled with fine mahogany furniture onto the back. For that dinner party, my mother had cooked their favourite meal. Pot roast and rice and peas and brown stew chicken and fried plantains. And because no party in Jamaica is a party without curry goat, they had said to hell with the expense and purchased a young kid, and slaughtered and curried the tender flesh. As she spread the table with the damask tablecloth Cleodine had given her as a wedding gift, and put out all her fine wedding things, remembering all the "daintiness" that her sister had taught her, my mother was overcome by the knowledge that this was the last time that she would ever spread a table in this house where she had come to be so happy. A realization so final that she had to sit down suddenly in her seat nearest the door through which she would come and go to and from the kitchen to the table.

My mother remembered the morning they had bade miserly Dorcas and her house of meanness farewell. She had woken and found herself singing, "The strife is o'er, the battle done; Now is the Victor's triumph won … Alleluia!" She and Marcus had carefully assembled their possessions and packed them into a truck belonging to one of their friends, on the day their house was finally ready to be occupied. "Thank you very much, Grandma Dorcas, for your kind hospitality," they had said to the wretched, miserly old woman, and then they had practically run outside to the truck and driven joyfully to their own house. Marcus blew the horn all the way from his grandmother's house to theirs. They sang a song that newly emancipated Jamaicans sang on the first of August 1838. "Jubilee, Jubilee. Me get full free. Me can stand up when me want, siddown when me want, liedown and gettup when me want, for me free." Yessir, they were free to laugh and talk and sleep and wake as they pleased, to cook big dinners and entertain any number of friends they wanted. "Why the hell would I spendup my money to feed a whole heap of hungry-belly people who should stay home and eat at them own table?" was Dorcas's response to a suggestion my mother once made to her that they invite some of their neighbours over for Sunday dinner.

She was well-acquainted with every corner of this house, every door, every window. "Brussels" and "tarshan." My mother had carefully stitched every one of the lace curtains that were now being taken down from the windows of their house. She could identify a Brussels lace from a Venice or chantilly lace with her eyes closed. She would rub a forefinger over the surface and correctly identify the lace in question. She had arranged every bed, chair, and table in that house, where they had kept the front door open from morning till night because they so loved to see their home filled with guests. They had planned to one day convert that house in Malvern into a paying guest house, for nothing gave them more pleasure than to see their friends and relations enjoying hospitality Doris and Marcus style. But they never did get around to it.

"Doris girl, your nice life done," said a voice inside her. She walked over to the table and stared and stared at her place setting before her, trying hard not to cry. To calm herself, my mother rubbed the crest of the bird perched on a limb at the centre of the dinner plate. She ran her finger along the limb on which the bird sat, and a voice rose up in her. It said, "Doris, this limb is now broken." She imagined at that moment that the bird on the dinner plate flew up and out through the dining-room window from which the lace curtains were now removed. "You soon come back man, Marcus, and you cannot live in town, you just going to pay Kingston a visit," said their friends. My mother would remember little about that last dinner party in their house they were about to lose because she deliberately kept herself busy tending to the needs of their guests. The friends who were talking and laughing too loudly. The people who kept hugging her and saying, "We don't know what we are going to do without you." Some of them were even crying openly as she remained resolutely dry-eyed, but she would always remember one incident.

"Time for a song now, Marcus." My mother felt her heart fall when their friends began to say that. "You know we can't let you go to Kingston before you drop two tune, Marcus." O God why they want him to sing, Doris thought to herself. Why can't they put themself in his place? How would they feel if this had happened to them? Would they feel like singing? O Lord no, Marcus just tell them you don't feel good, tell them you not up to it tonight, of all nights. She watched his every move nervously, rubbing the insides of her arms along the sides of her belly, which had become high and wide after she had given birth to four children. "Say no, you not singing tonight." She shook her head and tried to get him to catch her eye, but he refused to look in her direction. Instead he headed into their bedroom. She hurriedly put down the tray of cold drinks that she had been offering to their guests, saying in a "put-on" cheerful voice, "Have a last drink on Marcus and me." When she saw him come from the bedroom with the guitar, she made for the open front door and stood in the doorway with her arms folded. He took a seat in the living room beside his prized gramophone, the second thing that he had bought for their house after their marriage bed. She could tell that he was determined to avoid her look, which she had learned from her mother, Margaret, that cross between a cut-eye and a stare-down look that she'd brought with her from Harvey River.

What she did not understand was that his heart was so heavy right then, that if he did not sing, he was going to break down and bawl like a baby. He reached up and lifted the big heavy-headed needle off the seventy-eight record. It was Leadbelly singing "Goodnight Irene." Before that night they would always listen to that record together, sitting side by side on the loveseat, the third thing that he had bought for their house. He always wanted her to sit on his left. "On the heart side," he would say, "I want you always near to my heart." Always with one arm thrown around her neck and his long fingers stroking her rounded upper arm, they would listen to Leadbelly, and Marcus would say, "Wait, wait, the nice part coming now." This was how they liked to wait for Leadbelly to reach that part in the chorus when he sings, "Goodnight, Irene, goodnight, Irene, I'll *get* you in my dreams," for when he reached that part, they would both turn and face each other at the same time and laugh out loud. Every time, they laughed together as if they were hearing Leadbelly's lascivious tone for the first time, "I'll *get* you in my dreams." They'd laugh till she caught herself laughing at Leadbelly's slackness, and she'd stop and say, "Marcus, you are too out of order," as if she had not become a little out of order herself, now that she was a married woman.

But that last night in their house, she could find nothing to laugh about as she watched my father carefully sit himself down alone on their loveseat so that the seams of his trousers fell just so. She watched as he held his guitar close to his chest, just like he sometimes held her when they were alone, and she knew she would never laugh at that song again. She watched as he shut his eyes tight and began to rock back and forth, and with a lump-in-his-throat voice, took up where Leadbelly left off. When she heard his voice begin to vibrate and break up, she stopped clutching herself and balled her hands into two fists by her side. She leaned forward, gathered up her strength, and began to call out to him silently, insistently from her place by the door. She felt herself begin to haul up strength from her belly-bottom, until she was almost standing on her tiptoes, and she strained towards him begging, no, commanding him without words: bear up. Don't break. Marcus, don't you cry before them. Not even if they are our friends, don't make them see you cry. "Sometimes I live in the country, sometimes I live in the town, sometimes I take a great notion, to jump in the river and drown: Irene goodnight, Irene goodnight, goodnight Irene, goodnight Irene, I'll see you in my dreams." That night she gathered up her strength and force-fed it to him so he could part company with Leadbelly. When he switched to his repertoire of rude songs, she touched her open hand to her belly-bottom in gratitude to her woman strength. "Bredda Manny O mi find a Candy, Bredda Manny O mi find a Candy, Bredda Manny O mi find a Candy dash it wey you nasty bitch a puss shit." That night he did make them laugh, he made them laugh, he made them dance.

Later, as they lay on their marriage bed, without having bothered to remove the white candlewick bedspread, he had cried then. "How many times must I lose, Dor?" he had asked her. "How many times?" It was then he told her how his mother had lost her land. She had lost it, he said, because of him. He had gone as an apprentice truck driver at the age of fourteen to work in Port Antonio and there he had fallen sick with malaria fever. They had sent a message to his mother to come to him in the hospital and she had, in the emergency, used her house and land as collateral for a loan of thirty pounds from a Mr. Russell, the justice of the peace of that parish. Her son was sick, she was in a hurry, she did not read what she signed and that is how she lost her land, in the same way that thousands of poor Jamaicans have lost their land for nearly two hundred years. When she came back to Malvern, after a month of nursing her son, Russell had foreclosed on her house and land. She had taken her case to the authorities at Black River Courthouse, but Russell's friends who sat on the bench had found in favour of Russell. Everybody said it was the loss that had killed her.

"How many times must I lose, Dor?" And then it was she who was holding him close to her chest, saying, "no mine no mine no mine," and assuring him of the many opportunities that existed for him in Kingston, the businessplaces just begging for a good and capable man like him to come there and work. It was she who was saying that everything happens for a purpose and that one thing she was looking forward to (although she was not an idle sort of person) was going again and again to the Ward Theatre to see moving pictures and concerts.

The more she thought about it, growing up in Kingston would make the children grow bright and uncountrified. Barbara, their brilliant first-born, could go to a very good school like St. Andrews High School for girls. But she had also said, as he kissed her in gratitude, that if after experiencing all the wonders of Kingston, they still really didn't like it, they should move right back to the country, where they would buy another house after they had worked and saved enough money. That night she knew in her heart that from then on, she was going to have to be the strong one, the one who would have to adopt her sister Cleodine's straight-backed walk and grim determination to move forward, come what may. And then he said to her, "Dor, let us make sure we keep our business to ourselves." My father had learned his lesson from the early experiences of their marriage and the mischief-making of his friends, like the Cerassee sisters, and thereafter he always declared that what happened between a husband and a wife was strictly their personal business.

All the children in the Harvey household had grown up seeing their mother and father in agreement on most matters affecting the family. Sometimes if they disagreed openly and Margaret became loud and belligerent, as she was wont to do, David would suggest that they step into their bedroom and close the door and argue it out there. Sometimes as they lay in bed at night the children could overhear them talking about whether David should keep going to Cuba or not, or whether they should sell some of the land, whether David and his brothers should take a certain case, because everybody knew the accused had done what they said he had done. But before the children it was always, "Your father and me," or "Your mother and me think this or that." When Margaret did not get her own way, she would say, "Mr. Harvey and I think this or that so." And so Doris began to rehearse what she would say to anybody who asked her how could she leave the country for hard life in town. "We have decided to try our luck in Kingston." ...

———•◦•———

"I NEVER KNEW HARD LIFE until I came to Kingston," my mother would say as she gazed at her hands. "I used to have the most beautiful hands." Hard Life. When she sounded those words they became a fierce giant, a merciless enemy whom you had to struggle against. Hard Life was the hurry-come-up, ex-slave landlord who, now that he owned some property in the form of a tenement yard, wanted his turn to play busha, or slave master, to delight in lording his owner status over you, to extract exorbitant sums of money from you for the privilege of living in his dry-weather premises. To inform you loudly that he normally did not rent to people with children and that he would be coming every Sunday morning at 6:00 a.m. to beat upon your door and demand his rent, which you had better have or he would turn you out onto the street.

Hard Life was a levelling teacher, anxious that no pupil should ever outstrip him, who liked to shame you before your class, to expose your errors and mistakes and poor judgment to the mocking scourgings of those you thought were your friends before you got marked down. Hard Life was an ill-mannered visitor who came to call on you in order to search up your cupboards when your back was turned, so that they could go and tell everyone how things were bad with you. To lie about you, that you had no sugar for your tea and that you had to trust or credit food. It was a vicious old hige who liked to suck out the secrets of your broken heart and regurgitate them before your enemies. Hard Life was a pyaka, a cantankerous flying spirit who fed on the bitter seeds of the bad-mind tree, who lived only to fly about and broadcast to others that you mash up, mash up, mash up. Hard Life was a gravalitous grudgeful John Crow who kept pressing its black suit for the day when it would attend your funeral and give a eulogy which picked at your remains. A lamentation over poor you. Hard Life was a Cyclops whose cast-eye you had to blind with psalms in order to escape from the dark cave in which it wanted you trapped, and he would have trapped you were it not for your own strength and for the ties of blood, the generosity of some of your relatives, who as soon as they heard that you were now living hard life in Kingston, began to send you regular food baskets. Country baskets filled with ground provisions, yams, potatoes, vegetables, fruits, corned beef and pork, bottles of coconut oil, baked goods, peas, cassava, plantains. These baskets were the Jamaican equivalent of the manna fed to the Israelites by Yahweh as they wandered in the wilderness.

All over the city of Kingston, happiness and contentment would be generated in cramped tenements with the arrival of these baskets sent by friends and relatives in the country. Families would partake of generous oily-mouthed feasts, and children would be told stories about life in the villages where this food came from. Normally ill-tempered mothers, nerves frayed from hard life in town, fathers burdened by hard work or lack of employment, would become carefree children again as they enjoyed the sense of ease and plenty generated by the largesse of those back home in the country. "See this soursop here, it come from a tree that my grandfather plant and my navel string bury at the root." These food baskets were brought to Kingston on the backs of market trucks, or labelled and loaded onto the train and watched over by kind, considerate conductresses who knew they were doing a form of angel-work by delivering them. The conductresses knew how gratefully, eagerly, the people of Kingston greeted the arrival of the country baskets filled with fresh, life-sustaining things to eat. Our family began to receive regular baskets from Harvey River as soon as my mother's relatives found out that she was living in Kingston, and first thing that she would do when she opened one of them was to pass on some of the food to others who were even more in need.

MICHAEL IGNATIEFF

from

The Russian Album

A Memoir

REVOLUTION

I HAVE MY GRANDFATHER's diary for the year 1917. It is a pocket-sized leather-bound volume with all the printed information a gentleman of Petrograd would want to know: the Orthodox saints' days, the cycles of the moon and the Neva tides, the train timetables to Moscow, Paris and Berlin, and the four-digit telephone numbers of restaurants, hotels, ministries and Court departments. On a few days in late February, Paul has noted down his appointments; in early March there is a rather agitated calculation of family finance scribbled in faint purple pencil. After that, the fine cream pages of the diary are completely blank.

The depression that had descended upon him following his dismissal by the Tsar now turned into a complete nervous collapse, accompanied by a recurrence of violent asthmatic attacks and pains in the liver and chest. It was as if the symptoms of a neurosis suppressed but not confronted in Charcot's sanitorium twenty years before now chose the moment of the revolution to step out of the shadows of his life.

The revolution also accelerated a reversal in relations between Paul and Natasha. She had been first in her mother's shadow, then in Paul's. Now she came into her own. As Paul wasted away in the bedroom upstairs, it was Natasha who held the family together and protected him from the soldiers' and workers' deputations which began banging on the gates. She would let them in and have a maid serve them cucumber sandwiches. Most were just hungry and cold and they departed quite tamed. Natasha could not protect him from other deputations. Workers from Paul's cotton and glass factories arrived and stood in the hallway, their caps doffed, warming themselves against the radiators, politely listening to her when she said the master was ill but refusing to go away until she showed them up to the darkened bedroom where he lay in bed, white and drawn. He was helpless, unable to refuse them anything, but their demands were modest and they soon filed out, wishing him a long life.

Soon the revolution was less polite. In late March, a detachment of soldiers came to requisition the cars. They pounded on the gates while Basil the chauffeur struggled under the hood of the Mercedes to remove the distributor cap. When the soldiers found it was immobilized, they seized the Renault instead. The older boys were watching from the downstairs schoolroom window as one soldier took a red handkerchief out of his pocket, blew his nose, and then stuck the handkerchief on the bayonet out of the car window as it careered down the driveway. Demian managed to retrieve the Renault, abandoned and much the worse for wear, a few weeks later.

Throughout the revolution, Natasha was protected by her certainties: the provisional government were contemptible weaklings; the women who demanded bread in the demonstrations were deluded, for shortages were imagined, not real; the courageous police had been betrayed by officers who were half-witted and paralysed with indecision; the revolution was a crime and a blunder. What she watched from the window made her blind with anger. Years later, she wrote: "Till my death day will I have the same firm belief that it was only slovenly weakness and thorough absence of knowledge of the nature of Russian crowds that let go this first disorder. If only a strong man knowing the Russian nature had arisen with a nice stick or our wonderful Empress Catherine the Great had come to life (I always venerated her ever so much more than Peter the Great as he copied all just like the monkey copying the master and by that destroyed much of the genuine Russian). Our Catherine loving and understanding our country but with a stick would put back all in order at the first, not when things went dragging along from day to day getting worse from total absence of energy and authority."

When she talked like that Paul would always say half soothingly, half impatiently, "Natasha, calm yourself, calm yourself!" He thought the truth was more complicated than her simple anger would allow. He had been in the very heart of the regime, so he had seen the rottenness face to face; his disillusion was deeper than hers, and where she felt an anger that roused her to defence of her brood, he felt a despair that sapped him of the will to fight.

As for the children, the revolution was a wild street carnival they could not wait to get outside to see. The oldest boys were soon out in the street looking at the ruins of the courthouse and listening to the speeches on the steps of the Duma where a leaderless army had gathered to find leadership and absolution for its crimes. There was still a place for bourgeois boys like them at the fringes of a revolutionary crowd. Alec was eleven and was pissing against a wall near the Duma when a boy his age shouted, "Bourgeois, what are you doing?" and came towards him threateningly. An older worker shouted back, "Leave him alone—he's a kid like you." The boys mingled at the edge of the crowds listening to the slogans, each contradicting the other, which echoed above the din in the forecourt of the Duma:

"Fight Imperialist Germany!"

"Workers have not overthrown the Tsar to die for Capitalist Exploiters!"

"Secure the achievements of the Great Bloodless Revolution!"

"Down with the Imperialist War!"

Some speakers wanted to send the soldiers home to their villages and others wanted to send them back to the front. The soldiers shifted from speaker to speaker muttering, "True! True!" now to one side, now to the other. The revolution debated its future, veering now this way, now that.

In the household on Fourstatskaya, the servants began to take sides. Demian, Koulakoff and Roman were active supporters of the revolution, and while they continued at their posts there was a new edge in their relations with their masters. When Demian wanted a new suit, he pointed to one in Paul's cupboard and observed that it was worn out and needed replacement; he would then appear on his half day wearing it in the street. Koulakoff, the mild and inoffensive Cossack, acquired some backbone. When Monsieur Darier, the French tutor, observed that the bread was not a dirty grey colour in the house where his wife was governess, Koulakoff thumped another roll down on his side plate and told him what he could do with it if he didn't like it. Yet the same Koulakoff continued to wake the boys every morning, and supervise their washing and dressing; the stoveman kept piling the logs into the furnace; the serving girls kept bringing the dishes to the tables; and the milk churns from the Wassiltchikoff estate at Vybiti continued to arrive at the railway station and were picked up every morning by Basil the chauffeur. Even the bread eventually regained its old accustomed whiteness. There must have been moments in March and April when it was possible to believe the world outside would soon resume the measured order which had not skipped a beat inside the house on Fourstatskaya Street. But April turned to May and June. Lenin entered the city and began piloting the Bolsheviks towards the revolution of October.

Through the spring of 1917, Paul's condition worsened, and on 7 May a telegram arrived from Kroupodernitsa announcing the death of his mother. Father Nicholas was hastily summoned and Paul sang the *pannihida* in a broken voice. Natasha and the boys left him alone in his bedroom still clutching the telegram and hurried to the Church of Christ Walking Upon the Waters, where they lit candles and prayed for the repose of their grandmother's soul. A few weeks later Natasha moved Paul to a rented *dacha* in Tsarskoe Selo in the hope that the country air and distance from the downward vortex of the revolution in Petrograd would do him good. But he continued to lie in bed gazing at his inner wreckage.

On the front lines the disintegration of the army gathered momentum. In the Petrograd of May and June, crises and resignations followed each other at the heart of the provisional government; Lenin moved from house to house to avoid arrest. He spent several nights at the headquarters of the Central Trade Union, twelve houses away from the family home on Fourstatskaya. One of the boys is convinced that he saw him in the street or heard him speak from a platform. It is more likely that newsreels viewed in exile have seeped into his memory.

The family were safely out of the way in Tsarskoe Selo on the night of 3 and 4 July when Fourstatskaya again filled with a torrent of armed soldiers from the Bolshevik First Machine Gun

Regiment and metal workers from the Putilov factories and sailors from Kronstadt marching on the Duma. By evening troops loyal to the government had regained control of the city and put down the insurrection. For the moment the provisional government held together, but it was clear to Paul and Natasha that the situation in Petrograd was slipping out of control. Once late at night, listening outside his father's bedroom door, one of the boys heard his father whisper to Uncle Boria Wassiltchikoff, "I must get them out of here!" But when the children were assembled and told they were leaving for Kislovodsk, a spa town in the Caucasus Mountains, five days by train to the south, the reason given was that their father needed to take a cure for his liver. Yet whatever she told her children, whatever she told herself, Natasha went to the bank and scooped up some of her jewellery from the safe-deposit box; she packed the volumes of her ancestor Karamzin's history of Russia and her photo albums of Doughino into the trunk she had bought in Nice for her trousseau.

The family was at the station two hours early, Paul looking gaunt and haggard, Natasha wandering around certain she had forgotten something and making jokes about her family's comic-opera migrations. Koulakoff ran around the platform like a sheepdog with his whiskers flying, piling cases into the compartments. It was an expedition on a grand scale: nannies, tutors, cooks, ladies' maids, seventeen people in all counting the boys and their mother and father. The first bell sounded, then the second. Last-minute checks of hand luggage were made. The family stood at the open windows and looked down at the platform: a mournful Demian left with the keys of the house on Fourstatskaya, Father Nicholas, the family priest, and a cluster of colleagues from the Ministry of Education who had come to say goodbye to their chief. The third bell sounded and the Caucasian express began to move out. Through the crowd burst an old man—a singer of folk tales who used to sing for the family—waving a birch stick which he passed up to Paul. On it there was a note saying, "Be of good spirits and be sure of the results of your labour, as it has grown from a deep root." It was dusk, the train glided away, and they waved their last farewells. As the train gathered speed, they stared out at the fields in the summer light. The land itself seemed to comfort them with the message that Petrograd and the revolution were not Russia: in Ukraine the harvesters were out in the golden fields bringing in an abundant crop; the white convents of Orloff shone still in the summer evening and the country lanes were speckled with light through the poplars. They passed through Orel, Kharkov, Rostov, five days on the train. The little ones—George and Lionel—leaned out of the windows at every station, imitating the singsong of the vendors who wandered up and down beneath the train windows selling apples and pretzels and a bread called *bubliki*. Enveloped as they were in the calm of the countryside which passed their windows, it never occurred to the family to think they had left Petrograd for the last time....

THE CAUCASUS

IN THE AUTUMN OF 1917, Peggy Meadowcroft took a picture of young Nicholas sitting at his father's feet on the veranda steps, smiling and clutching his bare knees. Snow clings in wet clumps to the fruit trees in the foreground; in the background the hillside is white with snow. It is a bright day in late October. Paul is reclining in a deck chair, shrunken inside an overcoat, his face slack and puffy, the springs of energy in his body all run dry. He was slipping out of reach of his sons. If they asked him a question, it was minutes before he answered. He sat silently for hours, copies of his official reports to the Tsar on his knees.

In late October 1917, the local paper reported the storming of the Winter Palace, Kerensky's flight, the first decrees of the new Soviet power. In the last dismal hours, the only defenders of the frozen corridors of the palace had been the Women's Battalion, women like the one on the bandstand who had shouted through her tears in vain.

By the winter of 1918 Russia was plunged into civil war. White armies were in the field in Siberia, in the Crimea and in the north around Petrograd. But for the moment, the struggle was far away. For most of the autumn and winter the family went on as if the world beyond the green gates of their little house in Kislovodsk was still intact. The effects of the October Revolution did not reach the south Caucasus until a Soviet commissar, Kirov, proclaimed the advent of Soviet power from the balcony of the concert hall in the spring of 1918 and a Soviet of local workers replaced the old town council. But the lurid fears about what the Reds would do once they seized power did not materialize. The banks were nationalized but Paul managed to transfer his funds to a local cooperative society before his bank shut its doors for the last time. When the cooperatives were nationalized, he managed to withdraw his money and store it in an earthenware jar in the bathroom. Life kept on much as before. The boys began preparing for their gymnasium examinations with their tutors and managed to pass them in the spring. Paul kept up his routine of taking the waters, though with no discernible effect on his health or his mood. Natasha ran the little troop of servants. The mountain people still brought their food to the Friday market.

By the early summer of 1918, General Denikin and General Wrangel's White armies were doing battle with Trotsky's Red armies in the north Caucasus, seventy miles away. Yet workers from Paul's factories near Moscow kept showing up in Kislovodsk, having traversed the zones of the civil war with letters from Paul's factory manager in their knapsacks and hard cash in their boots. Some of these messengers melted away into the civil war with their master's money, but most made it all the way. They would eat in the kitchen and sleep the night in the servants' quarters and then they would set off next day with their master's messages, to make their return crossing of a country cut in two by civil war.

One day in the spring of 1918, a disagreeable old soldier, Sergeant Yankevitch, with four St George's Crosses pinned to his tunic, arrived at the green gates with some frightened-looking Ukrainian serving girls in tow. Paul's sister, Mika, had despatched them on a thousand-mile journey from Kroupodernitsa with potatoes and corn in their sacks and money in their boots. Grumbling all the way, Sergeant Yankevitch had carried out his mission and now wanted a good hot meal and a bed. He was the last of the messengers from the vanished life in the north, the last bearer of tidings from Kroupodernitsa and Countess Mika. She was now alone on the estate in the path of the German army marching into the Ukraine.

Paul pasted the money the old soldier had brought from Kroupodernitsa inside the upright piano in Peggy Meadowcroft's room. In the earthenware jar under the floorboards of the bathroom he hid Natasha's jewellery and his reports to the Tsar. Nothing had happened, but rumours told them searches and confiscations were about to start.

In early June 1918 they heard firing in the hills behind the town, then the grumbling of artillery and the screech of Red armoured trains on the railway lines. They learned that a party of marauding Cossack irregulars, under the command of a Tsarist colonel named Andrei Shkuro, was making raids on the Red defences at the edge of town. One morning, the family awoke to the chattering of a machine gun. Jumping up to his bedroom window, Nick saw a body lying in the roadway and soldiers in khaki advancing up the street. When it was safe to go out, Nick went into the garden, where he found spent cartridges and a bloody bayonet.

Shkuro's cavalry rode into the city. Tsarist officers donned their old uniforms and women held out money and clothing to the Cossack horsemen. Here at last, everyone thought, was the advance guard of White victory. But Shkuro did not have the troops to hold the town. He swept in to rescue his wife from a Red hospital and swept out again, leaving the Whites to repent of their rejoicing. As the Reds moved back into the city, servants betrayed their masters, and neighbours betrayed each other to the Red authorities. In the mountains the Red cavalry burned Cossack villages.

Food began to go short. The mountain people stopped bringing their produce to market, and on Fridays Tonia and Koulakoff returned with their shopping bags empty. Paul roused himself from his torpor and set to work digging a vegetable garden in the backyard. But he was too weak to keep it up: handing the spade to Vaclav, the Czech gardener, he limped back to bed clutching his back, the colour draining from his face.

In August, Natasha decided Paul should take the mud-bath cures at Essentuki, another spa town nearby. Savage battles were being waged between the Red and White armies only forty miles away, yet at Essentuki Paul spent a reflective week up to his neck in mud in the company of two old generals, wondering what had happened to the Tsar and his family. By then they were almost certainly dead. Paul returned to Kislovodsk, still no better, in time for Natasha's birthday. Five days later, on 30 August 1918, the head of the Petrograd secret police was assassinated, while in Moscow a Socialist Revolutionary assassin tried and failed to kill Lenin. In reprisal, terror was unleashed across Russia. The blacked-out cars filled with men in leather coats began making their nightly roundups.

They came for Paul on 6 September in the hours before dawn, pounding with their fists on the green gate, rattling the handles of the back veranda windows and hammering on the front door. Natasha shouted to Paul and the boys to stay in bed and rose to open the door. They swarmed past her through the house, twenty-five of them in all, led by a seaman from the Black Sea fleet named Tursky with a large diamond ring on his finger and drug-blurred eyes. Natasha felt herself shaking from head to foot, but she brought her voice under control and demanded to know what they wanted. The seaman asked her who lived in the house and he wanted to know whether her boys were of draftable age. She insisted that Nick, a tall fourteen-year-old, was really only twelve.

Then Paul appeared in the hallway, his greatcoat over his shoulders, gaunt and composed. The sailor handed him a search warrant signed by the Bolshevik Extraordinary Committee. They emptied his desk, took his ministerial briefcase and searched the high Dutch-tiled stoves. They found Natasha's housekeeping money, but when she pleaded that if they took it the family would be destitute, they returned it to her. One of the search party was a student wearing a cap from Moscow University. Paul remarked quietly, "What a strange meeting, colleague," and the student looked away. The leader of the search party then ordered his men to take Paul downtown for questioning. Paul kissed and blessed his children, and the men led him out into the street. Natasha dashed into the garden and called after them in the darkness, "When will I see him again?" As they loaded him into an automobile, she heard someone shout back, "Tomorrow morning early at the station."

The car had only proceeded a short distance down the street when it stopped and the men went into another house to make a search. Paul sat in the car between two guards listening to the shouts and screams and banging of doors as the search party went about its work. After Paul had waited an hour outside, a soldier rode up to the car and ordered him to get out. Covered by a young soldier from behind, Paul walked the mile and a half down to the railway station through the silent streets. After half an hour, the soldier let Paul stop and rest. Sitting beside him on the curb, the soldier said he had been a student at the Technical Academy in Petrograd and had joined the Red Army because he had nothing to eat. Then he added in a whisper, "This number will not go through."

When Paul reached the Kislovodsk railway station, the local trade-union guards lifted him up gently into the freight car. When the Red guards taking the roll got to his name, the sergeant muttered that there must be some mistake. He had been a student in the local primary school: he remembered the teacher had once asked the class to stand and sing a song in praise of Count Paul Ignatieff. Paul clung to these hopeful signs even when he heard shooting outside the railway car at dawn, and saw a Red soldier sliding his revolver back in his pocket and barking an order to bury bodies in the ditch behind the car.

At first light, Natasha was running along the tracks by the station. She found Paul at last lying with a few other prisoners huddled in his overcoat in a freight car that stank of motor oil. Natasha bullied the man standing guard until he allowed her to approach to within arm's length of her husband. Paul looked weak and exhausted. They only had time for a few words before the guard ordered her away.

Natasha returned with her son Dima that afternoon, carrying Paul's medicine for his angina, a syringe, some bandages and yoghurt in glass jars. The sentry rummaged through the bandages, driving Natasha into a passion of rage. Screaming that his filthy hands had contaminated everything, she seized the yoghurt from Dima's hands and hurled it into the ditch. Paul watched her from the open door of the freight car. He said, "Dearest, calm yourself, calm yourself." Natasha returned to the railway siding at night-fall, but the car had been shunted some distance away and she wandered across the tracks looking for it in vain. Exhausted and desperate, she returned home again and informed the family that she was going to Bolshevik headquarters to protest at her husband's incarceration. The family pleaded with her to stay where she was: it was curfew, she risked being shot. A family friend named Professor Nechaev—who was collaborating with the Bolshevik Soviet in the running of the city's schools—had assembled a delegation to plead for Paul's life before the town Soviet. Natasha refused to listen, said goodnight to her children and took a cab down to Bolshevik headquarters in the Grand Hotel.

Through the long hours of that evening, she waited alone in the lobby for members of the Bolshevik committee to appear. Around midnight, a commissar named Atarbekov, a stout bull-faced man in a Cossack uniform with a red armband, passed through the lobby on his way to bed. She leaped up and demanded to know what he had done with her husband. He waved her away: he had just finished a heavy dinner and needed to sleep. Next there appeared the drugged sailor Tursky, who had been leader of the search party that had arrested Paul. He shouted that she risked being shot for being out after curfew, and Natasha replied that if she didn't find out what had happened to her husband, she didn't care if they did shoot her. Tursky then seemed to relent. He hinted that he might be able to do something next day. The former mayor of the town was in the lobby and appealed to Tursky to let her go home. One of Tursky's bodyguards accompanied her home, drunkenly recounting his "work for the great bloodless revolution."

Natasha heard that the prisoners were being taken by train to the Bolshevik headquarters in the south Caucasus at Piatigorsk, a spa town about twelve miles away. The next morning she secured a pass from her friend Professor Nechaev to go to Piatigorsk, authorized as a schoolteacher sent to buy sheet music for the schools. After another fruitless exchange of insults with the Bolsheviks at the Grand Hotel, she walked to the station, where friends and acquaintances clustered around whispering that all the prisoners were being brought to the station to be liberated. Just then she saw her husband being led from a railway car. Accosting Tursky, who was strutting along the platform with his guard at his side, she asked him when her husband would be liberated. "He won't be liberated," Tursky said with a smile.

She screamed at him, "How dare you cheat me! You promised to let him go free."

"I promised nothing."

"Then I will accompany him."

"You do not have a pass."

"Yes I do!" she shouted. Reaching into her bag she grabbed a piece of paper and waved it in his face. He took it, examined it and returned it to her with a smile. She snatched it back. It was a shopping list. Aghast, she dug into her bag, found the real permit and handed it to him.

Tursky watched this comedy impassively. "You won't go," he said and turned his back on her.

At this moment, the doors of the station opened and the prisoners under guard were led to the train. Paul was among them; there were two Tsarist provincial governors she recognized and a party of Socialist Revolutionary opponents of the Bolsheviks who were carrying their bedding and singing revolutionary songs. Before Natasha and Paul could exchange a word the train moved out of the station towards Piatigorsk, which she knew had become a killing ground for White hostages. She felt like a stone dropped into a well.

Women on the platform comforted her, told her to be quiet, not to make a fuss. They told her to go home to her children. She did not go home to her children. All that day she sat in the lobby of the Grand Hotel, stunned and listless—half listening, half watching as the waiters passed to and fro in the lobby, as the Soviet committees argued behind the closed doors of the tea rooms and palm courts. Alone in her black dress and shawl, seated hour after hour of that long day, unnoticed by passers-by, she wondered in the unwounded part of herself how she would keep her sons alive now. She watched the September sun go down, distantly heard the shouts and clump of army boots in the marble hallway. Darkness roused her. She found a waiting cab and told the driver to take her home.

Her boys were all sitting in darkness: the electricity had been cut. In the silence and the darkness they sat together, stunned and motionless. To them, disaster had been a card always dealt to others. Everything their life had meant to that moment repeated the same reassuring message: you are immune. It will happen to others, but it will not happen to you. Now it was happening to them.

In the train to Piatigorsk, Paul was packed into the carriages with the Socialist Revolutionaries. As the blacked-out train crawled its way along the track, shunting around the edge of gunfire at the front, he sat muffled in his coat listening to the Socialist Revolutionaries sing the anthem "We Fell Victims to the Fatal Struggle," which he had heard as a governor from his office window and which he now heard as a fellow prisoner of the new power. He thought he was about to die. The Socialist Revolutionaries thought he was about to die too. But they were sure that the Bolsheviks would spare them as fellow revolutionaries. At Piatigorsk station, the platform was filled with Red Army soldiers who pushed towards the hostages threateningly. The Ukrainian trade-union guards surrounded Paul and their leader shouted, "The first one who moves towards us will be a dead man." An old soldier from Ukraine led him along the platform to a horse-drawn trolley. By this time Paul was scarcely able to walk. He leaned heavily on the soldier's arm. In the trolley that drew them along to the town prison, the old soldier, whispering, asked whether there was anything he could do to help. Paul just had time to reply: "Tell the schools."

Paul and the other prisoners from Kislovodsk were taken to a room at the entrance to the prison. Mr Gueh, chairman of the Bolshevik committee in Piatigorsk, a suave little man with bright intelligent eyes and a goatee, entered and asked in perfect French whether he could speak to Count Ignatieff. "Citizen Ignatieff, you mean," said Paul in Russian. Gueh seemed amused; the phone rang and Gueh went to answer it. Paul could hear a lady's voice inviting Gueh to tea and Gueh replying that he would be delighted to accept. Gueh excused himself and went back to the meeting to consider his prisoners' fates.

After a wash at the prison pump in the courtyard, Paul was led into a large room: provincial governors, Jewish merchants, judges, army officers, Serbs, Poles, Tsarists and Socialist Revolutionaries all lay against the whitewashed walls waiting. There was an old armchair in the middle of the room. The prisoners led him to it and sat him gently down.

Just before eight o'clock, the prisoners heard footsteps in the passage. The door opened and Atarbekov, the bull-like Bolshevik whom Natasha had accosted in the hotel lobby in Kislovodsk the night before, appeared with the prison superintendent and a guard. They pointed at citizen Ignatieff.

"You are free. Leave the prison immediately."

Paul said he would not leave without the others. Atarbekov pointed to two Tsarist former governors whom Paul had befriended in the railway car and said, "Take them quickly."

"You will give us a certificate that we are free?" Paul asked.

"I have no office here and no stamp so I cannot give you any documents," Atarbekov replied.

"Then I shall not leave the prison. The town is under martial law, and I prefer to be shot in the regular way to being shot like a dog in a dark street corner."

One of the prisoners was tugging at Paul's elbow urging him to make a run for it. But Paul was adamant. Why, he insisted, had he been arrested at all and why now was he being told to leave?

Atarbekov replied gruffly, "We did not know that you had been useful to national education." One of the prison guards chimed in, "You may not know, but we knew." In heavily accented Russian the guard explained that he had been a pupil at a textile vocational school in Lodz in Poland, funded and encouraged while Paul was minister. Paul said he would be willing to leave the prison with this man. He then demanded that Atarbekov phone the Kislovodsk Soviet to tell them he was free and to inform his family.

The Ukrainian trade unionists had done as Paul had told them: they had gone to the schools and had happened on a teachers' council in session. A local teacher named Oudariuk who had joined the Bolsheviks and helped them in map-reading in the Caucasus told the trade unionists to spread the word about the arrest of Count Ignatieff among the local schools. Soon teachers and students from all over town were gathered under the windows of the Bolshevik headquarters, standing silently in the autumn twilight. The Bolshevik teacher went into the meeting and demanded Paul's liberation. When Gueh began to protest, the teacher gestured to the crowd below and told him they would liberate the prisoner by force. The Bolshevik hold on the town was uncertain: the Whites were in the hills, and all available detachments were at the front. An uprising of the citizens of the town had just been suppressed. The only guards at Gueh's disposal were members of the Polish Legion and they had refused to do anything other than guard duty: they would not intervene against the crowd. Gueh's hand was forced. He ordered the immediate liberation of the prisoner. Paul owed his life to the capricious fortune of civil war, to some Ukrainian trade unionists and to a young Bolshevik geography teacher he had never met.

JANICE KULYK KEEFER

from

Honey and Ashes

A Story of Family

AN EQUAL SPILL OF BEAUTY AND BLOOD

IN 1927 MY GRANDFATHER Tomasz Solowski left the village of
Staromischyna and boarded *The Empress of France* in the Free
City of Danzig. He was as old as the century itself; he was leaving
his wife Olena and their four children, two of them newborn, to
find work in Canada, work that would buy more strips of black
Polish earth for his family. He returned to them in 1932, only to
leave again after ten months, finding it impossible to live under
Poland's repressive martial regime. Before he left, he pleaded with
his wife to bring their surviving children—my mother Natalia,
my aunt Vira—to Canada. It took my grandmother four years
to make up her mind, and even then, though she sold her house,
she could not part with the land she'd bought so dearly. She had

contracts drawn up between herself and the neighbours who'd agreed to rent her fields till she returned one day. And though she lost those fields in 1941, when the invading Soviets collectivized the land round Staromischyna, she kept the contracts, with their seals and stamps and purple ink, till the day she died, thirty-eight years later.

My grandmother never returned to the Old Place, nor did her daughters, who were fourteen and twelve when they abandoned their village and the narrow future it had dug for them. But in many ways they brought the Old Place with them when they crossed the ocean, hiding the past in embroidered shirts, the folds of woven rugs....

BLUE STONES, BANANAS, THE IMMIGRANT SHUFFLE

HOME, THE FIRST HOME, was Antler Street, one small room that Tomasz had furnished with two beds, four chairs, an enamel-topped table and the indispensable orange crates. Later they found better lodgings on Queen Street West, with another Ukrainian family. Somehow they all fitted into an apartment over a store—on hot summer nights the children would sleep on the roof, watching the stars rise or the sun come up through grids of telephone wires. "Which store was it?" I ask my mother. She can't remember: besides, it changed hands long ago. Walking back and forth along Queen, I try to guess which of these tall, narrow houses it might have been, houses at whose gingerbread gables I used to stare when having my teeth drilled in my father's office. It's hopeless. The street has changed so much even from the time I knew it best, working for my father as a teenaged receptionist, trying to interpret the Ukrainian and Polish of his patients, many of them old men with stooped shoulders and cloth caps, women bundled up in shawls and kerchiefs, a fragrance of poppyseed and dill about them.

Hopeless. Yet one day, only months ago, walking along Queen past Bathurst, past fashionable cafés and punk clothes boutiques, I happened to glance down a side street to find a large sign saying CHARLES G. FRASER PUBLIC SCHOOL. This was the very school my aunt and mother had attended more than sixty years ago. I walked down the side street and inside the school's front doors. The buzz of lights, the intimidating height and width of the corridors—this my aunt and mother would have recognized from 1936. These stained glass scenes of children having tea parties or flying kites— they would have been here, too, their content as opaque to Natalia and Vira as the lessons they were sitting through.

It's the end of the school day, most of the children are gone, there's nothing for me here. But still I walk inside the office, making my way past teachers, telephones, newspaper articles pinned to the wall praising the school for its success in acculturating immigrants— Asian, these days, rather than Eastern European. It cheers me to see these clippings and the photos that accompany them; they're a connection to my family's past. But when the secretary at the desk—a woman who wouldn't have been born when my aunt and mother first were students here—responds to my question by pulling out file cards from a cabinet, I am astounded. They are dated 1936, and they give me the very information that I need:

Solowska, Nataljia. Solowska, Irena Vera. Last School Attended: Poland. Present Address: I. 716 Queen Street West. II. 29 Manning Avenue. III. 94 Manning Avenue.

THE IMMIGRANT SHUFFLE, moving from rooming house to rooming house, apartment to apartment, each in a slightly better neigh- bourhood, with fewer roaches and more and more gestures towards gardens—pots of geraniums, even a patch of rank grass outside the front door. After Queen Street, two rooms on Manning, and then two larger rooms on Shaw. Tomasz and Olena, Vira and Natalia used the hallway as a kitchen and shared the house's one bathroom with half a dozen other families. Olena would take her turn lining up for the bathroom with the other women, lock herself in—it was the only room in the whole house where she could be alone—and cry her eyes out for the five minutes or so before a timid knock would signal the next woman's turn to go in and weep.

From a thatched and clay-floored cottage to a downtown rooming house; from the quietness of carts and horses to the screech and slam of city traffic—how do Olena and her daughters survive these sudden, stunning leaps? How do they know who or what they are anymore? Nothing here gives them back their true reflection. To those who own this place they are incurably foreign; if they're overheard speaking to someone in their own language, slurs like *bohunk* will be tossed their way. Not the colour of their skin, but the width and slant of their cheekbones, the very shape of their tongues mark them out as different, dangerous—why else would English people—the *Angliky*—go to such lengths to keep clear of them as they walk down the street? "It will pass," Olena's neighbours tell her. Or else, "You'll get used to it."

But for a long, long while they think they'll never get used to anything here. The first time Vira sees her father come home with a paper bag holding eggs, milk, bread, she feels a shock that sixty years haven't stilled. The shock that money must be paid out for the food you put into your mouth each day, money that's always been so scarce you're terrified to spend even a little of what you've struggled to save. At home the only things you needed to buy were what you couldn't make yourself: sugar and salt, coffee and tea. Soap you brewed from ashes and fat, oil you got from hemp seeds pressed at the mill. Even when paying the hired man after harvest, you gave him sacks of wheat, not money.

Not just at night, but all through the day, Vira dreams of home, the cow whose warm, frothy milk her mother would squirt from the teat straight into a cup for her to drink, the walnuts shaken from the trees, the deliciousness of sour cream dribbled over lettuce pulled tender from the garden. The fourteen fragrant loaves of rye bread her mother would bake each month, pulling them out of the oven with long-handled paddles; the *kvas* that was their version of a soft drink, made from fermented buckwheat flour. The pigs slaughtered after Christmas, every inch of their shaved, skinned bodies boiled or salted down to make sausages, blood pudding, headcheese. Home is the place where she never went hungry. But here, if her father's back doesn't heal, if her mother's eyes stay so inflamed from sewing that she can't go to work, what can they do but starve? The government offers relief in the form of free oatmeal for something called porridge, but Olena is too proud and too fearful to claim it: she's heard that those who sign on for relief are shipped right back to where they came from.

And so Olena walks her mile and a half each day to and from the shirt factory: partly to save the fare to buy bread, and partly because the jolting of the streetcar reminds her too much of her ocean crossing. Mr. Rosmaranovich, a neighbour who works at a dairy, brings them outdated milk, cream and butter for their table. Tomasz finds temporary work at a bakery, rescuing whatever's too stale to sell—I imagine the family sitting down to dinners of curdled cream and three-day-old chocolate cake and wonder what Vira and Natalia made of this new, forced luxury. Later, they'll live off soup bones and rhubarb; they'll even be able to laugh at things. Like the family downstairs, whose six sons play—most of them hopelessly—the violin. For exactly half an hour, each boy practises, handing the instrument to the next brother down as if it were a piece of chewed-out gum.

At first Natalia accompanies her mother to the shirt factory, but by the end of the summer Olena starts to earn enough—$3.50 a week—for Natalia to join Vira at school. This improvement in her wages Olena owes to the Russian woman who's the only person on her shift with whom she can communicate. "They're paying you less than anyone else," the Russian says. "They know you can't talk with the other women and compare wages. Don't let them get away with it—don't let them stick you with all the big sizes that take so long to sew." Somehow Olena makes herself understood, and the foreman, reluctant to lose such an expert seamstress, pays her the paltry sum per shirt that's considered fair. It's a small victory, but enough to give Olena the assurance she can hold her own here, just as she'd done at home.

It's the kind of assurance Tomasz lacks, by temperament and by experience. He had to borrow money to prove to the authorities that he could support his family once they came to Canada; now he's disabled and in great pain. If his back doesn't heal, he may never work again, even if by some miracle there's work to be had. He wanted to welcome his family to Toronto with a whirl of presents; all he can manage is to swear off cigarettes, after having chain-smoked all the years he was alone. But he quits cold turkey and manages to keeps his temper, too, the best part of the only gift he can offer his wife. As for his back, Olena contrives to save up the price of a chiropractor. After one appointment Tomasz comes back dancing; finding Olena sewing in their room, he swings her round as lightly as he'd done when they first met. Instantly his back gives out and Olena has to help him into bed. He returns to the chiropractor, who effects a more permanent cure, but never again does Tomasz trust himself, or fate, enough to dance up a set of stairs.

Nights are Olena's bête noire, literally. Of the four of them it's she who wakes at two A.M., covered with red, swollen bites. After airing the mattresses, they carry the iron bedsteads out into the yard, pour gasoline over them and light matches, listening to the bedbugs pop in the flames. But the next night the bugs are back, as bad as ever. Tomasz suggests his wife sleep on the wooden table in the middle of the room, but when they switch on the light the next morning, bedbugs are massed on the ceiling over the table; the hardier among them have, of course, dropped down during the night onto Olena. It's only when the Solowskis acquire a home of their own that Olena can sleep undisturbed once more.

What was it like living all together again? My mother once told me that her parents' reunion, after all the years apart, had been saddened by something that was other people's doing. In Staromischyna Olena held her head high in the midst of talk that Tomasz had abandoned her; in Toronto she held herself back from her husband. The signs of such holding back—how obvious and yet intricate they must have been in those conditions, husband and wife and children in one small room, haunted by other rooms unreachably distant and yet always there. Finally Tomasz persuaded his wife to tell him what had gone wrong. Again, as in the orchard sixteen years ago, his tenderness embraced her pride, disarmed it. But something, my mother says, was spoiled in her parents' first days together: a joy refused, to return only slowly, and in altered form.

There were no arguments, no scenes. Perhaps my grandparents were so busy trying to survive each day that they had no energy for shows of emotion. Except once, when a letter arrived for Olena. A letter from the Old Place, a rare enough event, but the handwriting on the envelope, the mere fact of the letter's having been written at all, makes it all the more conspicuous. Olena's at work when the mail's delivered. Tomasz accepts it from the postman's hand, takes it inside to their room, where Natalia's trying to make some kind of meal out of stale rolls and rancid butter. There's a look on her father's face she's never seen before, even when his back was causing him most pain. She sees the letter he doesn't open but keeps turning over in his hands. She, too, recognizes the handwriting, and only a fast wire of courage lets her keep her head when her father asks her, softly, what she knows. She shakes her head, and he, too, shakes his, leaving the room, the house, still grasping the letter in his hand.

When he returns, long after Olena has come home, he makes no mention of what has kept him, where he's been. He's as gentle as ever with his wife, his oldest daughter, who knows enough to keep the letter, and the wordless conversation she's had with her father, a secret.

COMMUNITY IS THE ONE luxury they possess. In this sense, despite electric light and automobiles and department stores, Toronto becomes an extension for them of the Old Place. Among Ukrainians, hospitality is a religion: even those just scraping by will offer guests a cup of tea, a spoon of sugar, advice on where to buy fruit at a good price, which butchers to avoid. One of the first things Tomasz does once his family joins him is to buy an enormous enamel pot. To repay the many meals he's been given here, he explains to Olena. Somehow, without telephones, without specific invitations issued or answered, up to thirty people come by after church, or after sleeping in on the one day a week they can do so. All Sunday morning Olena labours over two burners set up in the hallway, dropping the *varenyky*, for which her daughters have peeled and mashed endless potatoes, into the vat of boiling water. Lifting them out with a slotted spoon, dropping them into a pan glistening with buttery onions, and onto plates that empty faster than she can fill them.

ERNEST HILLEN

from

Small Mercies
A Boy After War

IT WAS EVENING. Some three thousand of us, bony women and children pocked with sores, in rags, stood assembled on a field of red mud fenced in by barbed wire while above us like a cloud hung the stink of our shit—and right then a trumpet should have blared, lightning should have cracked! After three and a half years of imprisonment we needn't bow to the enemy any more. The enemy, we were told, had surrendered! But, instead of joy, there was an instant shushing and the head of Camp Makasar, another prisoner, warned us not to yell, not to raise the flag, not to sing the national anthem. She said that, because our camp was so near Batavia (Jakarta, on Java), Indonesians living there might hear us. Indonesia may have been the Dutch East Indies when the Japanese invaded in 1942, but it was known that the moment the Japanese capitulated Indonesians meant to fight us, the Dutch, to get their country back. If we were attacked, our guards sure weren't going to do any protecting and Allied troops hadn't landed yet. So, to mark the war's end, we were permitted two minutes of silence.

A few people cried, but most, like my mother, just stood there, like stones. My best friend, Hubie van Boxel, who had golden hair (that's the word people used, golden) had died two weeks earlier absolutely certain—as I was—that the war would never end. It made sense. We'd simply been forgotten and those of us still living would stay in camp and die there, one a little faster than another, but everybody would get their turn, children, too, curled up in small bamboo coffins. Trudging back to our barrack with my mother in the dark I knew what she'd say next; they were about the only English words I understood then. And sure enough, inside barrack 4A, after she'd loosened her long red hair and we lay side by side on our narrow lousy mattresses scratching, she whispered, "Well, dammit—thank God for small mercies!" It's what she always said after a "fluke," a piece of luck, big or small, it didn't matter, and often included an English curse. She swore a little; I did, too.

Food rations had grown so small over the years, adults said, that the mid-August liberation had come none too soon; six months later we'd all have been dead. But, the very next morning extra rice was suddenly distributed, and then we raced back laughing into other line-ups for—unbelievably!—oil, fruit, sugar, soap, and *toothpaste*. And two days later a British plane thundered in low over Makasar dropping boxes swinging from parachutes—canned food, milk powder, medicine, cigarettes, *chocolate*. And the day after that, British officers, looking shocked, wandered around inspecting Makasar. And then, one afternoon ten days later, my father walked into camp.

Was it my father? I hadn't seen him since he and the other white men from our tea plantation had been trucked away to men's camps three and a half years earlier; women and children had followed a few weeks later, to other camps. A smaller man, round-shouldered, he hugged me and said, "I'm your father." "Yes, sir," I answered. His eyes tried to look inside my head like they used to, but it didn't work any more. He called me *jongetje,* "little boy" in Dutch, but I didn't feel like a *jongetje* any more. His last words to my brother, Jerry, and me had been, "Look after your mother." His blue-grey eyes had burned into our brown ones. Well, maybe Jerry, who was eleven then, knew what he meant, but I was seven, and had no idea. It was a strange thing to say. How could a little kid take care of his mom? Make her laugh? Bring her tea? It didn't make sense. She was there to take care of me.

"Jerry?" she and I wanted to know right away. My father said he was just fine. Jerry had been with us in women's camps in the city of Bandung (where she and I were interned longest) until, at thirteen, he and boys his age were taken away, we didn't know where, because the Japanese thought they'd become a "danger to the state." It had puzzled me that when the truck drove off Jerry was grinning: he would be "his own boss," my mother had explained. But by chance he landed in the same camp as our father. When we found out, my mother said lucky us: father and son, mother and son. Well, maybe. Our father liked "discipline," which, it seemed, just meant promptly obeying and not crossing him. Before the war he had taught discipline in many ways, mostly to Jerry as the oldest. So for about a year and a half Jerry had been alone with our father and I thought he might have taken in a lot of discipline.

By the time my father discovered my mother and I were in Makasar, British soldiers had landed on Java and begun policing cities and highways; Dutch troops soon followed. From his and Jerry's camp in Tjimahi, a small town near Bandung, my father had hitchhiked on military vehicles to Batavia. "I would have walked," he told my mother, and that was probably true.

We sat on our mattresses in 4A, my parents holding hands. With his free hand my father took something from an old children's schoolbag he carried, and handed it to her. It was a polished wooden box with lumpy roundings like women's thighs, and fitting inside it, exactly, a carved necklace of dozens of finely smoothed balls the size of peanuts; set apart by even smaller balls was a pendant of two maple leaves and an open acorn with, inside it, a third maple leaf. What my father had worked with, I'm sorry to say, I didn't ask—a razor-blade, glass-slivers, sand, who knows: he had no tools. He'd made these beautiful things from the roots of some hardwood bush, in secret, to give to my mother. "If, Anna," he said to her then, eyes blinking, "we lived." The maple leaves were because she was from Canada. My mother whispered, "Oh, John." I looked at her looking at him.

I wouldn't be missed, so I wandered outside. All through the camps she'd talked about him, stories, little details, also about Jerry after he was taken away, and about relatives in Canada and Holland; she marked their birthdays: "It's fun," she'd say. "This is how we'll survive." She'd told me how once upon a time the two of them had met. In the summer of 1929, two young Dutchmen, Jan Hillen and Gerard Röling, an artist, had crossed the Atlantic to make a long-planned Canadian canoe trip from someplace in southern Ontario all the way up to James Bay. They had been paddling for a month through endless hot mosquito-infested bush when the banks of the small river they were on suddenly changed to lawn. Then, high up one side, they spied two red-haired young women carrying a basket of oranges. The grubby, unshaven Dutchmen waved and shouted. The women looked over, one stumbled, the basket tipped, and oranges bounded down to the water. The Dutchmen raced yipping for shore. Sloshing after oranges, they learned they were in vacation country, in Muskoka, on a cottager's private grounds; the redheads were public-school teachers just starting a week's holiday. The men promptly hauled in the canoe and asked permission to pitch camp, their journey, it seems, done and over. The four had age in common, twenty-two, and by the end of the week Gerard Röling had become good friends with one redhead—and Jan Hillen had asked the other, Anna Watson, to marry him.

Perhaps it was the smell of Camp Makasar's open latrines—she and I were used to it—but my father told us we were going to take the first train back to Bandung next day, a three-hour run from Batavia: trains were probably safe. There was no discussion. Even though she was an adult and proud of her "common sense," my mother had always discussed decisions with us in camp. Now her serious brown eyes watched this restless man, blond hair combed back flat, often sighing—who knew why—and wordlessly she agreed. I had no say at all. Bring the minimum, my father instructed, all would be provided in Tjimahi. There wasn't much to leave behind: our mattresses, some grey worn-out sheets, a mosquito net covered in bug blood, two spoons, a fork, two mugs, and a lidded can for sugar. I owned a pair of shorts, a short-sleeved shirt, a harmonica, a khaki-cloth rucksack, and, especially given to me by his mother, Hubie's riding boots, a beret, and a toy soldier on a horse. My mother had a skirt and a shirt for working in, some underwear including a tea-towel-brassiere, one dress, and sandals.

Next morning, barefoot between my parents, I walked out of Makasar's barbed-wire gate. A whistling English soldier standing guard gave us a little salute. I was barefoot because I wouldn't wear Hubie's boots: his mother had hoarded them for *him* to walk out in. My mother wore the green dress and sandals she'd saved for this day—this day we'd pictured a thousand times. Just a short way beyond the gate, under a suddenly soaring sky, in air suddenly fresh and wind suddenly touching, there ran a wide pitted dusty road—bell-ringing carrier tricyles and bicycles, screaking horse-drawn carriages, honking trucks and, on the sidewalks, fluttery women in tight sarongs, children holding hands, yelling vendors, all moving unhurriedly, a few Chinese, mostly Indonesians. Lots of them thin, poorly dressed, even in rags, but all with purposes—and free. Unseen and unheard, that traffic had rambled to and fro all our dead days.

But this was just another day for the road—and we were the only whites on it. In camp, rumours had flared of armed Indonesians forcing *orang Blanda*, us Dutch, to stay in camps, of torture and killings. But no one on the road paid us any attention. My father waved down a Jeep driven by a soldier, a turbaned one called a Sikh, and asked in English for a ride to Batavia's railway station. The Sikh nodded without turning. We climbed in, my father up front, my mother and I in back, me behind my father—and I locked my eyes for dear life on the Sikh. A single look down that go-as-you-please road had been enough. For three and a half years, eight-foot plaited-bamboo walls had blocked my eyes, but in the Jeep I couldn't look. The road and then the city's hot streets sped by in a whir of colours and shapes—and smells: fried banana, roasted meat—but I fixed on the Sikh. The sun was nearly white, yet his uniform shirt was done up to the throat, sleeves buttoned down, beard pressed to his chin in a hairnet. On his left wrist he wore a copper bracelet; a walkie-talkie hung from an epaulet, a holstered revolver from his belt. Tall and lean with a thin, curved nose, he sat rigidly behind the wheel, black eyes ahead, never speaking. I didn't want to look at him any more, but didn't dare watch the world: it was too open. Outside the station my father thanked the Sikh, who nodded once and drove off.

Inside, Indonesians carting baskets, chickens, and babies scurried amidst whistles, shouts, and shrieking steel—and I homed in on the rear ends of my hand-holding parents. My father pushed into a line-up for tickets, then ran us to a far platform where we hoisted ourselves into a second-class coach, just in time; on two facing benches in the fourth compartment three seats were free. Five more people jammed in behind us, Indonesian women and a high-voiced man, the only other white I saw; they'd have to stand. During the trip, though, my father, or I at his look, would offer to let a woman or Mr. Bilt sit for a while. Doing strangers favours for free, I thought, was just dumb. The women, small and cool and neat, smiled but said thank you, no, *tuan,* "sir." Mr. Bilt always piped yes. In my mind I took the "t" off Bilt so he became *Meneer Bil,* "Mr. Ass" in Dutch.

My first train trip had occurred before the war, grandly alone at night in the locomotive all the way from Bandung to a depot near the plantation; the engineer had let me yank away at the whistle cord. During the war, my mother and I had travelled from Bandung to Batavia locked in a pitch-dark, fourth-class coach packed with other prisoners; the three-hour run became twenty, and we all did it in our pants. On *this* ride, we passed through tender-green rice fields dotted with farmers in conical hats driving water buffalo and, on higher ground, small bamboo houses, coconut trees, clumps of jungle growth. Glittering in the sun, the watery fields climbed terrace by terrace into hazy purple hills which, as we chugged further inland, swelled into hazy purple mountains. Our open window let in a little breeze, and soot and live embers. At the many small-station stops, my father leaned out and bargained with pedlars for water, bananas, papaya slices, rambutans; no cookies, cookies were expensive. A man with a big silvery tin hanging from his neck sold ice lollies, red, green, blue, white. Even after so long, I could *taste* them, but no, fruit was better for you. We passengers sat or stood rocking and bumping against one another, skin wetly touching skin, trying to doze.

Then, in the middle of nowhere, the train screeched to a stop. Eyes flew open and we lunged for the window. Up and down the train other heads poked out and in the sudden stillness we heard bird cries and the locomotive puffing. We sat or stood very straight, watched each other, listened. A door slammed at the end of the corridor, angry voices, yelling, a scream, scuffling, then slaps: familiar sounds—*stay calm; yield.* The commotion drew closer. Our compartment door slammed open and hard-breathing young Indonesians crowded in, *"Identifikasi! Identifikasi!"* Long-haired as women, they smelled wild and their skin shivered. Rifles hung from small shoulders, machetes from belts. Barefoot, they wore ripped, dirt-caked clothes but fresh white red-lettered headbands. The letters probably spelled MERDEKA! "Freedom!" the favourite slogan of what we called the Extremists. They at once picked out us whites.

"Identifikasi!"

My father stood up, bowed slightly, offered a pink card politely with both hands, and nodded towards my mother and me to show we were with him. Mr. Bilt, the idiot, had his card out but wouldn't pass it over—*their* identification first, he shrilled, a Dutchman not taking guff. For a moment it was very quiet—until my father jerked around, snatched Mr. Bilt's card away, and handed it over. *"Ezel!"* he said quietly to Mr. Bilt in Dutch. "Donkey!" The armed men studied the cards, tossed them back, and swaggered out to the next compartment. After a little while, the locomotive whistled and the train lurched forward. On a narrow dyke between rice fields the slender men trotted away single file towards the hills. Staring after them, my father, frowning, muttered something to himself. In the next few weeks I'd overhear him and other white men discuss the Extremists, in a soothing adult way, as rascals who simply needed discipline. They, the Dutch, were as keen as always, they said, to help Indonesians "mature" and, of course, as soon as Indonesians had done so, would be glad to hand them back their country. But first things first. Indonesia badly needed fixing and they, the Dutch, had spent 350 years doing just that. The fighting spread, though, and white patience ran out—the rebels simply needed squashing. There would be other adventures with Freedom Fighters, as *they* called themselves, but what stayed with me from what happened on the train was my father's fine quick action.

At one point, sitting swaying across from me, he leaned over and placed his hands on my knees, eyes glowing like a child's. From the time he'd walked into camp the day before, my mother had mostly absorbed him, but now, it seemed, it was my turn; my mother sitting back had her eyes closed. He was really a stranger to me though. Just as almost overnight the prison camp's crowded life had smothered the memory of our quiet plantation, so, too, had it pressed out the memory of him. My mother tried to keep it alive, sure, but soon I couldn't *see* him. I'd remembered his able hands—drawing or repairing things, spanking Jerry with a thin leather slipper, or oh so gently letting down the gramophone's needle on a record. He read a lot, like my mother and Jerry; and he had been keen on discipline. The rest was really information from my mother. He liked English (that's how Jerry and I got our names and why we called him "Daddy"); he loved his sons, music, painting, sailing, and motorcycling; he worked hard, was strict but fair, had travelled a lot, spoke fluent Dutch, English, German, and Indonesian, couldn't dance, and was sometimes funny—remember how on the plantation he and Uncle Fred at either end of the dining-room table had flipped fried eggs back and forth? I looked down at the short, strong hands on my knees; the right index finger was stained yellow. Boxes on parachutes had probably also dropped into Camp Tjimahi; he must have smoked a lot since.

Softly, warmly, my father said to me that he knew that I had had it tough, yes?

Wrapped inside his attention, I felt my face grow hot: it was the first time in years that a man was speaking to me, deep rumbling for just my ears. Aside from barking guards, the last man to talk to me had been Mr. Otten with the little moustache. Mr. Otten had shot a wild boar on the plantation and given me its head to bury and later, cleaned by worms, to dig up as a beautiful white skull to put in my room. That was just before we were interned; deep down in the red earth, teeth grinning, the skull had to be there still. My eyes stayed on my father's hands. *What* had been tough?

Oh yes, my father said, *tough,* and he sighed.

For his finger to get that yellow, he must've smoked a tin a day.

My mother, my father said, had told him that I'd grown up a lot as a person. A lot, he said again. He had been pleased—yes, even proud—to hear that. Of course, he had observed that himself the moment he laid eyes on me.

Meaning? A week ago she'd slapped my face; only the second slap in all those years, but still. "Don't you dare look at girls or women like that," she'd snapped. I'd been staring at bare legs and at breasts. She didn't blab though. So what *had* he noticed? That I could pass by sick and dying people and not *see* them? That I *knew* that pain was just pain and death just death?

Still, my father went on quietly, it was important that I not forget that I *was* a boy—the finger touched my chin—and boys, even boys who'd grown up a lot, Ernest, *listened* to their fathers, looked them in the eye.

The blue-grey eyes were waiting.

Even though I was young, my father said, it was important for me to know that the war had also been tough for *him,* Daddy. *Extremely* tough. As head of the family it had perhaps been *toughest* for him. He'd had Jerry to care for. He'd had my mother and me and the future to worry about. All that had been *his* burden. He sighed. Did I understand what he was saying?

I nodded.

He wanted me to think about that, my father said, his voice a little strained. Yes, I should think about how tough it had been for him. How lonely. I should think about it hard.

My God—*tears!* I nodded and nodded.

His wet eyes shone. Then he swallowed, took a deep breath, and said that the awful suffering was now behind him. And yes, behind *all* of us. We Hillens were going to be a family again. We Hillens were going to live good and normal lives and live them in a safe and quiet place. Now, he said, I should listen closely. What he was going to say was *very serious*. Was I listening?

I nodded, nodded.

He had already spoken of it to Jerry. He and Jerry, he said, had had many fine talks—Jerry listened; he wanted to have fine talks with me, too, of course. Did I realize that I was going to go to school one day soon? Well, I was. And when I was in school he expected me to work hard, very hard, no excuses, so that I would catch up fast after the years in camp with no school. And this—a light press on my knees—was the reason why: he wanted *me*, Ernest, to make *him*, Daddy, *proud* of me. But, he warned, it would take a lot—*a great deal*—to make him proud.

That was it. He'd had something to say in the shaking railway car that he'd wanted me to hear and then his attention shut off like a lamp. I didn't mind; hadn't minded when it was on either. I hadn't understood much, but that was all right: he might say it again. Smiling a bit sadly, my father slumped back on his bench and shut his eyes.

As we clattered through high country towards Bandung it grew less humid and less hot. The city lay in a valley but I remembered that you could shiver in the rain there, that at night in mountain homes people lit hearth fires. We'd lived in Bandung for short spells before the war and then in three camps—residential sections walled off by bamboo and barbed wire. Few city sounds had reached inside the camps and contact with the outside (mostly to smuggle food) was forbidden—the Japanese beat up, shaved the heads of, and killed internees for breaking rules. So, after a while, Bandung had stopped being real and we forgot we lived inside it.

We steamed into the city as an orange sun sank away and it promptly turned dark. Ours must have been the day's last train because, once the other passengers had scuttled off, the dimly lit station grew still; even small sounds rebounded from the high ceiling. Long neglect showed in cracked walls, broken windows, thickets of spider webs; a few human forms in rags sprawled in corners. My father at once hurried off to find transportation to Tjimahi and for the first time since he'd come to fetch us my mother and I were alone.

We'd been on our own a long time. She'd always had to work during the day—all adults and teenagers did—but evenings we talked or were quiet together until lights-out. I thought I knew her well. But, maybe not. She'd changed since my father's arrival. I was used to her eyes often looking, even in conversation, as if she were far away—thinking, dreaming. She'd give you lots of her attention, but not all of it. That was fine: the "look" was one of her ways "of taking care of myself." So, too, was reading into the night, when books were still permitted, and to hell with lights-out. Or insisting, when she came home from work, on being alone for a while—"That's how I restore myself." Or never sharing, as some mothers did, her food rations with me because, she said, those women risked illness, then death, and leaving their kids orphans. All through the camps she'd taken care by being cautious, accepting people and situations as they were, and using her "common sense" which was linked to her be-true-to-yourself rule (endlessly urged on me) which, really, meant being your *best* self. But when she saw my father the "look" went away. And, as the hours passed and the two of them laughed and talked, often in English to be private, and the three of us travelled, it didn't return, and it wouldn't in the days and weeks ahead. Her eyes were very alert. My father needed all her attention.

In the quiet station I felt his absence, how *there* he was when he was. I pulled on Hubie's boots, finally feeling it was okay now; stomped them down making an echo: a perfect fit. From the station's tracks rose the same smell as in Makasar; insects whirred and thrummed. The green dress hung on her; she'd worn it last on the first Christmas Day in camp when, the only non-Dutch person there, she'd ended up singing, alone and off-key, "Hark the Herald Angels Sing," and had run away crying. I hadn't seen her cry again. I clumped around dragging my feet, "sloff-sloffing" like Japanese officers did in their boots. She watched: yes, that's how they'd moved all right.

I asked her if Jerry would still be the same old Jerry.

She wasn't a mother who touched a lot, but then she took my cheeks between her hands and softly squeezed a fishmouth. Yes, she said smiling, Jerry would be same old Jerry when we saw him tonight. But he would be *more*.

How?

He would be wiser.

Why?

Because, she said, letting my face go, Jerry had been "his own boss" for a long time.

What about Daddy?

Daddy had been there, yes. And Daddy would certainly have kept an eye on Jerry. All the same, Jerry had been on his own a lot, too. He hadn't had me, or her, after all. Also, knowing Jerry, he would have kept an eye on Daddy, right?

True. Jerry had always watched out for me, even her.

Would he be awake when we got to Tjimahi?

Oh yes.

I had another question, not asked sooner because we hadn't been alone. Were we, I wanted to know, really free now?

She looked around the quiet building. The shapes in the shadows didn't stir. She swung her arms sideways, fluttered her hands, and like an airplane, but standing still, looped this way and that, as Jerry and I used to do playing pilots. Yes, she laughed, oh yes, oh hell yes, you bet, we really were damn well free!

I had to ask though: Weren't we going to just another camp in Tjimahi? With a fence? With rules?

Sure, but it would be temporary.

Were the English going to shoot the Japs? *All* the Japs?

No, she didn't think so.

Why *not*? They'd beaten us. Starved us. Killed us. Hubie was dead. We could've all …

She held up her hand, frowning—until the words were ready. That's just how she'd looked once very early on in camp. She'd had an important message then, and repeated it so Jerry and I would remember. "The Japanese soldiers," she'd told us, "have guns and they are dangerous. They don't like you, even if they smile at you. We are their enemy and if we disobey them or get in their way they will kill us. Always be polite, always be serious, always stay calm. Don't laugh, don't smile, don't joke. Don't look them in the eye. I am afraid and I know that you are afraid. But you'll be less afraid if you remember what I'm telling you." Now in Bandung station she said slowly, "We were at war, but it's over. Get it through your head—the war is over. Put it behind you. Get on with life. Get on to the next damn adventure! And understand: it was Japanese military men who made us suffer—not a whole nation." And in the days to come, in different words and every chance she got, she'd hammer this new message home—to me, to Jerry, to herself, and perhaps also to my father.

WAYSON CHOY

from

Paper Shadows

A Chinatown Memoir

THE WAR IN ASIA and Europe hardly interested me, though it seemed to me that everyone in Chinatown talked incessantly of it. Mother was involved in fundraisers, selling war bonds and collecting money, and volunteered to join the teams of women armed with pins and ribboned labels who trooped outside of Chinatown on tag days. They stood, rattling their tin donation cans, on the busiest corners in downtown Vancouver—on *low fan gaai*, on *white-people streets*, such as on Granville, near the Hudson's Bay, or on the hectic corner near the Bon Ton Shop and the Capitol Theatre. Signs in some merchants' front windows boasted: WE HIRE WHITE LABOUR ONLY.

The bustling corners west along Hastings near Spencer's and Woodward's department stores were also covered. Mother was to take up a corner with one of the actresses new to the Sing Kew company. The woman, one of a half-dozen players who had come up from a troupe stranded in Seattle's Chinatown, had a lean, stern face.

"Bring Sonny, of course," the actress had said when Mother asked her if I might come along. We were just leaving the mezzanine floor at Ming Wo's hardware store, where volunteers gathered to pick up their donation cans and assignments. As Fifth Aunty tells this story, the slender lady looked at her ageing face in her compact mirror and then looked at us.

"You stand between your mother and me, Sonny. I'll play the granny."

Mother asked whether she had heard any more from her family in Canton. There were rumours, she replied. Her two grandsons might have survived. But with the Japanese occupying the city, it was too soon to know what had happened. There were only the Pathé newsreels and the pictures in *LIFE*, images of panicked refugees and devastation in the bombed-out cities of Shanghai and Canton, and the eyewitness accounts of atrocities reported in the Chinese newspapers.

"Just as bad as Nanking, Sonny," Fifth Aunty said. "The Japanese bayonet live people. Toss the children in the air!"

"We fight our own way," the actress said, letting me carry her tin can. She helped me to button up my coat. She put her arms around me.

"If my family gone," she said, "you remember me, won't you, Sonny?"

According to Fifth Aunty, everyone at the store laughed because my eyes widened and I nodded my head so eagerly. She showed Mother and me a picture of her China family, her grandsons.

"Yes, yes, I remember," Fifth Aunty said. "A picture of her grandsons, *twins*, five or six years old, just like you, standing in a garden beside their mother."

Neither Fifth Aunty nor I could remember if the two boys survived. I remember putting three coins in the empty collection can so that they would make a good loud rattle, loud enough maybe to be heard in China.

TWO OR THREE MEMBERS OF the Women's Auxiliary of the China Salvation League of Vancouver covered each of Chinatown's busy corners, urging passers-by to surrender their coins:

"Small change for *Big Victory,* sir!"

Mother's and my job was to shake the tin can vigorously, taking turns, since we were both too tongue-tied to shout out *"Change for Victory!"* either in Chinese or in English. Mother hardly spoke English at all, and her Chinese habit of adding a last *ah*-vowel to any final word turned *Vic-tor-ree* into a plea for donations to the city of *Vic-tor-ree-*AHH!

"Never mind, Lilly," said the actress in impeccable Cantonese. "You and Sonny keep smiling."

Mother's job was to pin CHINA–CANADA VICTORY ribbons on bystanders; my job was to rattle the can. I also tried to shout the English words, but my voice definitely lacked volume. However, I was not entirely too shy to smile. There was a good reason to do that: the lady had promised me an ice-cream cone at the end of our stint.

If someone bent down to make a deposit, I stopped shaking the can, listening as the change *clinked* loudly at the bottom, and grinning as if it were falling into my own piggy bank at home. When Father stood with us for a few minutes one day, he noticed how I barely smiled, even looked disappointed, if folding money was pushed into the slot. I was like those Russian dogs trained to salivate at the sound of a bell: coins provoked a better response from me.

Evenings and weekends, the women of Chinatown folded bandages in church basements, packed first-aid kits in Tong Association halls, knitted endless socks and sweaters at socials, and boxed and shipped all these donated supplies to Kwong Ming Tong headquarters in the embattled homeland. For the war effort, everyone saved up balls of string and tinfoil, collected old pots and pans, bundled up newspapers, rendered lard and repatched old clothes.

There were no end of fundraisers, bake sales, church and school charity drives for the Red Cross, and the like. The grand Imperial Theatre was rented for performances of special operas depicting the war in China, with actors dressed up in copies of Chinese and Japanese military uniforms, uniforms as drab as Canadian ones, and having none of the flash and splendour I expected an opera costume to have. To my disappointment, when the Chinese soldiers began pursuing the fleeing Japanese, waving their olive-coloured sleeves instead of bright pennants, neither side seemed to be scaling a mountain, only a pyramid of chairs and benches.

I hated those modern shows. The acrobatics and the rifle fire kept me alert, but all the colourful sword-dances had disappeared, and the drama with them. Gone were the gem-encrusted robes, the spears and tridents. Gone, too, the quivering feathered headdresses, replaced by dumpy military hats. And these operas featured an oppressive number of arias.

Mercifully, these propaganda displays ended earlier than usual. Mother would wake me up, and we would have tea with friends at the Mount Shasta. Then she would take me into the magical world of the Sing Kew, in a storage room on the second floor, adjoining the building's common residential area.

The room was packed full of old stage props. The swords and spears hung on the brick walls. The *real* opera costumes reflected the dim light like scattered fireflies. The broad-shouldered robes were draped over stout dummies or suspended on wires in the air, like ghosts. By comparison, the drab Chinese and Japanese military uniforms stood like a dead forest. There, in cleared spaces, tables were set up and mah-jong sets spilled out. Meanwhile, an oversized wok was used to stir-fry the *sui yah,* the *late-night meal,* for the actors and musicians, and the cook used to let me taste a bit of stir-fried chicken. I hated bok choy or any kind of greens. Tea was poured for all, though sometimes it was hot water or rice-gruel water instead.

Mother played mah-jong with the theatre people and the ladies of the Chinatown auxiliary. Someone always herded the children into groups and entertained us in a room with a dark carpet and large carved chairs. There were old metal trucks with warped wheels and stuffed dolls and toy guns and spinning tops to play with.

I preferred to play with the opera dolls, the puppet-like minia-tures I discovered one evening in a small trunk behind some discarded scenery. The fierce-looking dolls, dressed in embroidered robes, gripped tiny swords and tridents or painted fans and wore jewelled headdresses. At first I was told not to play with them, but then someone tall, a man with a kind voice, showed me how to hold the heads of the dolls, as their necks were only stitched onto the costumes.

"Don't be rough with them," he said.

There were eight of them. I picked one up, held it in my hand, gently, gently. I believed at once that, when it was dark and everyone was asleep, the dolls in their majestic costumes came alive: stood up, bowed, and told elaborate tales in quivering small voices.

I soon discovered it was possible to prop them up with the stick stands in the trunk. I made opera music, pretending I could sing, and eventually attracted a crowd of adults to look at my "shows." Other children were allowed to watch me play with the opera dolls, but, when I asked them to join me, someone always came and said, "Only Sonny can play with these. You just watch."

Sometimes when Father came home from his seasonal sailings, I would play-act Cantonese opera for him. Aunty Freda gave me some old silk shirts whose long sleeves she slit and then restitched, so that I could swing my hands and have my own silk watersleeves cascade into the air. At first, Father was charmed.

Mother helped me set up pots and pans, and let me bang them with chopsticks and spatulas. I wore old hats and decorated them with lengths of ribbon and Mother's junk jewellery. Aunty Freda picked out multicoloured remnants from her sewing bags, and stitched and safety-pinned the pieces of silk and velvet brocade to the front and back of a flowery cotton shirt. Belted, the multilayered shirt looked, to me, like the splendid costume of the South Wind General.

To make myself fierce-looking, I slashed lipstick on my cheeks, rubbed rouge on my forehead and dipped into the stove for soot to outline my "beard." I ended up resembling a scruffy clown more than a warrior, and Uncle Wally's response was to dash into our hallway to stifle his laughter.

I didn't care. Serious theatre was not for everyone.

Father, however, no longer found my operas charming. He was angry with Mother.

"Why do you let Sonny have your lipstick?"

"I don't," Mother said. "He just takes it."

Father spoke of the notoriety that my costumed dramas, now performed publicly on our front porch and in front of our house, were bringing to our household. My cousin King had been seen running down Keefer, waving a toy sword that Third Uncle had bought for me. I ran ahead with a real red pennant tied to a bamboo pole taller than both of us, a pole given to me by one of the actors from the theatre.

"Now you can have your own army," the actor said, and showed me how to wave it so that its triple silk tails swirled like flames. Behind me, a hundred warriors would follow.

"Everyone's asking why a boy dresses up like that," Father complained. "Why do you let him behave like that?"

"I don't encourage it," Mother said.

Amused neighbours gathered. Mrs Wong applauded. Some grown-ups even threw me pennies and nickels; others walked away, shaking their heads.

Now and again, a friend or two banged on the pots and pans to accompany my screeching imitation of screeching arias. But often these friends, mostly my age, would be intimidated by the laughter of older boys and stop playing with me.

ONE DAY GUNG-GUNG left his Victoria family to visit with us for a week. (Grandmother refused to come with him.) He had come to Vancouver to see a doctor. The old man looked very tired and took a taxi everywhere, as he had trouble walking. Father told Third Uncle, "He has heart problems."

"Too much stress in Victoria," Third Uncle commented, and looked over at my big ears and said nothing more.

"He's going to move in with Freda," Mother said.

One afternoon, visiting with Aunty Freda, the old man witnessed one of my performances, and he said to Father in his formal Cantonese, his voice weakened by his mysterious illness, "What ... what will become of such a boy?"

"Oh, leave him alone," Aunty Freda said. "He's just got a good imagination. Take your medicine."

"Mother spoils him," Father said. "Spoils him too much."

I went on playing. I liked Aunty Freda. I didn't care what Grandfather or Father had to say. As Gung-Gung sipped his bottled Chinese medicine, I wondered for a moment why he looked so ashen. He didn't look like the man who was always bossing me around, telling me when to talk and where to walk.

"Ah-Gung," Mother said, looking worried, "please take more medicine."

When Grandfather coughed and held his side, the bottle shaking in his hand, I felt that I could do anything I wanted to. Just because I wanted to. And as I did not worry about happiness, I didn't know then that I was happy.

———•·•———

AFTER THE USUAL PLEAS for donations to the war effort had been shouted out over the squeaking microphone at the Sing Kew Theatre, a man in a suit stepped up to announce the Chinese and English names of enlisted men sitting in the audience.

"Soldiers of Chinatown, receive our gratitude," the man shouted in formal Cantonese. After each name was called, a soldier stood up. My opera aunties would swerve their heads in unison.

"Hai-lah! See!" Chulip Sim nudged Mother with her elbow. "There's the Lew boy! The other one *there,* Wong Sim's second son!"

The uniformed men looked shyly around, listening as their names rustled like autumn leaves through the hall. After the last soldier was introduced, the audience burst into applause. Mothers and girlfriends smiled and wiped their eyes.

"My oldest is talking of going to Burma," Leong Sim said, "maybe India." Mother held me tighter. "They need two-language soldiers who look oriental."

"Why?" Mother asked.

One of the men turned around in his seat and said, "Make good-looking Jap spies."

The soldiers sat down, their shapes like shadows around me. Unwanted and deemed undesirable before 1942, Chinatown's young men were now being sent to secret camps: for language training, to learn how to infiltrate enemy lines, to plant bombs and to deliver covert messages. They were to carry poison, in case suicide was the only option.

But little boys sitting on their mother's knees did not understand anything about the overseas battles or the desperate need the Allies had for spies. I did know that the war had placed limits on Chinatown celebrations, created inconvenient curfews for night society of the kind Mother enjoyed, and, most disappointingly, had banned the burning of firecrackers.

Any evidence I saw of the war on the streets of Vancouver was mundane: posters and uniforms. Mother would not stay to watch the propaganda films that were shown outdoors in the crowded alleyway between Hastings and Pender, off Columbia, the black-and-white images flashing across a taut cloth screen high above our heads. As she dragged me away, I glimpsed a vision of a panicked Shanghai street, heard the sound of planes and bombs, heard a Chinese voice speaking harshly, but saw nothing more.

"We visit Chulip Sims," Mother said, pulling me away.

I thought war should have been like what I saw enacted in the Sing Kew Theatre: there should have been silk and swords, the sound of drums and cymbals, urging my dragging feet to step lively.

THE CANADIAN MILITARY UNIFORMS were a disappointment, but I was impressed by the smart outfits worn by the Capitol or Beacon theatre ushers. Their braided-gold epaulets, perched on padded shoulders, appealed to me much more than the shine of brass buttons and the thud of heavy boots.

The military men who walked through Chinatown were mainly Caucasian sailors and soldiers, tall as giants. The city of Vancouver, with its crowded railway stations and packed harbours, was the last stop before soldiers and sailors shipped out; and the perfumed and powdered ladies from the back rooms of Gastown hotels and bars made Chinatown a favourite place to take shore leave. The military men and their dates elbowed each other and pointed at exotic displays of braised ducks in shop windows and wandered into Lucky Star Drugs for smokes. Once, while Mother was negotiating the price of a rare pair of stockings, I remember, a soldier pushed through the busy aisles of Kuo Kong Silk to outbid her.

By the winter of 1944, the curfews had been relaxed, and there were fewer air-raid exercises. The pages of war news posted on the walls of the *Chinese Times* building and stuck on the windows of the Kwok Min Tang Reading Room showed maps of Europe and Asia, where the Germans and the Japanese were retreating "like wounded dogs," the elders said; the men's talk across the tables of the Chinese Benevolent Association, even the sad letters from China, all spoke of oncoming peace, of an inevitable victory for the Allies.

Chinatown held its breath. Basement stocks of forbidden fireworks were unearthed from sand barrels, ready to be lit in celebration. Barbershops displayed more and more Union Jacks and Nationalist China flags. Chinatown was humming with expectation and jammed with tourists. The Japanese and Germans were everywhere being routed, beaten back. People were sniffing the air, waiting.

When noisier couples sauntered by us, Mother looked away, discomfited. She would clutch her purse tighter, and jerk me closer to her, so that I, too, stumbled. Thinking it was a game, I always laughed or jerked back. Mother's quick pull on my arm caused me a few times to fall, sprawling away from her. On the ground, I was the centre of street attention. Once, a soldier patted me on my head and lifted me up into the air. His lady, after she dusted my coat off, reached into her purse and handed me a shiny coin.

"New as a nickel," she said.

The soldier said, "You all right, Sonny Boy?"

I was staring, open-mouthed, astonished: the total stranger knew my English name. Mother forgot to tell me to say *"Doh jhay.*

Thank you." But after that incident, Mother seemed less worried about the high-spirited strangers that crowded Chinatown.

"They seem so *kai doy,* so *rough,*" Mother complained.

"Don't be silly," Chulip Sim said at the mah-jong table. "They're on our side." All the other ladies agreed.

I saluted some of the men who saluted me, and sometimes they gave me gum and candy. Then Mother made me stop because I was being spoiled.

To me, all of the outsiders looked perfectly ordinary, just part of the growing crowd of tourists who now ate at the affordable chop-suey houses. The round tables and high booths of the Yen Lock, the Chung King and the On Lock Yuen were nightly filled with as many white customers as Chinese.

Outsiders happily rediscovered the hand-made quality goods of Chinatown, buying inexpensive fitted shirts from Mr Wong's Modern Silk store near the corner of Main and Pender, or ordering jackets and pants ("Free pants!") to be made from pre-war bolts of cloth hoarded for years in Chinatown. At Pender and Carrall, popular Modernized Tailors, next to the Chinese Freemasons' Hall, blocked hats and made suits to measure.

And because they were featuring popular bands and local jazz singers nightly, the New W.K. and the Mandarin Garden Cabaret attracted exuberant, young crowds. Everyone wanted to swing and jive, to be part of the passing parade.

Up to the mid-1930s, Chinatown was an impoverished, undesirable place for tourists. The restaurants and tailor shops then were mostly empty of visitors, who came either for the New Year's fireworks or as part of a trouble-making gang. Perhaps Hollywood movies initiated the changing attitudes towards Chinatown. Films featuring Anna May Wong and Charlie Chan made Chinatown seem exotic and less frightening than the Fu Manchu opium-addict world of the silent era.

Chinatown was now seen as a friendly two-block exotic adventure, safe terrain in which to spend the extra wartime dollars pouring into West Coast port cities such as Vancouver.

WHILE THE TOURISTS WERE discovering Chinatown, I was discovering my own exotic landscape: East Hastings Street.

To me, not anything in Chinatown could prove as interesting as what I now worshipped: *c-o-w-b-o-y-s*. I thought that all the world's cowboys lived in the Hastings Street hotels. Nothing quickened my heart more than gawking at the rough, unshaven men who swerved out of barroom doors and loudly sang rude songs, swore openly, spat anywhere, and shouted at Mother, "Hey, good lookin'!"

Mother and her friends marched by these street corners, looking neither right nor left, the flowers in their bonnets bobbing with majestic indifference. As far as I knew, the ladies were never harmed; East Hastings was an everyday city nuisance that paralleled Pender Street, a gauntlet the ladies ran with cheek and courage.

"If any of those *kai doys,* those *louts,* try anything," Chulip Sim instructed my mother, "take your hatpin and use it. Like this."

She jabbed into the air to demonstrate. Long hatpins were perfect weapons. Chulip Sim had already taught Mother how to use a hatpin in dark movie houses, where the hands of strangers sometimes wandered onto a woman's lap.

"And like this," Chulip Sim said, jabbing downwards. "That stops them."

"I use my gun," I said, and fired a cap into the air. The *bang!* echoed loudly across the mezzanine of Ming Wo's. Mr Wong looked up sternly from his counter down below. His eyes were hard and piercing. Mother took my gun away and put it into her purse. Chulip Sim gave me a hard candy.

"Just walk quickly away, Choy Sim," Chulip Sim said to Mother. "Those *ngah-shee, cow turds,* too drunk to do any real damage."

"Haihn fie-dee!" Chulip Sim said. *"Walk quickly!"*

But these were the same street corners where I pulled back on Mother's hand, dragged my heels along the sidewalks and feigned an inability to keep up. My instinct was to take in everything cowboy-and-Indian that Mother avoided.

Walking that stretch of East Hastings Street, I had to be careful: if I dug in my heels too much, scraping them, Mother would tuck her purse under her arm and scoop me up, huffing away. Sometimes I got a knock on the head with her knuckles. If we were walking with Chulip Sim, each of the women would suddenly take one of my arms and yank me along, double-quick. It was a fine art for me to slow Mother and Chulip Sim down. Just to catch a glimpse of the colourful, churlish cowboy crowd in front of the hotel *Men Only* entrances, I tried everything. I wanted to be a cowboy, too.

My trump card was the discovery that some of my "uncles"—the bachelor men of Chinatown—loved the Saturday-matinée double-feature cowboy movies at the Rex and Lux as much as any kid did. Tagging along with them, starting from the age of four, I got to see as many horse operas as opportunity would allow.

———

THE UNCLES I GOT TO KNOW were descendants, not of the first Chinese who came in the 1850s to pan for gold, but of the Chinese who came during the railway and steamship days of British Columbia. Chinatown called them "bachelor men."

After the "Last Spike" of 1885—the end of the Canadian Pacific Railway contracts—the pioneer Chinese labourers' usefulness ended. Instead of finding themselves returned to China, as many had been promised, thousands of railway labourers, and some women who worked as prostitutes, were betrayed and abandoned in near-poverty. Left to fend for themselves in mountainside work camps and in ghost towns, hundreds travelled east to work in mines or to establish laundries and restaurants in the small towns and cities across Canada.

The majority of the men and women found their own way back from the Rockies to the ghetto Chinatowns of Vancouver and Victoria. Those who remained for whatever reason, often because they were too ashamed to leave, or were too poor or too sick, lived in Vancouver's slum tenements and shacks formerly occupied by Irish, Italian and Eastern European labourers along Water Street and Dupont–Pender.

When I was small, I remember seeing the last of these old men sitting on the steps of Chinatown, waiting to die, chatting and laughing at my toddling legs. Beneath street signs that read, in English: NO SPITTING, they spat out bad waters.

Of those unemployed men stranded in B.C., countless numbers died of malnutrition in Chinatown's rooming-houses; throughout the Depression, bodies were found in the makeshift shacks along False Creek. Suicide was not uncommon.

Those who returned to China by 1910 found that in the famine-struck villages of southern Kwangtung province a man could barely earn five cents a day—if he could find work, that is. In Canada, if there was work, Chinese men were being paid twenty-five cents a day. Before the 1923 Exclusion Act, other immigrants took the place of those returning to China. These men and women had to find work in Gold Mountain or their families would starve.

By the 1920s, the men were finding jobs in B.C. lumber camps and shingle mills, in the galleys of CPR steamships and in fishing camps. These men, like our kin-name uncles, Uncle Dai Kew, and Sam Gung, Third Uncle, all worked long hours and saved their money. The few women who came over took jobs as waitresses, slaved away in laundries, became the brides or concubines of wealthy merchants, served as house servants or worked as prostitutes.

The men and women spoke of the day when they would be reunited with their families. Tragically, the passing of the 1890s Chinese Head Tax, a tax raised from fifty dollars to five hundred dollars by 1904, had proved prohibitive for those who earned seasonal wages of twenty-five cents an hour. After Parliament's passing of the Exclusion Act of 1923, which forbade any Chinese from immigrating to Canada, except for a few merchants or scholars, Vancouver's Chinatown entered what historian David C. Lai has called "the withering stage." By 1934, the province of B.C. offered to pay one-way passage home for those Chinese wanting to go back to China, on condition that they never return to Canada.

In the ten years between 1931 and 1941, Chinatown's population was cut in half, to seven thousand. The racist Exclusion Act was made into law on July 1, a date my uncles and aunts always called "the Day of Shame."

MANY OF THE MEN REMAINING in Canada had to keep working in order to send their family remittances, becoming, in their isolation, "bachelor men." My family elders and uncles were among the last wave of Chinese immigrants from China. Until after the Second World War, no Chinese, even those born in Canada, like me, were given citizenship: I was a Resident Alien, forbidden to vote or to enter any profession, including law, teaching, medicine and engineering.

"Everything better after the war," Third Uncle used to say to my parents, like a mantra of hope.

Third Uncle's wife and son were in Hong Kong, living in a third-floor room on the remittances that somehow managed to reach them despite the war. He had not seen them for seven years. It would be another ten before they would reunite. Resident Aliens or not, Third Uncle's generation dreamed of one day sending for their wives and children, who would all have enough to eat in Gold Mountain.

By the onset of the Second World War, the bones of the dead Chinese who never made it back to China—who died of old age, of despair, of ill-health—languished by the ton in the Bone House in Victoria at Foul Point (Harling Bay), or were tagged and wrapped in gunny sacks piled up in damp warehouses in Nanaimo and in Vancouver.

"Spirits," Fifth Aunty called them. "Spirits wait for the war to end. Wait to go back to family."

Chinatown residents were never sojourners by choice. If they were buried in Gold Mountain, their coffins were packed into Victoria's segregated grounds at Ross Bay or triple-buried in the rocky headland at Foul Point. In Vancouver, the dead were interred in poorly drained land reserved "For Chinese Only."

"Yes, yes, many go back," Fifth Aunty told me, thinking perhaps of her own father and mother's bones.

"Why?" I asked. "They're dead."

Fifth Aunty gave me a puzzled look. Tears welled up in her eyes. When she spoke, at last, I could barely hear her words.

"Bones long for respect," she said.

"WE ALL DO what we have to do," my uncles used to say, when I asked them why they stayed so long at the tea houses. "You just be good boy and obey your grandfather and your parents."

When they weren't labouring, many of the bachelor men gambled, socialized, drank and fought, kept women or kept to themselves— did what men might do to keep their sexual and mental sanity, separated these five, ten, twenty years from their wives and children. With plenty of bachelor time on their hands between seasonal jobs, and haunted always by the family life they desperately missed, many became extensions of the families already established in Chinatown.

We shared meals with such men. The uncles would bring a pound of pork or some vegetables, sometimes a pound cake or tea cookies from the CPR galleys. Mother would be busy cooking in the kitchen, and Father would read his paper. I got to sit and listen to Old China histories, even watched a few weep over photos of distant families, of suddenly grown-up sons and daughters. Their Toisanese and other dialects sounded like music to me, instructional notes sung for my benefit.

"My boy smart as you, Sonny," I was told by one uncle. "You be sure to go to school. Be even smarter."

I have no doubt that many bachelor men would have been bitterly jealous of couples like Father and Mother who were safely settled in Vancouver. But a few of them must have felt that a surrogate-family life was better than no family life at all, and sought to balance the empty hours they faced in cell-like tenement rooms on outings with the children of working parents.

"You're going to have an adventure," Mother would announce. "You're going out today."

A tall man, who always seemed much older than Father or Mother, would be introduced to me. While Mother served tea and small pastries, I would shyly meet the new "uncle." I watched how familiarly he spoke to Father, listened as they chatted away about the war in China, the family, and, I suppose, about politics and the weather.

Finally, as if everyone had agreed upon this moment, Mother, looking at the clock, would say to me, "Are you ready to step out with Uncle?"

The very first time it happened, I was shocked to discover that she meant I was to leave the house with a stranger. Alone. Without her. Despite my concerted effort to cling to Mother, my arms were briskly threaded through my coat sleeves, and reluctantly I let the friendly giant take my hand.

"What shall we do today?" the stranger asked.

"See cowboys," I said.

By age five, I was a veteran, an opportunist.

DAVID MACFARLANE

from

The Danger Tree
Memory, War, and the Search for a Family's Past

BETTER OR WORSE?

HAMILTON, ONTARIO, IS AN unexceptional place. I was always fond of it. I grew up there. I learned to read and write and swim there. And year after year, in the classrooms of Earl Kitchener School, I seemed to embark on the same project there. My mother often complained about this. "Not again," she'd say when I brought home news of the assignment. "Don't they know that any place else in the world exists?" For every year another teacher instructed another class to put together another carefully underlined booklet of stapled foolscap. It was a social studies report about Hamilton, and I always called mine "The Ambitious City."

Usually, my pencil-crayoned maps showed Hamilton's convenient location in central Canada, and its enviable proximity to the fabulous sights of Niagara Falls and Toronto, and to the vast American market of Buffalo, New York. Cut-out magazine photographs of massive freighters—and once, by mistake, an aircraft carrier—illustrated the city's fortuitous position on the transportation routes of the Great Lakes. There were tonnage charts, favourably comparing the city's steel production to that of London, New York, and Paris, and there were carefully drawn pictures of dinosaurs to illustrate our colourful history. Hamilton, I stated half a dozen times if I stated it once, was situated at the hub of the Golden Horseshoe—at the very heart of Ontario's vast wealth, inexhaustible energy, exciting culture, and wonderful industry—and my projects always concluded with ringing civic pride.

Hamilton's stature in the world was obvious to me, as I'm sure it was to my teachers. After all, they'd assigned and marked dozens of nearly identical projects every year of their professional lives. But even if they hadn't, all they had to do to see the evidence of Hamilton's extraordinary civic success was to drive out of the city—an adventure that my mother suspected Hamilton teachers were not allowed to undertake. But there it was. During the 1950s, the population on the WELCOME TO HAMILTON sign on the Queen Elizabeth Highway seemed to increase every time our family car went past it.

In my memory Hamilton was a wonderful place to grow up. It had dusty, sprawling steel mills in the east end, and solid brick homes in the west. In the middle was the constantly aspiring but never quite succeeding downtown, a solemn statue of Queen Victoria ("Model Wife and Mother"), the YMCA, and, almost in the shadow of the Niagara Escarpment, the Medical Arts Building. My father, an ophthalmologist who was frequently called upon to remove slivers of steel from steelworkers' eyes, shared a cool, hushed office on its sixth floor with his father, an ear, nose, and throat man. I used to stop there, late on Saturday mornings, on my way home from junior swim at the Y.

At the Medical Arts Building, the parking lot attendant washed the doctors' cars and checked the oil. Inside the back door, there was an old-fashioned switchboard where the eggman always dropped off our family's eggs, fresh from the country. There were inevitable fox-wrapped old ladies waiting in the lobby. The elevator operators wore white gloves. On the sixth floor, the polished corridor smelled of rubbing alcohol. The place was as silent as a cathedral until suddenly a rattle of mail, dropped into the chute from the floor above, fell noisily past my father's office door while I sat in his waiting-room looking at *Life, Look,* and the *Saturday Evening Post.*

When I stopped in, my father was tending to his last patients of the day. "Better or worse?" he'd say. I could hear him through the closed door of his darkened examination room as he adjusted lenses and changed focal lengths. He clicked the lenses into place on the metal frames. "Better or worse?" Click, click. "Better or worse?" Click, click. By noon the patients were gone. Then, having asked enough questions for one day, my father would drive me cheerfully home for Saturday lunch without saying a word.

This was fine. But as I grew into a teenager these silences—my silences now—grew more ominous. My mother sat each evening at one end of the dinner table. She wore bright dresses, seemed always to have sunshine in her fine, light hair, and her voice was eager and touched with the faint music of a beautiful accent. She was pretty and lively and always wanted to know how we were and what we had done with our day. Her attempts at conversation usually came to nothing. At the other end of the table, my father calmly folded back the Hamilton *Spectator* and sipped his coffee. I sat between them, sullen as a rock.

"Nobody," my mother said. "Not a soul around here talks." This didn't come as news.

On my father's side of the family there are silences that are legendary. We don't talk about them, naturally. But among us they're legendary all the same. We think about them. Often we think about them during the stillnesses in which they occur. And we could, if pressed into speech, describe them in some detail. Conjured into visibility, they would probably look like a November afternoon in Southern Ontario, for that is the part of the country my father's side of the family is from. They would be extended planes of grey, marked here and there with steeples and the fine blackness of leafless trees. They would look like the bare limestone ridges of the Niagara Escarpment and they would sound—if it were possible to attribute to them a sound—like distant crows heard through the windows above the sherry decanters in the chill of a late afternoon, or like the pouring of ice water into Waterford goblets in preparation for Sunday dinner.

I believe the silences had their beginnings in the passage of my father's ancestors from Scotland to Canada almost two hundred years ago. Or so I conclude from the evidence of family heirlooms. Gloomy pieces of mahogany have come down to us. So have copper boxes to keep kindling in, and coal scuttles now used to hold old newspapers, and volumes of Walter Scott printed on fine, thin paper and bound in leather and used, as far as ever I could ascertain, to give book-ends something to do. Cookie tins, china figurines, antimacassars, recipes, baptismal gowns, gout stools, fire irons, and teaspoons have been passed from generation to generation. We keep things. We aren't careless with our history.

But we have little that predates the family's arrival in Canada, and nothing—no story, no memento—of the trip across the Atlantic. Or so I thought until one day, sitting in my parents' living-room, listening to the rush of warm air from the heat vents and bracing myself for the hourly uproar of the cuckoo clock, I realized that after the bald green bluffs of Scotland disappeared astern there was nothing more for my ancestors to see. Certainly, after a few days out there was nothing more to talk about. They didn't really know where they were going and they were happy to forget what they'd left behind. In Scotland, the rents for their farms had been raised to impossible levels, and where that hint was not taken, others were dropped: torches, for instance. Their crofts had been burned to the ground. Their land had been turned to sheep-walks. Whether things would be better in the new world, or worse, was anybody's guess. So they said nothing. Seasick and miserable, they continued to say nothing. And this was their souvenir. This is what we inherited.

THE FIRST LANDFALL OF my father's dour ancestors, and consequently their first subject of conversation in weeks, would have been the steep black cliffs of Cape Bonavista in Newfoundland. I may be the only person on earth who could imagine this an interesting coincidence. Certainly they didn't. Their first look at the new world wasn't promising.

A landmass of forty-two thousand square miles, the island of Newfoundland sits, all dark cliffs and muscled capes, like a rugged jigsaw piece of peninsulas and bays between Labrador, Cape Breton, and the cold grey seas of the North Atlantic. "A monstrous mass of rock and gravel," wrote the American missionary R. T. S. Lowell in 1858, "almost without soil, like a strange thing from the bottom of the great deep, lifted up, suddenly, into sunshine and storm, but belonging to the watery darkness out of which it has been reared." ...

———•◆•———

MY FATHER'S SEASICK ANCESTORS weren't expecting Eden. But they had no intention of settling in a colder, poorer version of Scotland. They sailed on, keeping the spindrifts and storm gusts of the Avalon Peninsula to their distant starboard. Not for them Petty Harbour or Witless Bay, Renews, Cape Race, or Trepassey. They weren't fishermen. They were farmers, and they sailed past the dark, surging crevasses of the Burin Peninsula, past the French islands of St. Pierre and Miquelon, through the Cabot Strait, and into the mouth of the St. Lawrence, on their way to Upper Canada. And they ended up talking as directly as they came: without the wayward tacks of complaint or entertainment or exaggeration. They sailed from the noun they'd left to the noun where they were going without digression, without anecdote, and without idle chatter in between.

They landed at Quebec and then, by cart and horse and corduroy road, headed west a few hundred miles to the clearings near Kingston, Ontario. Here, United Empire Loyalists had already settled, fleeing the American Revolution and displaying their selfless allegiance to the Crown by taking full advantage of the vast land grants offered to British subjects in Upper Canada. This wasn't Eden either, but it did have soil, and a generation later my family's silences began to lose their elaborate Gaelic bitterness. They incorporated the untroubled, empty views of Ontario into their temperament—the fields, the windbreaks, the circling hawks—and settled down to stay in the quietude of rising bread and in the chill fall of November dusks. Then the silences spread, like the shadows of a family tree, across the tilled and frost-ridden landscape. One hundred and eighty years later they came down to us like heirlooms.

And these silences were silences. There was nothing momentary about them. They were never just gaps in conversation. They had nothing to do with pausing for breath, or, in the midst of a lively discussion, providing a beat between subjects. They were full-blown marathons of speechlessness—and, as I eventually came to realize, they drove my mother crazy.

Once, my father's older brother presided over an entire Christmas dinner without, so far as I could tell, uttering a syllable. It was in 1962, and as the evening drew to its close—as a Lake Ontario snowstorm gusted around the house and my aunt passed a superfluous tray of brownies—I remember watching him closely and nervously, the way a crowd watches a pitcher on the verge of a perfect game.

"A white Christmas after all," someone said. A teaspoon tinkled against the china.

"The roads will be icy," someone else responded. Outside, the frozen branches of maple trees creaked in the wind. My diabetic grandmother—my father's mother—dropped two illicit sugar cubes, with two distinct little splashes, into her cup.

"Well," an aunt said, and sighed. No one else spoke. Eventually someone else asked if she could help with the dishes.

These weren't interruptions in the patter of life. These were lapses of speech that seemed sometimes as if they would go on forever. My mother fidgeted in the face of them, and from time to time mounted brave and hopeless assaults of small talk. Inevitably she was defeated. But she never surrendered entirely. For chief among my mother's peculiarities was that she wasn't from Hamilton.

"Like pulling teeth," my mother said after we had made our farewells that Christmas night and were all inside the car. Throughout the evening my uncle had maintained his silence with the same hospitable agility a graceful conversationalist uses to overcome it. He had gone nine innings without a slip. It seemed an impressive achievement—I was enough my father's son to admire my uncle's ability to say nothing when no one was saying anything of consequence anyway—but my mother's voice was taut as a tow-rope. "At Christmas dinner, if you can believe it. "Hardly. A. Single. Word. Doesn't your family talk to one another?" To which my father, who could hold his own with the best of them when it came to resisting pressure to speak, wisely and aptly said nothing.

I was ten years old, and I had never heard my mother criticize my father's side of the family before. In fact, it had never occurred to me until that Christmas night that our family actually had two sides. Somehow I had imagined that my parents' marriage had unified my various aunts and uncles, cousins and grandparents into a single, happy, indivisible dominion. Its capital was our house in Hamilton—more specifically, it was the bedroom where I kept my toy Mounties lined up along the windowsill, and where, once a year, I wrote thank-you letters to my relatives for their Christmas presents. ("Dear Gran and Gramp; Thank you very much for the socks. They will keep my feet really warm." For my mother's family always sent socks, heavy and cable-knit, always accompanied by ominous warnings about thin ice.) That my mother's family lived far, far away, that they came to visit only occasionally, and that we travelled to see them only on summer holidays, made them no less a part of this grand national scheme.

Now, for the first time, sitting in the back seat of a turquoise 1956 Pontiac, driving through the cold Ontario night along the Queen Elizabeth Highway, I began to realize what my parents had done. I tried to imagine their wedding. On September 12, 1950, in a small ceremony in Brantford, Ontario, that had been overseen by my mother's aunt—my great-aunt Kate, a woman who had also married an Ontario doctor and who had settled near the town of Brantford thirty years earlier—my parents had taken one another for better or worse.

The wedding wasn't held in my mother's hometown because my mother's hometown was so far away from everything—or so it must have seemed to my father's friends and relatives when the notion was first proposed. A rail strike provided a more politic excuse for holding the ceremony in Ontario. Because of the strike, my mother's father didn't attend the ceremony: he drove my mother from the house where she had grown up to the place where the road ended, at a rail trestle over a shallow, black river, and gave away the bride there. I imagine him standing on the bridge in his fedora—as dignified and proud as a father at the altar—watching one of his much-loved daughters disappear with someone who was waiting on the other side to take her to the airport.

I, like most children, had always assumed that my parents' marriage had been preordained, an inevitability. Now I wasn't so sure. Possibly it had been some kind of historical accident. Possibly it had actually been a reckless experiment. I leaned forward in the car and asked how they'd met. My mother told me that she'd met my father on a blind date at the University of Toronto.

I'd often heard the story of how, as a baby, bundled in a wooden box, my mother had almost disappeared through a crack in the river ice while being brought home from a lumber camp by her parents. Now I pondered the chances of a blind date working out very successfully. In a dizzying moment of what felt like motion sickness, I realized suddenly that the odds stacked against my existence had been overwhelming. I stared from the window of our car and wondered whether I was actually a boy in the back seat of a turquoise Pontiac or somebody else. Could I have been a boy sitting at the picture window of a suburban house, surrounded by blinking Christmas lights, watching a turquoise Pontiac pass through the night and wondering who was inside? How was I to know? And at that precise, unnerving moment I didn't know, but over the years I learned the awful truth: it had been a long shot, but I was the boy in the Pontiac all right. I am who I am because inside me is wedded the discomfiture of two societies as distinct from one another as night and day....

———•—•———

MY MOTHER WAS BORN in 1924, twenty-five years before Newfoundland, England's oldest colony, became Newfoundland, Canada's newest province. When she grew up, her music examinations were sent back to England to be marked. Everyone waved Union Jacks on Queen Victoria's birthday. Bonfires burned on the fifth of November. Anything purchased in Newfoundland that was any good had been made in Great Britain. My mother could play "There'll Always Be an England" at the piano without glancing at the sheet music. As a tourist, she once startled the guides at the Tower of London with her encyclopedic knowledge of British history. As a traveller, she once floored an officer of the *Queen Elizabeth 2*, who, at dinner, quoted a line of Rupert Brooke for his ill-educated North American table guests. "You've heard of Brooke?" he sniffed. She quoted back the entire poem to him from memory.

All this changed in 1949. On April Fool's Day, almost a year after a closely fought referendum, Newfoundland and Labrador became part of Canada....

———•◦•———

MY GRANDFATHER'S OPPOSITION TO Confederation, and the fact that I was the first issue of a marriage that began not in Newfoundland, where by custom it should have, but in Ontario—a wedding that was almost precisely coincidental with the island's union with Canada—has made me feel a little uneasy all my life. I was born and raised in Southern Ontario, the wealthiest part of the country. Newfoundland is the poorest: its unemployment rate is still twice the national average, and its fishery is, after centuries of crises, in its worst crisis ever. The island's dreams of offshore oil remain unfulfilled with each passing, inconclusive year. And its most recent government-sponsored industrial venture—a vast and fantastically expensive indoor cucumber farm whose special lights and transparent ceilings didn't do much for cucumbers but lit up the St. John's night like a landed UFO—was as unlikely and as doomed an enterprise as anything either Joey Smallwood or my great-uncle Roland ever dreamed of. When Newfoundlanders resent the rest of Canada, they zero their resentment on exactly the part of Canada from which I come. Up-Along, they call it. And strangers, like me, are called Come From Aways.

My uneasiness has never prevented me from feeling proud of my Newfoundland connection, however, and in the fall of 1963, at the age of eleven, I departed from the traditional topic of my relentlessly annual social studies projects. It wasn't a complete revolution, but it had a certain originality. My mother regarded it as a step in the right direction.

In a blue three-ringed binder I drew maps, traced charts, underlined headings with red pencil-crayon, and composed "Hamilton and Newfoundland: A Comparison." It was difficult to say which place came out on top. Hamilton had 273,991 people; Newfoundland had 438,000 but was, by my estimate, almost a thousand times as big and had more annual precipitation. Hamilton had two major steel foundries and dozens of subsidiary industries; Newfoundland had two paper mills, one international airport, and a seal hunt. In Newfoundland, sixty percent of the population lived in rural areas, whereas in Hamilton no one did. Hamilton had no rivers; Newfoundland, no air pollution. Anecdotal evidence seemed to suggest that Hamilton had fewer ghosts; Newfoundland, fewer industrial-related ophthalmological emergencies. Hamilton had no fishing industry to speak of, but it had less fog and fewer shipwrecks. In a paragraph entitled "Recreation," Hamilton was credited with having the YMCA and an exceptional football team, while Newfoundland had the Atlantic Ocean. The paragraph included a brief description of the time my grandfather took me cod-jigging. Hamilton, by my count, had eight movie theatres; Newfoundland, by my mother's, had just as many.

The social studies project was a great success. I received an A, and was even asked to read it over the P.A. system to a riveted schoolful of young social studies enthusiasts. I did so with quivering voice and considerable pride, but even as I stood at the silver microphone in the principal's office with the sheaves of foolscap trembling in my hand, I was aware that my report had a serious flaw. I knew that it made no mention of the most profound difference between Hamilton and Newfoundland. Nobody noticed my omission, but it was crucial. In fact, I could feel the difference struggling inside me.

Hamilton, I knew, had its legendary silences. Whereas in Newfoundland—as my mother still makes clear at every opportunity—they talk. They talk, as a matter of fact, like no one else ever talks. They never stop.

The humidity of Southern Ontario settled on my Newfoundland relatives like a weight of warm, sodden tissue when they came to visit us in Hamilton in the summer. I'm not really sure why they came, they all hated the weather so much. But they did come from time to time—my mother's sisters and her brother, her uncles, her aunts, and her parents—and when they showed up, with their huge, strapped suitcases and their summer hats, their pouches of tobacco and *Family Herald* magazines and the red bag of Purity biscuits with the yellow caribou on the front that they brought as a treat for me, they sat on my parents' front veranda and talked. They talked and they talked—about the First World War and the Bonavista North forest fire, German submarines and tidal waves, about business problems and sealing disasters, politics and ghosts. They talked about waiting at the airport to see Merle Oberon and about the time Frank Sinatra, when he was young and skinny and the girls were just starting to scream, played at Fort Pepperrell, the American base in St. John's. Or about how, when it was overcast on the Straight Shore, you could sometimes hear Dr. Banting's plane—the twin-engine Hudson in which the co-discoverer of insulin was killed in a crash in February 1941—pass overhead. They talked about the family company and the roads it built— from nowhere to nowhere, it always seemed to me—and the strikes in the lumber woods, and berry-picking parties, and about the time my grandfather called Harry Dowding back from the dead.

My grandfather and two of his brothers were partners in a construction firm called J. Goodyear and Sons. The family was also involved in lumber contracting and in operating a number of dry-goods and grocery stores throughout the island. But in the 1950s, the Goodyears' principal occupation was building roads, and Harry Dowding was the foreman on the job they had between Botwood and Leading Tickle. Harry was a good man and a hard worker, and one day, standing on the road's gravel shoulder in his boots and hunting-cap and quilted vest, he waved abruptly to the Caterpillar operator, took a few strange, faltering steps, and keeled over. He'd suffered a massive stroke.

He was rushed to the hospital in Botwood. My grandfather was called at the Goodyear office and told that all hope was lost. He drove to Botwood from Grand Falls. He was wearing his floppy fedora when he arrived at the hospital, and he made his lumbering way to the ward. He stood at the side of Dowding's bed. Then he did an odd thing. He shouted: "Harry!" He waited for a few seconds. He called out "Harry!"—more loudly the second time. "Harry!" he finally bellowed, so loudly a nurse dropped a dinner tray in the corridor. And, like Lazarus, Harry Dowding stirred from his stillness and blinked open his eyes. "Well, Skipper Joe," he said. "You were the last man I was just thinking of."

It was as if Newfoundland contained all the best stories in the world. Just when I thought they'd go on telling them forever, my Newfoundland relatives, briefly interrupting themselves, decided that, although it was too hot and sticky to sleep, it was probably time to go to bed.

What I liked best was that they talked in great, looping circles. I was used to people who spoke in straight lines, darting from subject to subject like foxes looking for winter cover. But my Newfoundland relatives set their stories going and then let them roll from one tale to the next until I—sitting on the steps of the veranda—was certain they had no idea where they had begun. Their plots and jokes and family legends possessed the same broad, meandering curlicues as their accents. Stories that began conversations were left unfinished—just as, in my grandfather's stories of the dreadful Bonavista North forest fire of 1961, the word "fire" was spoken, ominous and uncontainable, without its final consonant. Tales were abandoned in the telling in favour of other tales, but one story led seamlessly to another, spiralling like drifting pipe-smoke, farther and farther away from the conversation's beginnings. Yet somehow, without so much as a where-were-we, the stories found their way back, hours later, to where they had started: to the warm fresh bread served on a coastal steamer called the *Glencoe* that stopped in at places with names like Twillingate and Fogo when the Goodyears went to Carmanville for the summer, for there was no road to the Straight Shore until their construction company built it in 1958; or to the flyer who came back after the Second World War with the terrible burns that everyone pretended not to notice; or to the time my grandfather tried to buy his own car, an apple-green Chrysler New Yorker, because, having driven it over every stretch of gravel and mud on Bonavista—going salmon-fishing, going to oversee a road job, going fox-trapping, going to Musgrave Harbour for a glass of the fresh cow's milk he loved so much—he didn't recognize it once it had been washed; or to the night in 1943 when Pop Irish, who lived next to the Goodyears in Grand Falls, awoke to an exploding cellarful of home brew and shouted for his wife to fetch his Home Guard uniform, so certain was he that the Germans had landed and were storming Junction Road.

Or the stories found their way back to my mother, thirty years ago, on those hot, humid summer nights, sitting on our front veranda, passing the bowl of sweet, deep-red Niagara cherries, smiling indulgently at her silent, outnumbered husband and son, and telling her visitors—all of whom were capable of talking the devil's ear off, given half a chance—that whenever she opened her mouth in Hamilton she might as well be talking to herself.

Or they find their way back to me, in Toronto, remembering all this. Remembering how, years ago, I stood with my parents on the deck of a CN ferry called the *William Carson* and watched the bald green bluffs of Port aux Basques disappear from view as we chugged away from Newfoundland. We were steering the course which, on the map in my school atlas, was a dotted red line, linking Newfoundland to Canada. We were on our way home. I was ten years old, and school would be starting soon. Our summer holiday was over, and the little pale frame houses disappeared behind us, then the green, then the contours of the headland. Soon Newfoundland was just a dark shape against the sky.

My mother was crying. She wore slacks and a beige windbreaker. My father tried to comfort her. He wore desert boots and the hunting-shirt he wore on summer holidays. I was sure my mother's tears had to do with departure and, marked on the ragged grey sea by our wake, with the increasing distance between the ferry and the island and the family we'd left behind. Later I learned this wasn't the case at all; my mother was crying because it had rained every day of our holiday. She was afraid her children would hate Newfoundland. Still, for better or worse, the image has stayed with me. It returns at odd moments and seems to come from far away: the memory of my father holding my mother on the deck of a ship, and the taste of salt that may have been only the spray.

WAYNE JOHNSTON

from

Baltimore's Mansion
A Memoir

MY FATHER TOLD ME ONCE that the smell of a beach is not the
smell of the sea. Once you have gone far enough from land,
the sea doesn't smell of anything except salt water, he said, water
a hundred times saltier than blood. It isn't that the smell of
salt is masking other smells. There are no other smells. This is
why, unless you happen to be seasick, food cooked at sea smells
and tastes so good. The body, for so long deprived of it, craves
sensation. After your first prolonged stay at sea, you smell things
back on land that you never smelled before, things you thought
had no smell. Rock, for instance. He said that the first thing you
smell on approaching Newfoundland by boat is rock. You smell
it and even faintly taste it, a coppery metallic taste at the back of
your mouth.

My father, just back home after three weeks on the *Belle Bay*, walked around as though in a daze, eyes on the ground as though he were searching for something. He stood at the fence in the backyard, his hand on the rail, and simply stared at the proliferous landscape, as if it were all brand-new to him.

It was not just smells and sights but sounds too—birds chirping, dogs barking, cars going by on the road outside the house, the distant whine of a power saw or, from somewhere far off in the valley beyond the ridge, a rifle shot. The sound he missed most, he said, was the sound of the wind in the trees, the rustle of the topmost leaves as a land breeze moved among them.

He walked. What a novel sensation it must have been for him to walk, to propel himself more than a boat's length in one direction and feel the earth hard and motionless beneath his feet.

He walked up the road at a clip with no destination in mind. "I'm getting my land legs back," he said when he returned hours later.

The first couple of nights in his stationary bed he could not sleep—not that he minded much, for it simply allowed him to revel that much longer in idleness and in being back home, in not being on the water.

When he did sleep, he slept as he had not since he was last on land, before he set sail on the *Belle Bay*. A night at sea was at best one long dwall for him, a slumberous sleep during which his mind raced and he was always at least dimly aware of his surroundings and circumstances.

Even in winter, he spent as much of his week off as he could outdoors, shovelling snow, cutting a path in the driveway much wider than was necessary, pausing about every other shovelful to look around or relight a cigarette.

When my father was home from his trips, my weather-watching habits did not change much. He had become, from his time on the *Belle Bay*, an obsessive tapper of barometers. He couldn't pass by one without tapping it. We always had a functional barometer in the house, and often more than one. My father would cringe when the barometer registered a sudden drop in air pressure, and he knew bad weather was coming, as if it put him back on the *Belle Bay*, as if even during his time home he was vicariously on board with whoever rode on the *Belle Bay* when it was not his shift.

He would not sleep while a storm was raging, for the sounds of the storm were incorporated into his sea dreams and made them that much worse.

There was nothing I would rather do than watch a storm, so I kept vigil with him throughout the night, he sitting through hours of self-induced, nightmare-preventing sleeplessness, reading *The Reader's Digest* or doing crossword puzzles while sipping on a rye and ginger ale, while I, with my face to the window, kept him informed on the progress of the storm. "For God's sake, Wayne, get away from the window," he said, as if by watching it I was encouraging the storm, as if unless it was ignored it would never peter out.

Sometimes in spite of a storm he did go to sleep and spent the night thrashing about and shouting instructions to the skipper or one of the *Belle Bay* bunch while my mother lay sleepless beside him, afraid to wake him, for he always came roaring out of a nightmare when touched or spoken to as if such a prompt brought him in his dream to the brink of death, as if it sank the *Belle Bay* the last remaining inch below the waves.

TELEPHONES WERE RARE in the outports, so when my father was away, his only means to call home was the ship-to-shore telephone. We got about half an hour's warning from federal Fisheries that the call was coming, as it had to be patched through to our phone by some complicated series of connections. We took turns talking to him. The line crackled with static and his voice was very faint. He sounded as if he were calling from under water.

We had to say "Over" each time we stopped to let him speak, which we boys thought was great fun but my mother hated. While we fought among ourselves over what order we should talk to him in, each of us wanting to go last so that we could say "Over and out," my mother walked about arms folded, smoking, swearing that she was fed up with having conversations with her husband as if the two of them were in the Navy, having to say "Over" every fifteen seconds. But she always spoke to him.

Fearful that by not calling he would give away the fact that he had been drinking, he was most faithful about calling when he was least able to pretend that he was sober.

"You sound pretty pleased with yourself, over," my mother would say, a code phrase she need not have bothered with—we knew what it meant. He protested his sobriety, but there was no fooling her.

Her tone starting out would be reproachful, but perhaps because of having to say "Over" at the end of every sentence, rolling her eyes as she did so, she wound up laughing or making kisses into the phone as she never did when he was sober. My mother would make a long, drawn out smooching noise, then say, "Over," bursting into giggles, then into gales of laughter when my father did the same. "Other people can hear this call you know, over," she'd say.

"Where are you calling from, Dad, over?" I asked him. When he told me—Roddicton, Inglee, English Harbour—I wrote it down so that later I could find it on the map.

"I'm stormbound, Wayne, over."

"So are we. We're stuck in the house. Are you on the *Belle Bay* now? Over."

"Yes. We're tied up at the wharf in Ramea, over."

I could picture it, the *Belle Bay* moored and bobbing, my father's view of Ramea like that of someone on a trampoline.

"My God, Wayne," he said once, his voice suddenly breaking with emotion. "What a country we could have been. What a country we were one time."

I fell silent. My mother took the phone from me, went out into the hall and closed the door.

"I know," I heard my mother say. "We still are, sweetheart. I know. Try not to think about it, now. Don't be by yourself, all right? Stay with the others."

If they were docked and it was too rough to stay on board the *Belle Bay*, they found whatever accommodations they could. There were no hotels, bed and breakfasts or even boarding houses in most of the places they made port. If they were lucky, a priest or minister would take them in, or old couples who, because their children had moved away, had rooms not slept in for years. Otherwise, they displaced children from their beds, or slept on sofas, waking in the morning as a family of strangers began its day around them in self-conscious silence. The members of the crew would venture out from their various houses after breakfast and find some shed or flakehouse where they could pass the day together smoking and drinking the rum they had brought in case of such a stranding.

NEWFOUNDLAND IS AT THE end of the line weather-wise, the last stop for storms that come across the continent or up the Atlantic seaboard from the Gulf of Mexico. And stop they often do, especially in winter, giant low-pressure systems remaining stationary, generating northeast winds and snow that lasts for days. Night after night, a large encircled L appears in exactly the same place on the television weather map, the weatherman sheepishly explaining why, despite his predictions to the contrary, the storm has not moved on.

I remember my mother nervously smoking as she listened. She regarded the weatherman, Bob Lewis, with a kind of skeptical dread, owing to the inaccuracy of his forecasts. It was as though he was a symptom of some larger chaos that caused things to happen without reason or forewarning. "He can't forecast the days of the week," she said, staring at him on the screen as he described the track he believed some storm would take. But she watched him anyway. His forecasts, even if they were little more than fiction, gave to her anxiety some shape and substance.

We gathered round the set and watched with her, waiting for the L's to turn up on the map. It seemed that as soon as my father left on one of his trips, those L's popped up everywhere. Even if there had been none on the entire map of the continent the day before, there were swarms of them the next.

Troughs too shallow to be designated lows deepened as the *Belle Bay* headed west. Within their zones of influence, the barometric pressure dropped, the isobars of each low compressed to a vortex of concentric shapes.

Clipper storms stacked up like airplanes from east to west, destination Newfoundland; Gulf of Mexico storms hugged the coast until they plowed into the current south of Sable Island, banked off it and wildly veered northeast. The storms crossed three peninsulas, the Burin, the Avalon, the Bonavista, then stalled, brought up solid fifty miles off the northeast coast as if a mooring line with fifty miles of slack had at last run out. With the ocean to provide them with an endless source of moisture and the wind off the ice pack making sure the snow would never change to rain, there was theoretically no reason why they could not last forever.

For me, the map was a representation not of space but time. It was a time grid whose various sections could just as easily have been numbered as named, for the names meant nothing to me. The provinces and states, whose existence I did not really believe in, were preconfigurations of the next few days, the moods that would prevail in the house. The past was off-screen right, the future off-screen left and the picture on the screen was a photograph of now. Here comes next week, there goes last week. It was easy to imagine that the past was recoverable, that you could pull it back like a ticker tape, and across the screen would go the L's and H's that in code contained the past.

I imagined some giant L-shaped dirigible that would not move on until someone cut the rope by which it was moored to the island. Me trudging off through the storm, wading blindly through snowdrifts until I somehow found the rope that was thicker than a tree trunk and hacked at it with my axe until it broke and the ragged end of it trailed off across the snow as the storm withdrew.

My father was in some nebulous, electronic otherworld, in the phone, in the wind-whipped telephone wires, in the dust-covered workings of the radio, in the warm transistor tubes, in the worm-like filaments of orange light that dimmed and flickered when the wind was at its height.

He was wherever the voices on the air came from. He had not gone anywhere in space. He had been transported to this world of strange-sounding high-pitched voices in which storms of static raged like blizzards. He was out there somewhere in air as thick with static as a blizzard was with snow. And he was tenuously, invisibly there on the television weather map of Newfoundland. "That's where your father is spending the night," my mother said, pointing to some jagged little inlet or peninsula west of Baie d'Espoir, and often pointing to it the next night and the next, while on the screen Bob Lewis pointed elsewhere.

If the place where my father was stranded was big enough, Bob Lewis might say what temperature it was there now and with his marker write the number on the corresponding section of the map.

It was twenty-two degrees Fahrenheit in Ramea. That was all the verification of its existence we would get.

Sometimes in the middle of the night, the phone would ring, and I would hear my mother run to answer it. A crank call. A wrong number. Nothing on the other end but dial tone. She went to bed again in the vain hope of getting back to sleep. I would hear the click of her lighter and, soon after, smell the smoke of a cigarette.

During the worst winter storms, when she was especially anxious or upset and before it became impossible to go outside, she took us to spend the night at her parents' house, which my father referred to as "the world's most mournful dwelling place."

My grandparents, though they had electricity, used low-watt bulbs that lit the house about as brightly as oil lanterns used to do. The place was always dim and full of looming shadows that went up the wall and partway across the ceiling. Whenever we came to visit, my grandfather, knowing that we never said it otherwise, insisted that we join them in the kitchen to say the rosary. I couldn't help feeling that we were praying for my father's safe return.

My grandfather had spent at least half of every day from age ten to thirty-five fishing for cod off Petty Harbour, and he playfully teased my mother for being so worried about what, compared with the storms he said he had made his way through in a dory powered by nothing more than his arms and a pair of oars, was "barely a breeze."

I imagined him "sou'westered" as he called it, dressed in gleaming oilskin from head to toe, plying his absurdly tiny, inadequate craft up and down the sides of massive, slate-black waves.

The wind surged against the side of the house, the window panes buckled inward and the whistle in the wood stove rose to a shriek until the gust subsided, at which point my grandfather would look up from the paper he was reading and, wetting his thumb to turn a page, say, "Barely a breeze, Genevieve, barely a breeze, my dear."

It worked for a while. My mother would laugh at his teasing, encourage him. Then, when he saw she was past the point that his stories would do her any good, he went to bed while we boys were sent to watch TV with the sound turned down so low we had to sit within a foot of it to hear it.

My mother sat with her mother in the kitchen, the two of them talking softly, my grandmother reassuring my mother that the storm raging outside was not as bad as it looked—she had seen storms much worse before, and my father was doubtless safe on shore.

He was never more conspicuously absent than on those nights we spent in the world's most mournful dwelling place and from the kitchen came the murmur of voices while in the front room of the wind-besieged house my brothers and I huddled by the TV set, trying to hear, above the storm, some program like *The Big Valley* or *Bonanza*.

SOME SUMMER EVENINGS while my father was away, my mother piled us into the car and drove us down the road to Maddox Cove. We followed the flume into Petty Harbour, where the roads are so narrow it's necessary for a car to pull onto the shoulder to let another one go by.

The Catholic side, where my mother's parents had lived until they set out for the Goulds in the early 1900s, was on our right. Above the Protestant side on our left was the entrance to a long-abandoned mine, a dark door-shaped hole bored straight into the cliff. As a child, my grandmother had been warned not to cross the bridge to the Protestant side of town lest she be spirited away into the mine that led directly down to hell by "blacks," as the Catholics called the Protestants.

Beyond the breakwater, pink buoys marked the site of lobster traps. Fishing nets with large cork floats attached were spread out on the ground to dry. Dories being painted or repaired lay overturned beside the road. There were dozens of dories and skiffs anchored inside the breakwater, all linked by an elaborate network of ropes that kept them from colliding when the wind came up. Here, the water was like that of the pond below our house, so calm it mirrored the patterns of lights on the westside hill. But beyond the seawall, there were lozenge-like ripples on the water, the closest thing to calm the ocean that far from shore could get.

Maddox Cove is just up the shore from Petty Harbour. It's sparsely settled, just half a dozen houses on the north side of the cove that are owned by fishermen who moor their boats in Petty Harbour. There are no wharves, no breakwater, just an open, unprotected harbour, a horizon uncluttered by jutting rocks or islands, clear sailing all the way to the Old World.

We picked among the beach rocks for the remains of various shallow-water sea creatures that had been stranded by the tide. Sea urchins, crabs, tom cods, sculpins, jellyfish, even capelin, the last of which had washed ashore two months ago. We found cables of kelp, still wet, encrusted with little sea snails, and long tentacles of seaweed.

While we combed the beach for "skimmers," flat rocks that when thrown properly skipped along the surface of the water, my mother walked off by herself on the wet, wave-rippled sand near the water, her hands in the pockets of her jacket, her bandana tied beneath her chin. At a certain distance from us she stopped and looked out to sea.

I imagined that being at the sea's edge made her feel closer to my father, made her miss him less, or miss him more but in a way that felt good, as missing him sometimes made me feel.

Petty Harbour was not home for her the way Ferryland still was for my father, in spite of it being the birthplace of her parents. She had never lived there. By coming here, she was getting away from home, away from things that reminded her of him. Except us. And the sea, of course. There was no getting away from that.

The sea reminded her of where he was, but the beach, aside from costing nothing to visit and keeping us children endlessly occupied without much need of supervision, was a place where no one bearing bad news could call her on the phone or come by the house.

Once, as she was coming back down the beach, it was clear from her red-rimmed eyes that she'd been crying.

"What's wrong, Mom?" I said.

"Nothing's wrong," she said.

"Mom?" I said.

The others were out of earshot.

"What?"

"Do you know what happened on the beach?"

"What beach?" she said. "This beach?" She didn't sound as if she was hiding something.

"To Dad," I said. "On the beach in Ferryland. When he was going off to college. Before he went. I think him and his father were on the beach or something. Did something happen?"

"My love, I don't know what you mean," she said.

I saw that it was true. She didn't know.

"Never mind," I said. "I thought Dad said something happened, but maybe I got it mixed up."

I knew she would ask my father if he had put this idea in my head. And I knew that he would tell her no.

We went back to the others. She sat down on the beach rocks. We sat down with her, four boys suddenly, solemnly well behaved, fearfully watching her, dreading another loss of control, another sign that she was more than just our mother and had secret sorrows of her own.

There had been other times like this, times when in his absence she disappeared into her room for hours, or walked up the cartroad to the top of her father's farm. When she reappeared, her eyes were puffy from crying, though we never acknowledged it, never asked her what was wrong. We assumed that at the bottom of it all was this job of his, his long absences from home, the anxiety, the loneliness. We were partly right. But how exactly these things manifested themselves between them they hid from us as best they could.

We stayed there until past twilight, sitting on the beach rocks with our mother while she smoked, all of us facing seaward as if we were waiting for a boat to come ashore.

There was still no wind, but it was getting cold. She shivered.

"Snuggle up, boys," she said. It had been ages since she had asked us to. We used to "snuggle up" with her on Saturday mornings while my father cooked us breakfast. She took Brian on her lap. I knelt behind her and put my arms around her neck, rested my chin on her shoulder, and Ken and Craig, flanking her, each took one of her arms.

"Is everybody warm?" she said. We nodded. "Me too," she said.

Off to our left, above the hills behind the Brow, we could see in the sky the faint glow of St. John's, five miles of woods away. By boat, Ferryland was thirty miles south, ten miles closer than by road. Far out on the water, beyond the eastern point of Maddox Cove, came the periodic flash of the lighthouse at Cape Spear.

Every so often, as if the sea had shrugged it ashore, an almost silent swell broke on the beach.

"This is nice, hey?" she said. Brian said we should stay there all night. My mother laughed and kissed him on the top of the head. "We'll go camping when your Dad gets back," she said. "All of us, all night, okay?" Brian, who never forgot a promise, nodded.

We stayed a little longer, until my mother declared that it was time to head home. We left, scrambling over beach rocks that we couldn't see and that slid crazily about beneath our feet so that we had to hold on to each other to keep from falling, my mother shrieking with laughter as the four of us all but dragged her to the road. When we reached the car, I looked up. The sky was full of stars.

MARIAN BOTSFORD FRASER

from

Requiem for My Brother

BLESS THIS HOUSE

JOHN DAVIS BOTSFORD WAS BORN in the Kirkland Lake Hospital on April 28,1949. Delivered, as all three of us were, by Dr. Tom Armstrong. People in small towns always know, or did then, who delivered them. Our parents were American: our father, Jack, came to northern Ontario as a mining engineer in the late '30s, served in the Royal Canadian Engineers, and returned to northern Michigan in 1946 to marry a young woman from his hometown. Our mother, Louise, visited Canada once before their marriage, and, famously in the family, Dad drove her quickly past the house where they would live only as he took her to the train station at the end of the visit. I was conceived during the camping trip that was their honeymoon journey, from Michigan to northern Ontario.

Dave (or Davy, as we called him until he married) was two years younger than me, and for the first few years of our lives we lived in that small pleasant house, unusual still in its sharply pointed roof over the porch, in the row of five staff houses on the Upper Canada Mine property, a row known as "the hill." The hill was about 2 kilometres from the village of Dobie, called "the townsite." Our childhood was contained by the gently rolling topography of a small piece of bush with a radius of about 5 or 6 kilometres: the hill, the townsite and the railway tracks and the reason for it all, Upper Canada Mine—a rambling mill for processing the gold, a water tower, modest offices, and the tarpaper-clad head frames over the two underground shafts (#1 and #2) about a kilometre apart. A circular network of gravel and tarred roads joined the mine, the hill, and the townsite, but there was only one road out to Highway 66, a bleak stretch of blacktop whose terminal points for us as children were Kirkland Lake to the west and the town of Rouyn-Noranda to the east on the Quebec border. Dobie and Upper Canada Mine were invisible from the highway, unsigned....

———•◦•———

FOR AS LONG AS WE lived in Dobie and Dad was the manager of Upper Canada Mine, the price of gold was fixed at $35 an ounce. The mine and employment in it were guaranteed, it seemed then, forever. The rhythms of work underground determined patterns of life on the surface. The mine whistle blew at noon each day, and the familiar rumble of daily underground blasts and the dreaded occasional rock bursts marked time for us. The mine bus that brought workers out from Kirkland Lake for every shift doubled as the school bus, which took us into Kirkland Lake for school after the sixth grade. But until then our frame of reference and the locus of our feelings and imagination was Dobie. My best friend, Susan, moved away when I was ten, and I thought that was the end of the world. Davy's best friends, Lorne and Donald, never moved. Sara's best friends, Pat and Susan, moved in next door when she was ten. Davy and Sara were defined by these Dobie friendships until they left home for university.

But mingled with the coherence, the sweet sureness of the seasons that rolled over the landscape, the certainty of school and friendships, there were dark currents. These were cruel times. A Dobie friend, still living near Kirkland Lake, remembers going out to pick blueberries one summer afternoon and discovering the old black spaniel that belonged to Mr. and Mrs. Connors up the row from us on the hill, dead—tied to a tree and shot. Two boys who lived across the street from the Dobie school would be "beaten home" at lunchtime by their drunken father brandishing his belt. Houses burned down in the night. Children went in and out of foster care. There were Dobie families we referred to casually as "DIPS"—displaced persons. There were children in the Dobie school who smelled of neglect. These things we knew and took for granted.

Other things too were more subtly destructive, insidious over time. Environmental hazards were incidental, the stuff of daily life; PCBS were carried home from the power lines in swinging, open pails. In spring, a small tractor came and sprayed the lawns and the bush around the houses on the hill and on the streets of Dobie with DDT to kill the blackflies, and we ran after the tractor like the children of the Pied Piper and jumped and twirled in the billowing white clouds of poison. Although Dad was justly proud of the impeccable safety record of Upper Canada Mine, almost every second family in Dobie sooner or later was afflicted by cancer or chronic disease. If you named everyone who lived there in one year, say, 1960, and asked what happened to them, there would be an exceptionally high incidence of early death, illness, suicide, misfortune, and alcoholism. My best friend's mother had MS. Sara's best friends' mother had Parkinson's disease. As adults, we would have cause to ponder this thicket of afflictions.

In our house this dark current took the form of jokes. One April Fool's Day my parents left a trail of red food colouring in the snow and told me that my beloved cat, Gray Boy, had been killed. One Christmas Eve, Dad put a glass of water on top of a broom handle up against the ceiling, gave the broomstick to Sara to hold, and then made the rest of us walk away. The joke was that she had no way of getting the glass down, and when it finally fell and broke, he made her clean it up. These "jokes" were signals to us that perhaps we should never feel fully secure, or unconditionally loved. We all had our version of feeling like the different or unwanted one—the dark side of being the oldest, the boy, the baby—thanks to our father's tendency to throw out the kind of thoughtless, jocular remarks about such things that children are haunted by. Mine surfaced every time we went out to Crystal Lake in summer, to the funny small mine cottage that was always ours to use. It had a fragrant outhouse, beside the woodpile at the end of a covered, wooden walkway, where I pondered his deliberately offensive phrase "nigger in the woodpile," which seemed to apply to me (or, somehow, the milkman?), as I was dark and brown-eyed and my brother and sister were both blue-eyed redheads. Sara grew up believing she had been born under a cabbage leaf because by the time she was born, Dad wasn't taking so many pictures and that was the reason he gave her. Davy was mocked as a sissy.

People like our parents, who married after the war and settled down and quickly had children, felt in the immediate postwar years a brief sense of liberation and release. But in that bubble of illusory affluence and certainty, in the late '50s and early '60s in northern Ontario, there were deep traditions of silence in all classes and ethnic backgrounds. Secrecy was the dominant social code, ingrained during the war and abetted by a crisscrossing net of hierarchies based on religion, ethnicity, income, and job status; it was only in school that these barriers were erased, to be replaced by others, mainly scholastic and athletic aptitude. Many things, many forms of emotional or physical violence within families, were never discussed or admitted to or revealed in Kirkland Lake. Silence was the glue of our society. My family had secrets, things that remained unspoken. But it was only as an adult that I learned that other families had terrible secrets too and that the habits of emotional rigidity were common.

The violence I remember in our house as a child was verbal, and late at night, from around the time that I was eleven. Our parents would come home late from parties, arguing and drunk. Kirkland Lake was a hard-drinking town, in beer parlours and hotel bars and taverns, and at house parties, where my father and his friends mixed up gallons of a lethal mixture of brandy, rum, sherry, lemon juice, and soda water known as Boston Fishhouse Punch and served it ice-cold in small glasses that were never allowed to be empty. (I am lying in my bed, suddenly alert—the creak of tires in the snow, car doors slamming, stamping feet on the front porch, voices clashing in the vestibule, the hall, the living room. I pull the pillow over my ears and shut my eyes tight to drown out the sound of my pounding heart.)

It was when I was a teenager that Mom began to drink secretly. A pall fell on all of our adolescences. We became tense and wary, ashamed. Complicity encouraged a fierce sibling bonding, even as our natural tendencies at this age were to drift apart. Nothing changed, but everything changed.

In my midteens Dad's parents lived with us, causing disruption in routines and in our living space (I ended up in the basement for a while). My grandfather's senility, as we called it, was very hard on my mother; he would follow her incessantly, all day long from room to room, not knowing who she was, and he would try to enter her bedroom, which resulted in a lock on that door. She would retreat there in the early evening, with a gin and Tab. Ah yes, the gin and Tab.

None of us had a sanctioned or formally, happily recognized relationship until we left home. I had unrequited crushes on boys, but never a boyfriend, only hearty friendships. In high school, Davy tentatively, briefly loved a girl who was killed in a car accident. Sara remembers going to her funeral, but I never even met her. Sara had a long love affair, never approved by our parents. What were the barriers? In Davy's case, shyness. We were all afraid to bring anyone home, in case Mom had been drinking. We were terrified of embarrassment or shame.

WHAT SURFACES: looking for gin bottles hidden in the bathroom, counting the Tab under the kitchen counter. Mom never drank pop or soft drinks (ginger ale was the only one permitted to us), so it was very odd that Tab (an early diet coke) became her cover of choice. Our searches were always done surreptitiously, as if they were the terrible thing, opening doors so quietly with a sharp intake of breath, running the water in the sink to cover the sound of rustling objects. She had sharp ears and unerring instincts. Usually finding nothing, and hoping to find nothing, but not relieved when nothing was found. Knowing something had been missed. We all did this, independent of one another, and not reporting to one another. Parallel furtive vigilance.

Her aqua-covered chair moved from house to house to house, but it always represented the same thing. Dad in his corner with the beer that smelled so wonderfully of hops (martinis came later); Mom in hers, with a glass of clear liquid (Tab was for upstairs, never officially a mix), sometimes hidden on the floor, at hand's reach, the ashtray slowly filling with half-smoked cigarettes, one lit from the last, long inches of ash, the scars over time that pocked the waxed wooden table, and latterly, the chair itself. Mom never drank and knitted at the same time. She knitted in the afternoon, fast and furious. She could and did knit in the dark, at the movies. She could knit and read at the same time. It was always a relief to come upon her knitting.

There is that wrenching theme in Eugene O'Neill's *Long Day's Journey into Night,* the father and sons gathered in the room downstairs, hearing the mother moving around overhead. Clocking, with increasing dread, the barely audible indications of addiction. That is how I recall this time: when she would retire and drink, and then get churned up by something and emerge belligerent, with a grating, flattened voice and eyes hard as buttons. "Go to bed, Louise," Dad would shout from in front of the television, when she would open the door to the basement and stand there, glaring or crying, swaying. And she would retreat, and come out again later, sometimes apologetic, sobbing, and he would tell her again to go to bed. What was she angry about? Why did we never know?

Some things: the early death of her younger brother, Jim, whom she had mothered from the age of 14; her virulent dislike of her own mother; her sense of uselessness, once we were past childhood. Self-loathing (she hated her body—she dressed and undressed inside her closet—the length of her arms, the colour of her eyes) exacerbated by becoming an alcoholic, this secret that everyone knew, but that she could talk about with no one. For many years we did not use the word alcoholic when describing our mother. We allowed the phrase "nocturnal alcoholic" when pressed, or to one another. We may have said, our mother has a problem with alcohol sometimes.

What drove us wild was the Jekyll and Hyde nature of this furtive beast. There was the public, daytime, fun-loving and immensely capable Mom, with whom each of us had sweet and goofy times. There were days or weeks of being "good" and then she would become this other person who cried, railed against life, stumbled and fell, was incoherent, and then the next day it would be as if nothing had happened.

I avoided the worst years by being absent. Davy expressed his disapproval by viciously imitating her behind her back. Sara lived with it as a teenager and under its shadow afterward because she was closest, geographically and emotionally. Dad's attitude in front of us was irritation at most and a fierce protectiveness if we dared to criticize. When I was 21, I wrote him a letter from university. I apologized for bothering him, "so busy with mine business." I said I spoke for Davy and Sara as well, about "the extent of Mother's drinking ... I hate to call it what it must be...." I sent the letter "confidential/ special delivery" to the mine and lived in terror that Mom would find it. The next time I was home Dad took me for a walk down to his vegetable garden, and said gently, "Your mother doesn't drink, but sometimes she's affected by what are called barbiturates."

When Dad died, in November 1991, that letter, carefully folded back into its envelope, was the only personal artifact in his dresser drawer, hidden under a box containing his war medals.

Why did he go on making martinis, night after night, year after year? Why could she sometimes hold her alcohol and at other times not at all? This went on, in varying degrees of awfulness, for thirty years. We would watch her, with despair and yes, contempt, sitting in her chair, with a cigarette in one limp hand and the drink, being sipped slowly, silently, and one slim, stockinged leg sliding slowly up and down the other, an almost sexual movement in a body otherwise still, the hated half-smile on her face, the slur and repetition overtaking her speech.

There was a game we played as children, in the basement of the Dobie house. The record player was plugged into an outlet that could be turned off with the light switch. We would put on "Ghost Riders in the Sky" and at a certain point in the chorus—"yippee yi yay, yippee yi"—right there, exactly, we would flip the wall switch and the music would go into a descending fall and the light would go off and there would be silence and darkness. We were in charge of this repetitive little drama in the basement. We could do and say absolutely nothing about the one in the bedroom upstairs.

IN THE LATE '50S, an entrepreneurial portrait painter travelled around northern Ontario, coming to middle-class houses to do formal portraits of the children, a deal that included identical, thickly gilded gesso and wood frames—$25, fitting extra. The three of us sat for this painter over three successive summers. It is impossible for me to say even now if these were good paintings; the likenesses were accurate, the backgrounds moody and atmospheric. The eyes were disconcerting, because when you entered the living room where all three portraits eventually hung, you were trapped by the gazes of all three of us hung on different walls, following you around the room.

My portrait was the first to be done. I wore a short-sleeved, pinkish-red blouse, very plain. Davy was next, and I suspect the artist talked my parents out of a shirt and tie; Davy wore a short-sleeved, collared, white polo shirt. Sara was painted in the beautiful pale turquoise silk dress that our parents brought back from Paris when they made their once-in-a-lifetime voyage in the *Homeric,* across the Atlantic.

When the artist came back to do Davy, my portrait was already hanging over the piano, where I looked at it every morning as I did my scales and arpeggios and Hanon exercises and Royal Conservatory pieces like "The Avalanche" and "Für Elise." I had decided my lips were too pale, too small, too *babyish*. When the painter was out of the room smoking a cigarette, I dipped the end of a toothpick into the colour I preferred and made my lips a slick cherry-red. No one but me ever noticed this.

It was the end of childhood.

We still have our portraits. They travelled with Mom and Dad from Dobie to the mine manager's house at Macassa and then to North Carolina when they retired. When our parents died the portraits came to the summerhouse we three shared on Lake Simcoe in Ontario, where they again hung together on the living room walls, observing.

I brought the portraits of Davy and me up from my basement recently, dusted them off, and leaned them side by side against a wall. We look like conventional, middle-class children of the '50s— the children our parents hoped that we were, and to a considerable degree we truly were, before the rowdy onset of adolescence. We are caught in unlikely repose, with a half-smile on our lips, and my hands are neatly clasped in my lap. Davy is thin, his pale arms held awkwardly away from his body, his eyebrows pure white, his thick curly red hair cut short and slicked into a neatly parted, crisp cap.

The gesso on the frames is chipped and broken in places, the gilt worn, the paper backing is brittle. I tried to decipher the artist's signature—a scrawl in the same red as my lips—but I could not read it.

WARREN CARIOU

from

Lake of the Prairies

A Story of Belonging

OUT OF PLACE

I BUILT UP A long list of fears over time: bees, large dogs, horses, bears, hypodermic needles, bombs, Mrs. Carter, God. There were stories behind each of these terrors. Bees because of the hornet stings; dogs because Uncle Eddy's yellow Lab, Butch, had snapped at me and taken a chunk out of my lip; horses because I had seen a stallion kick the boards out of a corral at Marion and Wade's place; bears and needles because everyone was afraid of them; Mrs. Carter because of the carrot. God because—well, because I was raised Catholic.

Bombs were probably my most justified fear, given the continuing escalations of the Cold War. I was vaguely aware of the arms race and its potential consequences, through news reports and popular post-apocalyptic science fiction shows and novels. But in addition to the generalized Cold War dread of nuclear annihilation and my knowledge that Cold Lake would be vapourized in a first strike, I heard and felt *real* bombs every summer. Our cabin at Jeannette Lake was only a few miles from the eastern edge of the Primrose Lake Air Weapons Range, which was—and is—a training site for NATO bombing missions.

Sometimes we saw the jets streaking across the northwestern horizon, or heard the oddly disconnected, directionless roar of the engines. Once when Glenn and I were fishing on the far side of the lake, an F-18 appeared just above the treetops, not 200 yards away. It was utterly silent, and we were so surprised that we both stood up in the canoe, poised to jump overboard, to seek cover. For a second I thought it might be a Soviet plane, the first wave of an invasion. The NATO pilots weren't supposed to fly outside the boundaries of the bombing range, and certainly not so low. When I recognized the tiny American flag beneath the cockpit, it was only a minor relief. No matter whose side it was on, this thing was bristling with danger. The massive bombs clung to the fuselage like parasites, jutting out in front of the wings.

As we stood there in the wobbly canoe, the plane flew silently out over the water and then banked sharply to the right, fully displaying its malevolent, arrowhead shape. Thinking back, it seems like no coincidence that F-18s are called Hornets. It was as if someone had designed this plane specifically to terrify me. Inside I could see the insectlike form of the pilot, with his helmet and face mask and strangely mandibular, quick-moving arms. Before we had even said a word, its afterburners flashed with a pink glow like a car's cigarette lighter, and it disappeared over the treetops on the far side of the bay. We were left with the belated thunder of the engines.

That's how it was: always by surprise, always when you had just forgotten that the planes and bombs existed, when you were napping in a lawn chair or bouncing a yellowtail jig along the bottom of the lake or wading in for a swim. The unpredictability magnified our unease. We flinched at the sight of loons and swallows in the air.

Far more common than close-up sightings of the planes was the sound of the bombs. Most of the time they used "dummy" bombs made of lead or cast iron, which we couldn't hear from the cabin, but several times a year they practised with live ordnance. Sometimes the explosions were almost indistinguishable from thunder, but if the targets were closer to our end of the bombing range, the effect was far more jarring. They sent shock waves through the sand that were like brief earthquakes. The cabin would heave and shudder momentarily, or the beach would shimmy beneath us. It was as if the ground had been changed into muskeg for a second.

The noise would hit an instant later: a thick, heavy sound, not at all like a gunshot. It seemed to come from deep in the earth. Then there would be a moment of absolute silence, like after the firing of the cannons on Remembrance Day. Soon came the other sounds: dogs whining, children crying, men swearing, parents offering words of comfort. Sometimes people had to talk their dogs out from underneath the crawl spaces below their cabins. One of the neighbour kids was so terrified by the bombs that he became almost catatonic. He would fall to the ground clutching his ears and stay there in a heap until his parents came to get him.

I wasn't as frightened as that. Sometimes I even thought the bombs were funny, like the time when Mom stepped into the outhouse and a few seconds later a whole planeload of ordnance exploded in the distance, shaking the cabin. Mom herself didn't find this so amusing.

I never worried that the bombs would accidentally hit us. I was simply shocked by their existence at all—their interruptiveness, their incongruity in this place where we went barefoot for weeks on end, and threw ourselves into the water a dozen times a day, and hiked out to the secret berry patch to pick raspberries or blueberries or pin cherries straight into our mouths. That this should also be the site of bombs and warplanes was hardly comprehensible. Every time we heard the bombs it was a reminder that something was wrong, something was out of place in the world. Either those planes didn't belong or we didn't. It was impossible that the two realities could coexist in the same place.

I ALSO HAD ANOTHER FEAR, a secret one. I never mentioned it to anyone, even though I felt it in my stomach every time I stepped outside the boundary of our yard. I was afraid of Native people. Not so much the women, and certainly not the girls, but the men and especially the boys. They were the most visible. There were always a few Native men standing outside the Stampede Hotel and the Empire and the Hub Café in their plaid shirts and jeans, smoking roll-your-own cigarettes or chewing Copenhagen. Many had braids, but some had flat-top brush cuts, and others kept their hair hidden under their caps. We also saw them in Pete's Billiards Room and Dickowicky's Modern Billiards, where we went to play pinball and Space Invaders and Defender. They talked among themselves, and laughed often, but always quietly. They never spoke to me and they certainly never made any menacing gestures toward me. They rarely even looked in my direction. But still I felt vaguely threatened by them, though I didn't know exactly why. They were different, they seemed to set themselves apart, and I suppose that was enough. That and the stories about tomahawks and scalping and eyes pinned open in the sun.

Of course it wasn't entirely their own decision to be set apart, though I didn't realize this at the time. I didn't know that for many years the people of Flying Dust were required to get the Indian agent's permission to leave the reserve for any reason. I didn't understand the function of the residential schools. If I had looked more closely I would have seen that the Cree people on the street corners often had a sheepishness about them, which had probably been learned through generations of discrimination. It was as if they *expected* to be denigrated, perhaps even to be feared. This was probably why they seemed to talk only among themselves. It was the solidarity of the oppressed, and it led to a kind of voluntary segregation of the streets: the Native people stood and visited while everyone else walked by them as if they weren't even there. This separation extended to the church, where the Natives always took the pews at the back, as if intuiting their place in the town's social hierarchy. The beer halls in town were surprisingly like the churches: the Indians sitting at the back, in the corners, the most poorly lit places. Even the buses were the same. Maybe they chose to do this, but something must have governed that choice, something must have made them feel they belonged only on the perimeter of these gathering places.

I took that separation for granted when I was a kid. I didn't wonder where it had come from, how it had developed. I didn't think about the exceptions: my friends Gilbert and Jimmy, and Mrs. Bear, who went to our church and was famous for her beaded mitts and mukluks. There were also Native men who golfed at the course in town and who seemed to be accepted in the clubhouse. But on the streets and in the bars and churches, the separation was largely maintained. And I suppose that division was what reinforced my fear of them. I knew the Native people were different from me, but it was more alarming to recognize that I was different from them. They made me feel uneasy, like I didn't belong in my own hometown.

It's clear to me now that there was a vast history to my fear, one that began generations before my birth and that I would not become aware of for many years. It was built on stereotypes of savages and heathens that dated back to a time when Meadow Lake was known only as Paskwâw Sâkâhikan. The whole western culture has always been afraid of Indians, at the same time as it has cheated them and infantilized them and distorted them into jokes and caricatures. I think that simply by being who they were, aboriginals made everyone else question their own belonging, and that questioning tended to raise the most fundamental kinds of fears and insecurities.

I absorbed those fears unconsciously and began to enact them, to give them my own personal reality. I had, after all, like almost every kid of my generation, played cowboys and Indians. I loved *Gunsmoke*. I had heard, and sometimes repeated, the stories about Indian givers, drunk Indians, stupid Indians, lazy Indians, thieving Indians, dead Indians. No aboriginal man had ever threatened me, but I'd heard about the fights in the bars, the number of Native people in jail, the terrible living conditions on some of the reserves. That was all the threat I needed.

With the Native boys it was somewhat different because I knew them from school. They weren't just silent presences on the sidewalks but individuals who knew my name and who had good reasons to resent my place in the community. Everything about my relationship with them was conditioned by the environment at school, where I was often favoured and usually the Native kids were not. I was hardly aware of the racism in school because I wasn't the one singled out for mistreatment. But boys like Clayton Matchee were, and Gilbert Lachance, and Kenny Laliberte, and my friend Jimmy Sinclair. I remember that Clayton got in trouble with the teachers regularly, but not for anything substantially different than what other boys did. He was only a low-grade troublemaker—a prankster, a teaser of girls, a kid who got into tussles at recess—yet it seemed he was punished more often and more severely than some of the white boys who got into more serious trouble. At the time I didn't question it much; I still believed that everyone got what they deserved. Even in grade one when Mrs. Goodman took Gilbert up to the front of the class, pulled down his pants, and paddled his ass with a yardstick in front of us all, I didn't think her unfairness had anything to do with Gilbert being Indian. I just thought it was strange and arbitrary that she should humiliate him this way for such a minor transgression as playing soccer with the grade sixes. She didn't know that he would later be welcomed among the white kids because of the very thing she had punished him for: his skill at sports.

Some of the teachers had obvious prejudices, but the racism in my school was even more visible among the kids. As usual, they were less subtle about it than the adults, less aware that there might be anything wrong with what they were doing. I wish I could say I wasn't involved in it, but that would be a lie. I was racist too. I took part in the name-calling, the jokes, the exclusion. I felt it was my natural place to be respected by the teachers and by my peers, but when anyone else was treated unfairly, I didn't come to their aid.

The white boys taunted the Native girls mercilessly, even though most of these girls did their best to remain inconspicuous. I remember Melody Kahpeepitow, with her ill-fitting glasses and stringy hair and perpetual shy half-smile that was offered to the world as a sign of supplication, a plea for treatment less cruel than what she expected. She said nothing in class and kept to herself at noon hour, chewing her balogna sandwiches and paging through the teacher's collection of *Tintin* cartoons, but still somehow she attracted the attention of Darcy Carlson, the class jock. "Melody, you black thing," he would say to her almost offhandedly, with a snarl of emphasis on the last word. "What're you doing by my desk, you black thing, you?" She never answered him, but she flushed sometimes, and her face took on a faraway expression, the classic if-I-ignore-him-he'll-leave-me-alone look. The rest of us gazed on, wondering if she would ever say anything. But she didn't.

The Native boys were taunted too, but usually at more of a distance, and more obliquely: name-calling across the hallways, jokes at the back of the classroom. These boys could be expected to fight back, and they were known to be good at it. The cleverest tormentors stood near a teacher for protection and whispered their epithets as the Native kids walked by. "Hey, Nitchie. Want some Lysol?" If a fight broke out, the instigator would turn to the teacher with a look of puzzlement. "What? I didn't do anything...."

It was after school and at recess that I understood there were dangers to being white, if you were caught in the wrong situation. In the elementary grades, a boy named Billy Tootoosis used to follow me and my friend Andrew every day after school. I'm not sure Billy understood why he hated us, but he knew I was scared, and I suppose that was good enough for him. He used to come up beside me on the sidewalk and inflate his bony chest and squint at me through the convex lenses of his old-fashioned black-framed glasses. "Wanna fight," he would say. It was a command, not a question. Every time he said it I answered, "I'm your *friend*, Billy." And every time, he accepted this stupid assertion—not because he believed it, but because his question had served its purpose.

I never did fight Billy, but sometimes Andrew did. During their struggles on the lawn of the boulevard, I feigned impartiality by holding their glasses for them. I remember looking down on their fights with one pair of glasses in each hand, like some myopic statue of justice—a self-appointed referee of the battle between the races. As if I could opt out of the battle myself whenever it was convenient.

I didn't always find the neutral ground so easily. There were many other dangerous places in my neighbourhood, many other people to avoid. The Fiddler boys frightened me the most. They travelled together in a little gang, and I often saw them lurking near the T. C. Confectionery or hanging out in the labyrinthine hallways of the hockey rink. Once, when I was in grade one or two, they chased me halfway across town, from the old hospital down to the low-rental housing units and out toward the stampede grounds. They had managed to position themselves between me and home, so there was nothing for me to do but run farther and farther into dangerous territory. I remember glancing from one strange and decrepit house to the next, wondering which of them might contain someone who would protect me. But I believed none of them would.

I kept running. I heard the Fiddler boys laughing as they followed, and sometimes shouting phrases in Cree. The silver jackknife in my front pocket bounced against my leg as I ran, and I remember resolving to use it when the time came. I almost looked forward to the confrontation, imagining the looks on their faces when I waved the blade in the sunlight.

But then, miraculously, the time didn't come. They must have grown bored with the pursuit, because they stopped running and eventually turned down another street.

At the time, I didn't wonder why they had been chasing me in the first place. It seemed inevitable that they would. I wonder now if it wasn't just my fear that made them want to do it. I was never good at disguising fright. I always believed that I could make myself look tough by squinting my eyes and breathing through clenched teeth, but it never worked. I don't suppose the Fiddler boys thought much about why they pursued me either, but if anyone had asked them they might have said it was fun to put a scare into wimpy little white boys. They always gave up the chase before catching me. I suppose to them I was just a bit of entertainment, a sideshow: *let's watch the white kid run!* I think they might even have said I deserved a bit of a scare. I had been blessed with all kinds of things that they were excluded from: relative wealth, the respect of teachers, an expectation in the community that I would make something of myself. And I took it all for granted. I can see how blithely annoying I must have been.

It was all about belonging for them too, I think. In Meadow Lake, belonging was written on our skin. We all shared a knowledge of the difference between brown faces and white, knowledge that came complete with a whole series of lessons in racism: rules about whom we could associate with, where we could feel safe, what we could become when we grew up. Everyone lived by those rules. I knew I belonged in school and in our backyard, whereas theirs was the kingdom of the roadways, the stampede grounds, the reserve. We all patrolled our territories, watching for each other....

———•—•———

BORN IN FORGET

MY GRANDMOTHER, Marie Clemence, died in 1991, and in the following few years the family began to talk about her history. The information came gradually, and at first it took the form of nuances, unfinished sentences, suggestions. Eventually one of my aunts came out and told me—almost nonchalantly, in the midst of other family reminiscences while we were cleaning raspberries from the garden—that her mother had been of mixed Native ancestry: that she was Metis.

"You mean from the voyageur's wife?" I said, thinking back to what Dad had told me about our ancestor François Beaulieu in the eighteenth century.

"Oh no, they were all Metis," she said. "Her mom and dad both, and all their families way back." She went on to tell me that Grandma had learned Cree as a young girl, and that our ancestors had been part of the Red River Settlement.

As I listened I felt like I was standing on muskeg. *Where do I come from?* The story I had been telling myself all my life was incomplete, incorrect. Norway, France, Germany, my mother's belly, my hometown, yes. But Indian? How could that be?

"Mom's mother was born in a place called Forget," my aunt added, "and one time I asked Aunt Josephine how come my grandma was born so far away from Ituna, and she said, 'Oh, they were on a buffalo hunt.'"

My aunt said all this as if it were a historical curiosity rather than something that might have a real effect on Grandma's descendants. But to me, having grown up in a community that was hypersensitive about the divisions between Native and white, this information was unsettling, to say the least. What did it mean about me? I remembered the Fiddler boys chasing me through town, yelling in Cree. At the time we all thought we knew what sides we were on.

So *Grandma* was the Indian in the woodpile, the one my family had been speculating about all those years. I had known that her second husband (not my grandfather) was Metis, but somehow I had never considered that Grandma herself might be Metis as well. I was white, after all, and so were my parents. Everyone in Meadow Lake would have said so.

Grandma would have probably said so too. I had never heard her deny having Native ancestry, but I had certainly never heard her proclaim it either, and I think the silence of her children on the subject indicated that she was not interested in spreading the news. This is not at all surprising, given the prejudices against Native people and against the Metis in particular during her lifetime. She was born within a generation of Louis Riel's execution, and raised in an era when Metis people had many reasons to disguise their heritage if they could. For a long time after the North West Rebellion, to be Metis was to be considered traitorous, untrustworthy, savage. Officially, the government treated the Metis as if they didn't exist, saying that they should choose to be either white or Indian and should deal with the government as one or the other.

Many Metis were pushed off their lands after the rebellion, by soldiers and then by settlers. After this, most of them had absolutely nothing: no home, no pride, no status in the eyes of the nation. They were at the absolute bottom of the social scale, lower even than the Status Indians, who had at least some land and the dubious honour of treaties. In the great dispersal of Metis people after the rebellion, it was no wonder that many of them chose to suppress their Metis identity when they moved to new places. Passing as white was a survival technique; those who couldn't do that would often try to pass as Cree. The result was that generations of Metis were born into a vast canyon of forgetting.

Now that we have been shaken into remembering, everyone in my family has dealt with the knowledge in their own ways. Some would rather not acknowledge it at all, while others see that the Native heritage is there, but they don't see how it matters, why it should make any difference to who and what we are now. A few have gone so far as to claim themselves as Metis and to announce this publicly by becoming official members of provincial Metis associations. It is a source of great controversy in the family, and one measure of the strength of this controversy is the fact that it is still seldom discussed.

For me, the knowledge did matter. I started to wonder if I really was the person I had thought I was, if I really belonged where I had always assumed I did. I found myself in a between-space, a location that the logic of Meadow Lake didn't allow. It was impossible to be both a Native person and a non-Native person; the two notions were mutually exclusive.

I didn't discuss this quandary much at first. I thought most people would scoff at any claims I might make regarding aboriginal identity—and I wouldn't really have blamed them for scoffing.

I felt a certain amount of guilt about the fact that this Native heritage had been hidden for so long, and about the possibility that I had unknowingly benefited from that secrecy. I had never been subject to discrimination on the basis of my hidden Native ancestry. Now that it was becoming more socially acceptable to be a Native person—at least in the cities where I had lived for several years—I wondered if it was hypocritical to announce this discovery about myself. But to keep that aspect of my family's past a secret also felt wrong, was a perpetuation of the racial divide that had existed for so long in Meadow Lake and across the continent.

I also wondered what Native people would think about such claims. For generations, they have been the focal points of impersonation schemes by Europeans. Grey Owl is the most famous example of this, but there have been many other non-Native people who have tried to supplement some missing aspect of themselves by attempting to become Native. The last thing I wanted was to be seen as one of these contemporary Grey Owls, who often unwittingly cause offence to the very people they seek to emulate.

As some other members of my family began to go public with our family secret, though, I started to feel a little more comfortable with it. One of my cousins informed me that she had joined the Manitoba Metis Federation, and my uncle Vic started to become active in Saskatchewan Metis politics. Most of my friends in Toronto were quite excited to learn about my Metis ancestry. Some even treated me with a certain amount of awe, perhaps because they had only met a precious few real Native people, or because they believed that being aboriginal was somehow inherently valuable. Others were confused by the contrast between my appearance and the revelation of my background. I don't "look Native," if there is such a look. Nonetheless, some of my acquaintances claimed to be able to see it in my cheekbones.

Once I had mentioned the family secret to a few people, it began to take on a life of its own, and I started to wish I had kept it to myself. People seemed to be unable or unwilling to accept the idea that I could be Metis *and* Norwegian *and* German *and* French. For some of them I became simply "the Native guy," while others insisted, "Yeah, but you're white; I mean, look at you." At the same time I was, as always, privy to racist comments against Indians, made by people who assumed I had no connection to them.

I never did talk to Dad about all this, though I heard him acknowledge his Metis ancestry a few times after the fact became established in the family. I didn't ask him how long he had known about Grandma's origins, or whether he had always known. I didn't ask if he had ever thought that he was keeping a secret or that others in the family were keeping one from him. I wondered if he felt the same kind of destabilization that I felt, the same sense of self-division. He had lived in Meadow Lake for longer than I had; he must have sensed the weight of the community's contradictions within himself. Did he think of himself as Metis, or as white, or as something else—a hybrid of a hybrid? I wanted to know all this, but the subject had such an aura of taboo about it that I couldn't bring myself to ask him.

A few years later, when I ended up being called "a Metis writer" in the national media, I realized that I had to think seriously about the ways I would advertise my identity. And the more I thought about it, the more it became clear to me that I simply don't feel like I am exclusively an aboriginal person. I have some Metis ancestry, and I have been raised among many Native people, but I didn't grow up with the sense that I was one, and I have never learned their cultures from the perspective of an insider. I feel closely connected to Native people, and particularly to the Metis, but it doesn't seem quite right to claim that I am one. I am instead a little of this and a little of that; a child of the heterogeneous multitudes. I come from half the globe, and I come from Meadow Lake.

DIONNE BRAND

from

A Map to the Door of No Return

Notes to Belonging

ARMOUR

I AM ALWAYS IN the armour of my car in these small northern Ontario towns. They are unremittingly the same. There is a super-market, a liquor store, a video store where there is also milk, bubble gum, and Coca-Cola, and inevitably a pickup truck parked in a lot. There is sometimes a garage with a greasy man or two and a harassed guard dog or an old dog suffering from hip dysplasia. The small town to which I drive every morning and which I never become so familiar with as not to think of my car as my armour, my town is the same as the rest. And yes, there is also a cemetery and a church, two churches for a population that can hardly divide into two. The garage in this town has a mechanic who hates to talk. He keeps a dog tied up on a filthy mattress inside the garage. One day

I see this dog who has also been cultivated for fierceness and I want to let him go, even if he will bite me. The mechanic who is also the gas attendant is a middle-aged man. He has been burned by wind and snow and gas fumes. His face is scaled red with white patches. His mouth is a tight thin wire. His jeans have grown small, but he hasn't disowned them. Sometimes I am not sure if he will sell me gas. Sometimes I am not sure if the corner store will rent me a video. Money is not always the currency here. Nor books, which I could offer. There might be no way of exchanging even the things that strangers might exchange. Here I feel that I do not share the same consciousness. There is some other rhythm these people grew up in, speech and gait and probably sensibility.

THERE ARE WAYS OF constructing the world—that is, of putting it together each morning, what it should look like piece by piece—and I don't feel that I share this with the people in my small town. Each morning I think we wake up and open our eyes and set the particles of forms together—we make solidity with our eyes and with the matter in our brains. How a room looks, how a leg looks, how a clock looks. How a thread, how a speck of sand. We collect each molecule, summing them up into flesh or leaf or water or air. Before that everything is liquid, ubiquitous and mute. We accumulate information over our lives which bring various things into solidity, into view. What I am afraid of is that waking up in another room, minutes away by car, the mechanic walks up and takes my face for a target, my arm for something to bite, my car for a bear. He cannot see me when I come into the gas station; he sees something else and he might say, "No gas," or he might simply grunt and leave me there. As if I do not exist, as if I am not at the gas station at all. Or as if something he cannot understand has arrived—as if something he despises has arrived. A thing he does not recognize. Some days when I go to the gas station, I have not put him together either. His face is a mobile mass, I cannot make out his eyes, his hair is straw, dried grass stumbling toward me. Out the window now behind him the scrub pine on the other side of the road, leaves gone, or what I call leaves, the sun white against a wash of grey sky, he is streaking toward me like a cloud. Frayed with air. The cloud of him arrives, hovers at the window. I read his face coming apart with something—a word I think. I ask for gas; I cannot know what his response is. I pass money out the window. I assume we have got the gist of each other and I drive away from the constant uncertainty of encounters. I drive through the possibility of losing solidity at any moment.

PINERY ROAD AND CONCESSION 11

THE WATER PUMP chortles and the car stops abruptly. I am in a great field of snow at Pinery Road and Concession 11. In the summer here the trees form a cathedral over the road. Today they are frost-bitten, their summer communion broken, their branches brittle.

THE CAR STOPS. I try several times to turn the engine over, but nothing. It is three kilometres back to town where there is a post office at which perhaps the librarian who is also the post mistress might allow me to use the phone. I have been living out here in the bush for two years now. This place fills me with a sense of dread but also mystery. I fear the people more than the elements, which are themselves brutal. Winters here are harsh and long. I spend mornings getting the house warm. The house is still six kilometres away from Pinery Road and Concession 11 where my car has stalled.

I HAVE INHERITED this fear of people from my grandmother. She never went outside the house except on the rare occasion when some bureaucratic necessity, some official order, warranted it. She was a fearful woman, a private woman. To ask a neighbour for anything, which straightened circumstances necessitated, caused my grandmother much anxiety and shame. She would have the family wait until the last possible resistance gave way before sending a carefully worded message to a neighbour for help. I am the same way. I sit and panic and wait and wait until the last moment before calling for mercy. Then I compose my plea, then I agonize about the composition—is it too brief, is it too long, is it overweening, is it too dignified to warrant sympathy? When I am sure, deciding most times on brevity, I approach the telephone three or four times. Sometimes this last process takes a whole day, sometimes two. I wait again to see if I cannot do without what I need. Does it really matter? Can I not find it another way? Is asking for help really the only thing I can do?

SO I SIT IN THE car at Pinery Road and Concession 11 wondering how I can get the car to move without going for help. Help exposes you to people's disdain was how my grandmother saw it. In this way my grandmother assumed nothing of anyone, nothing good, perhaps; she only assumed her own acts. What will the librarian say when I walk into town and ask her for the favour of using the phone? What foolish act of mine caused me to have to ask? I contemplate leaving the car there in the middle of the road and walking deliberately into the snow and the forest.

ALL AROUND ME IS forest, except to one side there is an open field where cows graze in the summer. There are few houses along the three kilometres to my house—lone buildings on acres of forbidding forest. In the winter they are for the most part empty. Like my grandmother, for me the outside is treacherous. This is country where people mind their own business; they are as cold and forbidding as the landscape. They live out here free of the city, they guard what they call their "property," they eschew city life, they love country music's lonesome and outlaw tenors. They are suspicious of strangers. I can only imagine nightmarishly what they think of me. I am grateful for their sense of privacy.

WHEN YOU LIVE out here, six kilometres from Pinery Road and Concession 11, you become impervious to the cold. The winter is thermal. You go out on your "property" only in jeans and a flannel shirt. Granted, your feet must be well shod for the wetness, but you gradually do not need a jacket. You need a dog and you need a gun, but not a jacket or a coat. I have left the dog at home. Unfortunately I do not have a gun or perhaps walking the six kilometres home could be easy.

SNOW IS QUIET. It is not like rain. It has the sound of nothing happening. It is like a deep breath held and held. I sit in the car and the cold of it begins to creep in. There is a way that land defeats you, just the sum of it. In a cold car at Pinery Road and Concession 11, you notice its width.

WHEN IT'S COVERED in snow you know that it is hardly sleeping. It is like a huge brown-backed being waiting.

IN THE SNOW every distance is long. At Pinery Road and Concession 11 there is a peace, except it is too much peace. I imagine remaining in the car until all this peace and snow covers me and I melt into the forest. I settle into eternity. I would prefer the world to stop now, or at least my part in the world at Pinery Road and Concession 11. But it doesn't, so I contemplate the walk to Burnt River.

BURNT RIVER IS WHERE the librarian doubles as the post mistress. I cannot say how I have managed to live in this country place.

Summers and winters. Like my grandmother I hardly speak to anyone. I keep to myself. Each morning when I am not sitting in my dead car at Pinery Road and Concession 11, I go to town, Kinmount, about ten minutes by car along Highway 121. I buy a newspaper, bubble gum from the gum machine, and on occasion any supplies I need for the house, my bunker on Concession 11. Gradually, but it has taken me months, I exchange a few words with Mr. Dettman at Dettman's Store, where I buy my newspaper and bubble gum. Dettman's also rents videos. It would not be too much of an exaggeration to say that I've seen every video Dettman's has in stock. Mr. Dettman, no more talkative than I, manages something approximating civility when I enter. A nod. I nod back but I am much more eager to please or not to cause offence here in this town, which is all white except for the Chinese people who took over the restaurant in my last year in the bush. So I not only nod but also say good morning and take some time looking over the movies for anything new. Nothing, so I buy my paper, my bubble gum, and on the mornings when I feel that I must show Mr. Dettman a loyalty, a bottle of distilled water. Then I get into my car and head to Concession 11. I enjoy my bubble gum on the way home. Sometimes I buy two pieces. I like to put my quarter in the machine and wait for the routine surprise of colour. I like the reds and the blues. I never buy more than two pieces or else there would be no reason to go to town except the newspaper.

IF THE RED FLAG ON my mailbox is up I am delighted. It means that there is news from away. My grandmother's "away" was England. Mine is Toronto or Ottawa, sometimes England or the United States. To be sure, one of the benefits of living in the bush is that it gives you distance. A lovely distance from everything. There is no urgency, as when you live in a city. It does not matter if you do not return a phone call or get some very important thing done. Very important things do not need to get done. Very important things do not happen. Except for the porcupine climbing the pine in spring, or the moose crossing the river one winter, or the snowplow plowing me into the driveway after all my shovelling. Or the wood I have to fetch and pile near the stove to be dried and the other pile I have on the veranda. All right, all the stages of wood I have to arrange, the pile under the tarp I have to shake the ice off of, the pile near the doorway. The whole business of ordering the wood in the fall from the farmer who does not have a phone. Sound man. I drive to his place down Highway 503 and call to him. He comes out up to his arms in blood. I hope that he hasn't killed his wife, but I am already out of my car and cannot retreat. She appears a few seconds later to put my mind at rest. Calfing, he says, explaining his hands. I order two cords of wood; I give the money to his wife and leave. When he brings the wood several days later his arms are blistered. Poison ivy, he says. He drops the wood in the driveway, and we talk about wood: how much I'll need; when the cold seems like it's going to come; no, I might not burn any wood till late October this year counting by the *Farmers' Almanac;* oh yes, this will do me fine this year, not like last year when I ran out.

THESE ARE THE very important things of living in the country. There is a drought each year in midsummer. The river up the road recedes; my well water is not even two feet high. In May, June, and July you can hardly go outside for the mosquitoes and black flies. I have a green cylindrical hat with netting for walking; I have a white mosquito net draped around my bed. I bought it second-hand somewhere. There were a few holes in it I had to mend. It's very good lying under it, making sure no mosquitoes get in when I do. I lie there at night in the very, very dark of the country, the smell of pine and cedar around me, the very quiet of the bush pressing in, and I listen until I fall asleep.

BUT NOW I AM sitting in the car at Pinery Road and Concession 11 deciding to make my way to Burnt River and the post mistress. It is mid-afternoon. I've left the dog at home alone all morning. She'll be needing to get out by now. She's a good dog. Aggressive and unfriendly. I get out and lock the car. There's really no need here, even if it wasn't stalled. There is no one here who would steal it. This is not a desperate place. It is a still place. To steal a car requires a kind of quick desperation. If there is desperation here it is the kind that is slow burning, the kind that drinks beer and smokes cigarettes and is overwhelmed by the bush or the river, the kind that makes the body grow large and lumbering and listless. There is no one on this road today. Only me. I stand in the middle of the road and take in my choices: to the left along Pinery Road where I've never turned; to the right six kilometres of turns and bends and possible surprises to my house and the dog; to the north into the bush of deep snow or to the northwest into the open field where I can lie down and be swallowed up by tonight's snowfall and wind; or to the post office. Cautious, I head for the post office.

WHAT I AM DOING out here I do not know. I mean of course in the sense that I did not know I would end up here. *End up* is not the right phrase. My life is not over. *Land* may be a better word. Landing is what people in the Diaspora do. Landing at ports, dockings, bridgings, stocks, borders, outposts. Burnt River is another outpost, another destination. Conrad was a seaman who had his darkness; I have Burnt River. But I had no destination in mind. I am without destination; that is one of the inherited traits of the Diaspora. I am simply where I am; the next thought leads me to the next place. I have come to Burnt River to write. I have ended up writing a few books in Burnt River. I landed in Burnt River and I am writing a few books. I had no money so I came to Burnt River. I left somewhere else and came to Burnt River. I am in Burnt River. I am lucky that the name of this place is beautiful, though it is beautiful in that same oppositional way as everything else. River and Burnt. The history of this name I do not know, but it is like all names in the New World cut through with something terrible that happened. Altered, as River is by Burnt. And what this place was called in its own language I do not know. But River must have been in it. One night, one of the rare nights that friends visited, sleeping in the upstairs of my house someone had a dream of something with a great wing passing over the house. The next morning one of those friends who was Six Nations asked, "Whose land is this, I wonder?" Whoever's it was, they had passed over the house. I thought of this winged being when I was alone. Sometimes at night I felt it pass and linger at the tops of the scrub pines. It was not a peaceful thing, though it meant no harm to me, I think.

YOU WOULD NOT KNOW it to look at me but I am like my grand-mother a person of sure perimeters. Though I have arrived all the way here in Burnt River I am not adventuresome. Burnt River is just below the forty-fifth parallel, and I have arrived here—well, to be sure I have meandered here—from the tenth parallel. But that is not to say much. I still take the small steps of my grandmother; I lift my eyes only to the immediate area of the house I live in, the small bit of road I can see from the window. Though I look intently and I know each dead weep of grass within my view. I pore over the spindly shrub pine clacking together in the wind. One winter I shovelled the hundred-foot driveway, three feet deep in snow, the whole winter long, crying at my misfortune, before I got the idea to call a snowplow. I always had the idea that while my grandmother did not move much she observed well. So, hunkered in my house in Burnt River I scrutinize each window's drama of trees and sky. But in the beginning I did not notice wildflowers. So intent on the hardship of living out here and missing the city and missing friends. I never bathed in the river, I never jumped off the bridge in town. Life was always something waiting to happen later. Until one day at this same spot at Pinery Road and Concession 11, when it was fall and all the grass had turned brown and wilted, I saw something violet. I thought, "What a fool!" struggling up like that with winter coming. And all through the fall I thought, "Well, I never!" when violet kept appearing on the side of the road. Finally I thought, "Well, what else is possible? Nothing but to make a go of it, I suppose."

AFTER A HUNDRED METRES or so, I turn and look back at the car. Its hulk is already embraced by the snowy road. The road knows that wherever you find yourself you are.

SHARON BUTALA

from

The Perfection of the Morning

An Apprenticeship in Nature

DREAM COYOTE

THE DAY I LEFT SASKATOON for good, I had sold my house, abandoned a promising job teaching at the university as well as my nearly completed master's degree, and said farewell to a circle of good women friends and to my mother and three of my four sisters and their families who lived there. I was both rather proud of my own daring and a little appalled at it; the image of a burning bridge was strong in my mind, and I stoked the flames gleefully, with a feeling close to triumph.

Although they said nothing, I knew both my friends and my family thought I was making a terrible mistake. Such is the prestige of a university job, the sense of those who make a life there as being the anointed, that my fellow graduate students and lecturers must have found my abdication from it very hard to understand. If my mother and sisters were collectively holding their breaths, not wanting to pass judgment and hoping against hope for the best, I knew my friends expected me to be back, newly divorced, in a year if not sooner, for marriage breakdown was happening all around us at the time—divorce, separation, reshuffling of couples, more split-ups, more divorces, more unhappiness.

And the truth was, in that first two or three years of my new life, I often said to myself that if I'd really understood what I was getting into, I'd never have done it, not realizing before I left that if my own family and friends had their private doubts about our marriage, the same was true of Peter's family, his friends, even his hired man. In my new life I would have to learn to deal with, at the least, skeptical glances, and for every person who was welcoming, there would be no shortage of people who, though they ought to have been at least silent, if not kind, on the subject of my suitability as a wife for Peter were neither.

Peter had been born and had never lived anywhere else but on the remote family ranch in the Old Man On His Back range of hills, south of the Cypress Hills, and north of the peaked, purple line of the Bears Paw Mountains in Montana. Unlike most of the city men I knew, he didn't nourish in secret bitterness unfulfilled dreams about another, better life; he loved his life as a cowboy-rancher and rural man. And, too, he was secure in his community, surrounded by men he'd gone to school with, cowboyed with, had good times with as far back as he could remember, who'd married and whose wives he'd known since childhood, and whose children were being raised into the same rural, agricultural world as their parents and grandparents and sometimes even great-grandparents had been.

Maybe it was his calmness, engendered by the deep sense of security stemming from a life lived all in one place, and of his sense of the rightness of his life that attracted me. But looking back, I see such a complicated mix of factors: the man, yes, but also the greenness and beauty of the landscape, and the smell of the air, the cool, sharp wind that swept away those things that in my city life I had thought were inevitable and unavoidable.

I first visited this place eighteen years ago on a twenty-fourth of May weekend when I drove down with my son, Sean. Peter had invited us months before, but I hadn't wanted to come, thinking that a ranch held no attractions for me. Peter repeated the invitation and Sean, all boy, had been begging me to go, till I finally gave in. Through a mix-up about dates (the twenty-fourth of May weekend didn't fall on the twenty-fourth that year), the day we arrived at the hay farm Peter was taken aback to see us. He and some other men were hard at work rounding up his cattle, sorting them, and loading them into huge trucks (called cattle liners) to haul them south to the ranch for the summer, since for a variety of reasons, including uncooperative weather, it was too late in the year to trail them on horseback the forty miles as he usually did. He explained to us that the cattle spend most of the year on the ranch, but winters they're trailed to the hay farm in the Frenchman River valley where the supply of winter feed is grown. This is a more economical alternative to moving the feed to the cattle. Peter was embarrassed because he couldn't leave his work to act the proper host and had to leave us pretty much to fend for ourselves.

I spent the entire day perched on the corral watching the men work. There is a snapshot of me sitting there, my hair well down below my shoulders, wearing jeans and a thick siwash-like sweater, which always reminds me of B.B. King since I bought it the same day I heard him perform at the Montreal Forum, in what was one of the highlights of my life (overshadowed only by the time in 1965 when I'd heard a young Bob Dylan perform in a half-empty Queen Elizabeth Theatre in Vancouver).

I was so fascinated by what I saw that the day flew by, even though all I did was sit and watch. Sean sat with me at first, but then he helped in the chute loading cattle into the trucks, and was nearly trampled by a steer when it backed down the chute, turned around, and was about to run over anybody who got in his way.

"Climb the corral! Climb the corral!" the men shouted at him, as Sean and the thousand-pound steer faced off and I watched, too dumb even to realize his life was, quite seriously, in danger, since the steer might avoid him, but more likely wouldn't. Sean, twelve at the time, leaped to the side of the chute and scrambled up the corral rail with the agility that marked him as a young athlete, so that my heart swelled with pride. Later there was a branding, and Peter invited Sean to help wrestle calves, an invitation Sean eagerly accepted. When Peter teasingly invited me to do the same, I laughed and said no thanks.

I think now that if there hadn't been that confusion about which weekend we were to arrive, and Peter had taken the days off to do as he usually did for visitors—drive them around the countryside, show them the ranch, saddle horses and take them for a ride—I would have said, Ho hum, gone away and never come back again. But the privilege of actually seeing the real work of the ranch and all the things that went with it had a different effect on me. I remember afterward laughingly telling my mother we'd spent the weekend in the middle of a Roy Rogers movie, but if I joked with her about it, and if Sean viewed it as an entertaining but not-to-be-repeated adventure which he soon forgot about, I was actually stirred so deeply that everything in my old life—friends, job, family, politics—paled beside it.

It wasn't just the scenery or the novelty of everything that captivated me. I was struck also by how comfortable those men had seemed, how at ease they were in their work, and how unassuming and casual in their skill with the animals and with the tools they used to manage them. I was surprised to see they were actually enjoying themselves. They laughed, cracked jokes, kidded each other while they worked in the corral or on horseback, roped, or cut out cattle and chased them in. I was used to a world perpetually fraught with tension, with competitiveness so extreme at times as to seem really crazy, where the only constant was steady but, nonetheless, gut-wrenching change and the resulting mad scrabbling for position. As I sat on the rail watching and listening that day a new world was washing slowly over me, seeping in without my noticing, a slower world, and a timeless one that resonated with a sense that it must always have been there in just this way and always would be.

It had been an unusually wet spring, and although it wasn't warm, the hills and grassy plains were as green and inviting as Ireland, so that my first look at the area was, to this extent, deceptive. As I look back to that weekend such a long time ago, when my world changed forever, the memory is dreamlike: the men riding their horses at a walk through the tall green grass and wildflowers on the riverbank, the wave of sloping green hills behind them, the clarity and the veracity of the light, in the lulls between wind gusts the music of birds, the splash of the shallow brown river running by below the corrals, the click of the cattles' hooves, the cowboy ululations of the men.

I HAD NEVER LIVED on a farm. Both my parents had come from farms, though: my mother from southern Manitoba and my father first from a farm near Magog, Quebec, and then from near St. Isidore de Bellevue, Saskatchewan, about seven miles from Batoche, the site of the Riel Rebellion in 1884–5, the trenches of which may still be seen, as well as the bullet holes in the little church. I have sometimes wondered if my father, who didn't speak English himself till he learned it at school in Bellevue, had heard from his

French-speaking teachers in that French community about Louis Riel, Gabriel Dumont, and the battle fought just down the road from where they sat. Even though we have no Native blood that I know of, I do remember him mentioning Dumont more than once in a way that suggested the name and possibly the events were a part of his community's folklore. In those days, around 1912, there would not have been Native children in school with him, although many of the children must have been Métis, since Batoche was the heart of the Métis community in the old Northwest. But all that is an aside. It was a farming community and the Le Blancs, too, having come as farmers to Acadia in mid-seventeenth century, were still farmers.

My sisters and I came from pioneering families on both sides: both sets of grandparents had homesteaded, as had our parents, so that "the homestead" was part of our basic vocabulary, a term we must have learned along with "mother," "father" and "bread." Our Irish-Canadian grandfather, Francis Graham, was even said to have been born under the wagonbox near Portage-la-Prairie, Manitoba, as his family trekked, in the early 1880s, from their home in Ontario to the West. Their original Manitoba farm was established in 1884, a Centennial Farm, a fact of which the family is inordinately, and justifiably, proud. On that side of the family our children are fifth-generation westerners.

This is how it was that my sisters and I grew up with the notion of the farm as a mythic paradise from which we had been expelled, by drought and bankers, and could never return. Basic as it was to us, though, having never lived on a farm much less a ranch, which belonged to some other tradition than our family's, we viewed the notion as city dwellers do, quizzically, with a touch of apprehension, possibly even a little distaste.

In the years since the summer I turned thirteen and we moved to the city, I had become so urbanized that I knew nothing about farming, or about the daily life led by people who made their living in agriculture. I thought of myself proudly as a sophisticated city woman, but even that first weekend with Peter, strangely, I kept having flashes of déjà vu. They were incomplete, vague and unformed, and yet carried with them a puzzling tug of recognition, of memories that were more visceral even than images or fragments of conversations. Bewilderingly, I felt comfortable when I should have felt ill at ease; I felt at home when I should have felt lost. The can of evaporated milk on the table we used for our coffee, the orange offered me for dessert, the denseness of the air, the smell, the feeling of being close to the earth in the log house where we stayed were all *just so* to me; I felt transported to a familiar way of being and to a familiar place. Yes, I thought, and then, but how do I know this?

Gradually, over the year of our courtship, I began to remember what I had deliberately forgotten, how I had spent the first four years of my life in wilderness, living in log or hastily thrown together frame shacks in what we call the bush in northern Saskatchewan. I was conceived there, carried for nine months in my mother's body there, knew no other place for those first formative years. My earliest memories are of nuggets of sunlight glinting off shoulder-high, damp emerald grass, of playing in the roots of trees, of the ephemeral, terrifying beauty of the northern lights, of the soul-stirring wail of timber wolves, of our mother setting coal oil lamps in windows to keep bears away, of mountains of snow and impass-able, muddy or "corduroy" roads, boggy stretches which settlers covered with unpeeled slabs of trees for wagons or cars to bump over, and the richness of the texture, scent, the vibrant colour of the air of northern Saskatchewan.

For a time my mother's parents rented a farm somewhere north of Prince Albert or Nipawin: the feel of the hot sandy road on our bare feet as Cynthia, my older sister, and I whiled away the interminable summer afternoons while our grandparents napped, having been up since dawn, playing in our grandmother's garden where with our cousins we built bowers and planted cities and made celebratory avenues out of plucked pinks, pansies, bachelor's buttons and daisies, waiting for our mothers to come and collect us. And the violent northern storms where we sat indoors with our feet up off the floor as lightning cracked and thunder boomed all around the small log house, the swaying yellow lanterns, the feathery legs of our grandfather's big work horses, their huge feet and their quiet steady air, our grandmother smiling and silent, as if meditating, as she sat moving the paddle of the butter churn up and down for hours in the kitchen, morning after morning spooning up the breakfast porridge from her blue willow bowls till the sad lovers and the weeping willow between them were revealed again.

In that setting at the hay farm, the colour and feel of an orange in my hand, the can of milk on the table were suddenly freighted with meaning beyond the immediate circumstances, meaning that at first I could not quite decipher. I was now beginning to remember the early childhood I had chosen to forget as both value-less and unsuitable for the person I had been trying to become. As I remembered it, I began slowly to reclaim it in surprise and delight, for in this new context it was valued, something to be proud of, a treasury of meaning, facts, knowledge. I didn't consciously think so at the time, but in some ways it began to seem that instead of coming to a new place, I had come home.

As time passed and I visited the hay farm occasionally, the rural setting with the Frenchman River running past the house, I remembered too the Saskatchewan River from a later time in my childhood when we'd lived in a village on its banks before the damming of it. I remembered the crash and roar of the ice going out in the spring, especially the spring it almost took the great black iron bridge with it, and our father (with the Mountie's permission) bravely walking out onto it, just to feel the power of the river, I guess, as we waited, breathless and awestruck, on the bank for him either to be swept away forever or to return to us. The river's great, wild presence came back to me, its spirit which hovered over it and around it and in it and which affected everyone who came near it touched me again; I could even recall its heavy, scented odour.

What I could remember about that natural world from which our family had been separated by so little was a combination of smells, the feel of the air, a sense of the presence of Nature as a living entity all around me. All of that had been deeply imprinted in me, but more in the blood and bone and muscles—an instinctive memory—than a precise memory of events or people. I remembered it with my body, or maybe I remembered it with another sense for which we have no name but is no less real for that. As I returned to the ranch and hay farm to visit, the sense of this memory grew; I found myself inexorably drawn to it although I did not understand this at the time, preferring to accept the obvious romantic scenario of marrying and living happily ever after.

If I could recover my powerful early connections with Nature, there was still the reality that as I became a town and then a city child, I had stopped thinking of Nature as people raised in it do and began to think of it as urban people do: as a place to holiday—the mountains, the seaside, a quiet lake somewhere in the country—as a place to acquire a suntan, have a summer romance, paint a picture of, enjoy a change of atmosphere. For a long period in my late teens and early twenties, I actively avoided picnics, complaining bitterly that they were stupid since there were always dirt and bugs and leaves in your food and insects to bite you, and although they were supposed to be a holiday, picnics were more work for us women than cooking a meal in the kitchen would be.

Besides, for a girl born in the bush into relative poverty who, for whatever reasons, had learned to aspire to a more glamorous lifestyle—at six, never having seen a dancer other than my father stepdancing late at night at a farmhouse party somewhere—I wanted to be a ballet dancer; I wanted to wear satin ballgowns, go to the theatre, have movie stars for friends. I did not want to go back to the bush, a place so terrible that my mother, once we were gone from there, wouldn't even speak of it. When I asked about it when she was an old woman, she told me that she tried never to think of it, and on her deathbed, when I asked again, her response came in a distant whisper, her eyes dark and fixed on something I couldn't see: "It was so cold ... the wind was always blowing ... in the morning ... the men would ... put on their things and go out...." She fell into silence and I regretted asking her, and yet I wanted to know, I truly wanted to know.

There was indeed a whole other story, a narrative, our family history transformed into our family mythology, which was what I had grown into since the other—the compelling, intense beauty of Nature and our lives lived in the midst of it—was never spoken of, never even conceived of in any concrete way in all the years since we'd left. Our father said nothing; our mother painted golden pictures of her girlhood on the prosperous farm in Manitoba, which I at least doubted, although I never dared say so. (And a good thing, too, because long after her death, when I paid my only visit there, I saw that they had all been true.) We had come from better things—land ownership and wealth, ancient heroism, blood links to the aristocracy in Ireland and Scotland—our fortunes had fallen, but we as people had not fallen with them, and consequently we did not dwell on the hardships, the misfortunes, the demeaning struggles for survival, refusing to accept them as anything more than temporary conditions to be met with courage and disdain.

I think, in accepting about our family history what I was told, I was often confused by the contrast between it and the life I had lived. I couldn't doubt what my mother said, yet these ancient family memories were no more to me than fairy tales. (As I grew older, in fact, I persisted in identifying with my father's family.) I was too young at the time to have been able to keep clear mental pictures of my own of our life in the bush into which I was born, but from my own diffuse memories in combination with our few ragged black-and-white snapshots, and eventually our mother's mother's memoirs, the images I knew were not inviting. The family stories, not often mentioned, were about hardship: people hurt or ill or losing or having babies, doctors miles away over bad or impassable roads and stories about survival in the cold; about the hard, hard labour of the men to provide the most meagre kind of existence for us under conditions that were often heartbreaking, the most instructive of these being how, according to our grand-mother's memoirs, during the Depression when our families ran out of cash, our father and our mother's father would spend an entire day in the bush cutting a couple of cords of firewood which they would take to town and sell for one dollar and fifty cents a cord. And once our grandfather had to carry one hundred pounds of flour on his back a mile and a half through the water and bog that had swallowed the road into his and our grandmother's log house.

But there also had been much laughter. Our mother and our aunts sometimes talked, when we were young, about the funny things that had happened, the practical jokes, the visiting with neighbours; there was even much laughter about the hardship, trailing off into muted smiles and finally silence freighted with a painful and, it seemed to me, confused nostalgia.

Even though that past which had become somehow shameful was hardly ever mentioned—such a fall it was for our mother and her family—as I grew up this was what I remembered. It had become far more important than the other—the life lived so close to Nature—which also was never spoken of. (Although I remember our mother, in her seventies at the time, saying in a dreamy voice with a faint smile, how our father "used to shoot ptarmigan." "Really? Ptarmigan?" I said. She looked at me, her distant smile vanishing, returned to her small house in Saskatoon where we sat together. "I think it was ptarmigan," she said. "I think it was your father.")

By the time I was twenty I had developed contempt for those who wanted to return to Nature, believing they were all romantic dreamers, nitwits from the city, people raised in the lap of luxury who did not know about Nature's nasty side, who had never done a day's real work in their lives and thus had no idea of the grinding labour a life in Nature demanded for mere survival. I liked to look at Impressionist paintings of Nature, having once harboured the dream of becoming a painter, and I was not averse to sunsets or moonlight on water, but I was just as happy to look at pictures of them while seated on a soft couch, with my feet on a thick rug and a well-insulated wall between me and the thing itself.

Yet driving home from some errand in Regina, late at night on a deserted and lonely highway, I often looked out my side window and saw above the hills a few small white stars, points of light in boundless darkness. Once, as I gazed up at them, my heart, a live thing in my chest, leaped, cracked and then hung there, aching. At that moment it seemed a thing apart from the *me* I knew, and it yearned with an intensity that was deeply sorrowful to go back to the immensity from which it declared itself to have come.

And, driving down for short visits in the year before our marriage, I used to wait for that first moment when I neared the ranch, when the country seemed to open up, and I saw again the wide fields of native grass cured, very quickly even after that wet, green spring, to a pale yellow by the sun, for with that sight came the much longed-for lifting of my heart, a metaphorical unfurrowing of my brow, the easing of my muscles, and the city life, my studies, my urban concerns fell away from me. It was as if in that magnificent spread of pure light across the grassy miles I could breathe freely for the first time since childhood.

PETER AND I DECIDED very soon after my first visit here that we would marry, but we both agreed, each for our own reasons, that it would be better to wait till the following spring. The winter was a long one, and at Christmas, leaving behind the round of parties and my long, silky dresses, I drove down with Sean to spend the week with Peter on the ranch.

It was my first lesson in the realities of ranching life. Although none of this made clear sense to me at the time, every winter the Butalas, on horseback, trailed their cattle the forty miles from the ranch northeast to the hay farm where there was shelter in the breaks of the Frenchman River and a winter's supply of hay and grain bales. Every spring they trailed them back south to spend late spring, summer and fall on the ranch where the great fields of grazing land were. Each move took three days, and sometimes four, since they were willing to travel at a pace comfortable to the cattle.

Peter took it for granted that I would do this without questioning it, and since I had no idea what I was getting into, I naively didn't. I got up one morning and soon found myself, with Sean beside me, driving the half-ton loaded with square bales behind a four-hundred-head herd of twelve-hundred-pound range cows and two- and three-year-old steers and heifers. Between the half-ton and the herd were four men on horseback, and out of sight up ahead, another led the way in the four-wheel-drive ton truck.

I had never seen anybody move cattle before, and I knew nothing about range cattle. Peter's cattle were (and are) horned Herefords, beautiful, powerful animals whose strong white horns can kill with one well-aimed thrust, but I hardly knew enough to be afraid of them. Except in the most vague sense, I did not know where we were going—to a road allowance somewhere where we'd pen them for the night—or even very clearly why. I was in a kind of culture shock, at once bewildered, frightened, excited.

That winter there was an unusually large amount of snow which was in places, even out on the open and windswept plains, very deep. Since we were crossing uninhabited grassland that first day, our progress was slow because of it. All that first day, I drove through that frigid air, in the middle of what seemed to be nowhere, far from houses or barns or people, picking my way carefully through the deep snow, getting stuck occasionally when, recognizing by the roaring motor I was in trouble, Peter would ride back, dismount, and drive the truck out for me. After three or four rescues, I learned from him how to do it myself. It had been cold when we started out in the morning, but as the day wore on the temperature began to drop and it got colder and colder.

Darkness came in the late afternoon and we hadn't yet reached our destination. The wind had begun to blow, and snow drifted across the backs of the cattle and the hood of the truck and swirled up around the riders hunched on their horses, sometimes blotting them from view. I discovered that if I stayed too close to the back of the herd—they had never "strung out" that day, but moved in a clump—my headlights would throw their own shadows over the cattle, which would frighten them and make them run, bad for their lungs in that intense cold. I tried to keep far enough back to prevent that from happening, but in that directionless, timeless darkness and that inexpressible cold, if I could not see the riders between me and the cattle, I grew frightened. I struggled to keep the truck neither too close nor too far away.

By now it was about thirty-below Fahrenheit, completely dark, and we had still not arrived at wherever we were going. Picking my way carefully so as not to get stuck, I shone my headlights on what looked like a safe, flat spot and drove through it only to discover that the level snow hid a deep depression. I was stuck. I shifted into first and tried to roar ahead, and then through neutral into reverse, then back again, till I'd set up a rhythm, the old prairie trick of "rocking" my way out. But we were in too deep, and in a minute I'd stalled the motor. The riders kept moving on into the blackness out of the range of my headlights and were gone from view. Sean and I sat helpless, alone in the stalled, cooling truck in the darkness.

Before I had time to feel fully the fear that was threatening to swamp me, out of that blackness Peter came riding toward us, icicles hanging from his horse's mane and muzzle and clinging to his own eyebrows, lashes and beard. When he saw how deeply we were stuck, he told us to wait and he'd get the four-wheel-drive and pull us out.

"We're there," he added, as he rode away. I peered ahead and, at the place where the truck lights melted softly into moving, black emptiness, I saw a fence corner. How the men had found a mere fence corner, and the right one, in the blackness and blowing snow, I had no idea. I imagine there'd been consultations between them I hadn't heard, about how the fencelines ran in that field and, relative to them, what our location at any moment must be.

Peter was back in a minute in the four-wheel-drive and pulled us out. All the riders but one piled into the two trucks, while Peter and the remaining rider, using the trucks' headlights, held an intense conversation about what to do with the four horses, which were tired, hungry and very cold. The image is forever imprinted in my mind: sitting in the cab of that truck in that black and frigid winter night with snow all around us, far from succour of any kind, watching Peter and the other man unsaddle all but the lead horse, throw the saddles on the back of one of the trucks, and change their bridles for halters.

Then, as we watched, one by one they tied the tails of each of three of the horses to the halter of the horse ahead of it, till there was a line of four horses tied tail to halter, together. The other man mounted the lead horse and leaned down from his saddle to hear better while Peter gave him precise, careful instructions about how to find a ranch house almost three miles away across the frozen fields and through the blowing snow that obliterated landmarks. All of us knew, even I, that if the rider got confused in the darkness, or if the fences which he would be following had been changed from the year before, there was a good chance he might pass that shelter by and freeze to death.

The men closed the gate on the cattle, threw off the feed for them, settled them down for the night in a low spot out of the wind, and we went around by a prairie trail, with Peter driving my truck, to the ranch house where we found our rider had reached safely. The horses had already been fed and stabled, and the woman there invited us in for coffee. Not even trying to hide her surprise and what might have been a touch of awe, she said, "We expected you through one of these days, but we sure didn't think it would be on a night like this."

It was an overwhelming experience which afterward I could hardly find words to describe adequately to my friends and family. My mother must have been alarmed, although she was careful not to say so. Her memories of her hard years in the bush must have been strong, and I think she wanted to advise me to give up the idea of marrying Peter because of the hardship she was sure I would have to endure. On the other hand, if the Butalas were far from rich, having succeeded in wilderness where we had failed, it was clear they had at least a considerably more financially secure life than we had had when we were enduring those years of privation in the bush country, and this would make my life much easier than hers had been. And she must have seen in Peter the same qualities

I saw: his strength of character and physical strength, his stability, his integrity and his quiet competence.

The draw was powerful and it was not mitigated by the obvious physical danger of such a life; it may even have been enhanced by it. I saw nobody in my city life doing anything more physically dangerous than walking to work, and in Saskatoon that wasn't much of a risk. I'd had enough of my windowless office at the university and the endless manoeuvring for advantage, not to mention the incredibly hard work people of my lowly rank had to do for distressingly low pay; I'd had enough of the men I was meeting, each one of whom seemed to be more insecure, convoluted and uncertain than the last one; I couldn't wait to put it all behind me. The winter cattle drive had been more than memorable—it had been invigorating, simple, firmly tied to a physical reality that I had been missing and, without even realizing it, longing for.

ISABEL HUGGAN

from

Belonging

Home Away from Home

THERE IS NO WORD FOR HOME

IN THE COUNTRY WHERE I now live, there is no word for home.
You can express the idea at a slant, but you cannot say *home*. For
a long time this disconcerted me, and I kept running up against
the lack as if it were a rock in my path, worse than a pothole,
worse than nothing. But at last I have habituated myself and can
step around it, using variants such as *notre foyer* (our hearth) or
notre maison (our house) when I mean to say home. More often,
I use the concept *chez* to indicate physical location and the place
where family resides, or the notion of a comfortable domestic
space. However, if I wish to speak of "going home to Canada," I
can use *mon pays* (my country) but I can't say I am going *chez moi*
when I am not: for as long as I reside in France—the rest of my

life—this is where I will be *chez moi*, making a home in a country and a language not my own. I am both home and not-home, one of those trick syllogisms I must solve by homemaking, at an age when I should have finished with all that bother.

In the foothills of the Cévennes I live in a stone house that was, until only a few decades ago, home to silkworms, hundreds upon hundreds of them, squirming in flat reed baskets laid on layered frames along the walls in what was then the *magnanerie,* a place for feeding silkworms, and is now a bedroom. For the duration of their brief lives, these slippery dun-coloured creatures munched mulberry leaves, fattening themselves sufficiently to shed their skins four times before they'd stop eating and attach themselves to twigs or sprigs of heather on racks above the baskets. With a sense of purpose sprung from genetic necessity, they'd then spin themselves cocoons in which they'd sleep until they were plucked from their branches and dunked in huge kettles of hot water. Perhaps some luckier ones were allowed to waken and complete the magic of metamorphosis— there must be moths, after all, to furnish next season's eggs—but silk manufacturers preferred the longer filament, which comes from whole cocoons. There are sacrifices to be made for beauty, and if the life of a lowly and not very attractive segmented grub has to be that sacrifice, perhaps that is the Lord's will.

The Lord's will rests heavy on the high blue hills of the Cévennes, for here God has been imagined in Calvinist clothes, a moral master whose plans for man and beast alike are stern. This little-inhabited part of southern France (the mountainous northern corner of Languedoc, much of it now a national park) has long been the heart of Protestant opposition to Roman Catholicism. From the mid-1500s, revolt against Paris and the Church continued with appropriate bloodshed on all sides until the *Édit de Tolérance* in 1787 finally allowed those few Huguenots who remained the right to practise their religion.

The rugged terrain, hidden valleys and craggy cliffs are geologically congenial to the Protestant mind—in the back reaches of the Cévennes there have always existed stubborn pockets of religious and political resistance. This is an austere landscape where, even now, life is not taken lightly and where pleasure and ease are distrusted. The puritanical harshness of Reform doctrine seems also to show itself in the fortress-like architecture of Huguenot houses such as mine: angular, stiff-necked buildings, tall and narrow with small windows shuttered against the blasts of winter or the blaze of summer. Nevertheless, graceless and severe though it may appear from outside, the cool, dark interior of the house is a blessing when you step in from the painful dazzle of an August day. It is not for nothing that the stone walls are well over half a metre thick, or that the floors are laid with glazed clay tiles.

Sometimes I wake in the early morning before it is light, the still, dark hours of silent contemplation: how have I come to be here? But there is nothing mysterious, the reason is mundane—it is not the will of God, but the wish of the Scottish-born man to whom I have been married since 1970. The first time we came hiking in these mountains—more than a decade ago, while we were living in Montpellier—he said, immediately, that he knew he was *chez lui dans les Cévennes*. His experience was profound, affecting him in some deeply atavistic way I did not understand until later, when I felt the same inexpressible, magnetic, and nearly hormonal pull the moment I first set foot in Tasmania and knew myself to be home.

When it happens, this carnal knowledge of landscape, it is very like falling in love without knowing why, the plunge into desire and longing made all the more intense by being so utterly irrational, inexplicable. The feel of the air, the lay of the land, the colour and shape of the horizon, who knows? There are places on the planet we belong and they are not necessarily where we are born. If we are lucky—if the gods are in a good mood—we find them, for whatever length of time is necessary for us to know that, yes, we belong to the earth and it to us. Even if we cannot articulate this intense physical sensation, even if language fails us, we know what home is then, in our very bones.

I sometimes say jokingly that I have become a WTGW—a whither-thou-goest-wife, an almost extinct species, but one with which I have become intimately familiar in the years we have lived abroad because of Bob's work in development. I have met many other spouses—men, as well as women—who have done the same as I: we have weighed the choices, and we have followed our partners. Our reasons for doing so are as diverse as our marriages and our aspirations and the work that we do. In my case, writing is a portable occupation: I can do what I do anywhere.

And so it follows that I shall learn, as I have learned in other places, to make this house home. Over time, I shall find out how to grow in and be nourished by this rocky foreign soil. I early learn the phrase *je m'enracine ici,* which means "I am putting down roots here," in order to convince myself—for this time, we are not moving on. We are here to stay, *définitivement.*

The house, Mas Blanc, is one of ninety other scattered farms and hamlets that constitute the commune of Latourne. The property we bought includes a stone barn and a hectare of land beside the little river Ourne—a few old olive trees, a field we're making into an orchard, and part of the bush-covered hillside along our lane, where we gather deadwood for kindling. Mas means "farmhouse" and can designate either a single dwelling or a collection of buildings grouped together: over a couple of centuries, the central house, which is ours, extended itself in a manner not unlike the Mennonite farmhouses in Waterloo county where I grew up, with various stone outbuildings attaching themselves as part of the whole. Possession of this property has changed hands many times, until today the house and its various parcels of land are divided among three owners. We know, from a document dated 1646, that this was one of nine farms belonging to the Duchy of Latourne for which the family seat was a hilltop castle, now in ruins, about two kilometres away. Along with the others, Mas Blanc still bears the name it was given then, and we could never change it, even if we were so inclined. By chance, the stones from which the house is built are a light creamy colour, but we believe that the place was named for a family called Blanc, and not because it is white.

Within Latourne, various sections of the commune have specific names, some of them springing from location and others from historical connection. Our portion is known as La Grenouille, probably because the nearby Ourne and its two millponds are a perfect breeding ground for frogs. Big, plump, noisy frogs. Beginning in April and continuing through the summer, the nightly racket they make is less than charming if you are trying to sleep, but as the presence of frogs indicates an absence of pollution, we philosophically bear their creaking and honking. When we first bought the house, we were so amused to have something froggy as part of our address that we included it on everything—only to discover that the word *grenouille* is hellishly difficult to pronounce correctly. We've given it up, although the phone book continues to list it properly after our name.

The Ourne separates us from vineyards that once belonged to the nearby monastery, an assemblage of tall stone buildings divided long ago among four families who have left part in ruins and renovated the rest for their own use. Church records in Nîmes at the end of the eighth century mention the Monastère de St-Étienne and in 808 A.D., when Charlemagne was passing through this region, he is said to have stopped by and taken mass. No doubt one of those "X slept here" tales, nevertheless the fact that it could possibly be true is enough to cloak the entire area in the rich sauce of history. Why should this make living here more palatable? But it does.

One winter's day last year I noticed a man with a metal detector in the vineyard along the road and, when I asked what he was looking for, was told, "Roman coins." Although he appeared to be a rough type—shaggy hair, ruddy face, ill-fitting old clothes, the sort of fellow you see selling junk at flea markets—he was kindness itself and took time to give me a pocket version of local history, the ebb and flow of Celts, Greeks, Romans, Goths, Saracens—you name them, they were here, and they left their mark everywhere. He lifted a chunk of rose-brown brick from the soil and gave it to me: "Roman," he said. No more Roman than I am, I thought, but I took it graciously and carried it home, a reminder that everywhere around me there are bits and pieces of the past, visible and invisible. In *Lives of a Cell,* Lewis Thomas said, "We leave traces of ourselves wherever we go, on whatever we touch." Perfume lingering in the air, letters in the attic, the pressure of your hand on the small of my back as we danced, tears on the pillow, a shard of pottery, a piece of brick.

There's an apricot-coloured brick above the doorway of our barn, on which is carved 1853, the same year a boatload of my poor Scottish ancestors began settling themselves down on the shores of Lake Huron, thrown off their heathery land in the Hebrides for the sake of sheep. Seemed a long time ago, 1853, when I was growing up in Canada: seems yesterday, here. The barn is considered relatively new, and even our house, built well over a century before that, is not considered *old:* old is reserved for the Château de Latourne, built over the remains of a Roman tower and in ruins since being burned at the beginning of the Revolution. Old is St-Baudile, a stone church built for the parish of Latourne by the monks of St-Étienne in the twelfth century: I can see it from my window, plain and chaste in the middle of vineyards, a perfect little *église romane* guarded by a stand of cypress.

Time passes unevenly from place to place, has different weight and value. Here, it seems to have collapsed, folding in and compressing itself into something deep and dense, a richer, thicker brew than I, a child of the New World, have been accustomed to. The air I breathe as I walk by the Ourne is full of old souls, the noise of the water falling over the dam is like the sound of distant voices. Layer upon layer of lives come and gone.

In Canada, it is easy to keep one's childish illusions of primordial nature intact when out in the woods, whether canoeing through the bush in Algonquin Park or taking a Sunday stroll through autumn-stained maples in the Gatineau hills. In our heads, even as adults, we can continue to play "explorer" and deceive ourselves that we are surrounded by untouched wilderness. Hiking in the Cévennes, one finds different games to play, games of retrieval, understanding one's place in the context of others. Just a few metres from the path, a ruined stone wall will emerge, moss covered and beautiful, in the midst of forest that, until this moment, has seemed pristine. There have been so many other people here before me, and the tangible evidence of that raises questions, gives me pause, thrills me to my boots.

Why should bits of brick and stone be so seductive? The people who passed through this land have nothing to do with me: this is not my story. Nevertheless, I am touched by the past and stand with tears in my eyes reading a plaque at a mountain pass commemorating the deaths of seven local partisans in the Resistance: the heroes in the Cévennes have been *camisard* and *maquis,* resistance fighters in every century. Near Anduze, the village where we go to market, there stands a memorial to the destruction of a German Army brigade in 1944 by local *maquis:* courage, death, victory, freedom. All the big notions, over and over again, on the same ground.

In much the same way as I read Susanna Moodie's 1853 memoir *Life in the Clearings* when we moved from Toronto to Belleville, because I passed her old stone cottage every day on my way to work and felt I should pay literary homage, I spend much time reading books about this region to learn who was here when, and why, slowly getting a sense of how things fit together. And just as the Victorian sensibilities of Moodie's prose had little to do with my life in 1972, nothing I read now seems directly relevant to my immediate task. Nothing I read will ever make me fit here. I will always be an outsider, no matter how much history I swallow. Nevertheless, I persist, imbued as I am with the belief that reading is the way to salvation.

Throughout this region, emptied of people for reasons as various as war, famine and financial failure, there are terraced hillsides on which mulberry trees once flourished. Although some terraces are used today for growing olive trees or onions, most of them are abandoned and overgrown, melancholy testimony to change and loss. In the rafters of our barn we found bunches of old mulberry branches, the leaves dry and brown, left behind after the raising of silkworms was no longer profitable even as a cottage industry. Most of the silk factories in the Cévennes had already closed by the end of the nineteenth century but some farmers continued to use the upper part of their houses as *magnaneries* until the 1940s, when silk was still used for parachutes.

Measuring time by the remembrance of Fanette, one of five elderly local women who once came for tea, it seems that was true in my house. Fanette, well over seventy, recalls being in this house as a child—she was born round the corner in the monastery—and when I took her and the others on a tour of the house to see our renovations, she threw up her hands in astonishment as we entered the bedroom, recalling how it had looked when the *vieille dame Augustine* had lived here and kept her *vers à soie* upstairs. *"Alors, quelle différence,"* she said, shaking her head in disbelief.

The ladies came to tea with my friend the widow Germaine, as I'd suggested she bring the companions with whom she walks for exercise on Tuesdays. When they arrived at the door they were buzzing with curiosity, as if an electric current were lighting up their lovely old faces: unheard of in this rural community to be invited in and allowed to look through someone's house. What a grand opportunity! How amazing is this Canadian! In the village the week after, I heard it was said, in tones not of censure but delight, *Elle est très ouverte!*

Germaine is very fond of me, she says. Two years earlier when I arrived in June for the summer, she met me on the road and told me that over the winter her husband, Armand, had died. Surprised by the news, I burst into tears and we wept together, arms round each other, both of us moved by the other's sadness. At that moment, she says, we became friends. He was a lovely man, Armand, with bright blue eyes, a big white moustache and wine-red cheeks, and he kept the little mill, just the other side of the stone bridge that leads to our long lane. He, and his father and grandfather before him, had turned out whole-grain flour for well over a century until the mill was ruined in the flood of October 1995, when the Ourne, normally a shallow stream, overnight roared swollen and crazy and turned into a torrent carrying trees and horses and cars in its rushing course. The horses are dead and gone, but uprooted trunks and rusting fenders lodged for years along its banks, like mournful memories, reminders that flood and drought are a double scourge in this countryside.

I met Germaine and Armand the first summer we arrived to work on the old house—we were living in the Philippines then. Although we didn't bother getting a telephone for that short time, it was no hardship as there's a public booth at the *mairie,* only a ten-minute walk away. One evening, on my way to make a call, I came upon Germaine with her old bicycle on the road by the monastery. After my polite *"Bonsoir, madame,"* she struck up a conversation, evidently curious about who I was and what we were doing at Mas Blanc. Once her questions were answered, she offered the use of the telephone in her small apartment in the monastery.

Somewhere in her sixties, with short hair hennaed that deep purple shade favoured by Frenchwomen, Germaine has a sharpness to her features I now recognize as typically Cévenole but at the time found slightly forbidding. She insisted I meet Armand, who was in the monastery gardens, planting beans. We shook hands and then I offered to help and he accepted, after being assured that I knew the right way to plant: three beans to a hill. As darkness fell upon us and the stars came out and bats joined the swooping martins overhead, we worked up and down the rows, me chatting away in cheerful high-school French, sticking beans in the soil, patting them down, planting them and myself in this place. And now Armand is dead and the mill stays ruined and empty, for his son never learned the trade, and Germaine has given up their section of the monastery and lives alone in a nearby hamlet.

Everything, for me, dates from that hour of planting beans. The familiar rhythm, the smell of damp earth, somehow knowing where I was because I was in a garden. Lines from a poem by Margaret Avison, memorized more than thirty years ago, resonate with new meaning now: "When day and life draw the horizons, / Part of the strangeness is / Knowing the landscape." There are moments I startle myself nearly witless because I sense so acutely where I am, know exactly the curve of the road and where to slow down, or when to expect the sunlight to catch itself in the crystal prism hanging in the window, or which way to turn to find Orion's Belt in the clear night sky. Emotional geometry, physical knowledge of the deepest sort, the kind that resides under the skin beneath history, beyond words.

During these years spent outside Canada, I've lived by something I read in an interview with surgeon Chris Giannou: "Home is not a physical, geographic entity. Home is a moral state. The real home is one's friends. I like to think of that as a higher form of social organization than the nation state." With my parents dead and no home to return to in Canada, I found this gave me great comfort in our expatriate years abroad, for I kept in mind the idea that we were "only renting temporarily" because of Bob's work, and my real home was somewhere else, invisible but enduring—and permanent.

But something in me is changing. I am burrowing down into an actual place now, my hands in the dirt, planting tulip and narcissus bulbs under the spreading branches of the old *micocoulier*, the wild nettle tree that stands by the house. It is the feel of the earth I desire, this most primitive need finding expression in an act as simple as digging holes and plunking in bulbs. Has this to do with growing older, approaching the earth itself on new terms? Perhaps. Bent on one knee, I let the leafy humus run through my fingers, wondering if I might be buried here someday, whether I want to be, or not. We are told there are already three dead Protestants under the barn, interred two hundred years ago according to a local ordinance that allowed home burial for non-Catholics. If I still lived in Canada, would I occupy myself with questions about where my bones or ashes will go? This is a sign, no doubt, that my heart feels in exile, no matter how I try to force these bulbs into the ground. But I do not dwell on such foolish thoughts for long—it is autumn and I am busy preparing for spring. What better indication of an optimistic spirit could there be?

Much of my effort here so far has gone toward supervising interior renovations, such as the installation of a bathroom and a kitchen, making the place habitable and, more than that, homey. Good plumbing and carpentry are required, but small things matter too, like bouquets of wildflowers on the table. And in the first months, it is less the house than the surrounding hills to which I attach myself, walking daily and learning to name those wildflowers. I am discovering this small truth: to feel *chez vous*, you need to know the proper names for things. Thus I must rename daisies *marguerites,* call the swallows *hirondelles* and the chestnut tree *châtaignier.* It is work, pure and simple. And it is daunting. My mouth cannot produce the liquid sounds required by the French language, my throat cannot give up a rounded *r,* my tongue cannot do arabesques around the word *heureuse,* my lips purse up to no avail.

And my ears! I live in a muddled state of mild incomprehension, often uncertain if I have properly grasped what has been said: my public stance is one of brave bewilderment, my tone of voice inquiring, apologetic. In some ways I exist at a level beneath language, where words do not touch me, but at the same time I am forever trying to "catch on," to know and be known. I am not myself, at the same time as I am more myself than ever, for there is also constant clear definition. I am visibly not French. I am sometimes taken for Dutch or American, and then I explain that *je suis Canadienne anglophone.* I will always be foreign, alien, *toujours une étrangère.*

When I am in Toronto on my annual teaching visit, sitting in a subway car amused and amazed at the wonderful way the faces of the city have changed since I lived in a boarding house on St. George Street in 1965, I think how hard it is to learn another language, to get it right, to make yourself fit to the shape of different sounds in your mouth. I want to tell the woman beside me—Cambodian, Peruvian, Ethiopian, Croatian—*I know how you feel. It's not easy. It's lonely and tough. But trust me, start with little things: flowers, trees, birds. Make a little garden, if only in your head. Get to know your neighbours. Dream of home and it will come to you.*

But then I think how incredibly presumptuous it would be to offer such platitudes, and I do not reach out, I stay silent. What can I possibly know of her plight? Why should she care that I, who appear to belong in this city, also know what it's like to be an outsider? What earthly good might it do? What works for me may work for no one else.

Get to know your neighbours. For me, that's made easy because Mas Blanc is divided in three and we all exist within its walls. My house is the central one and, jutting off to one side, rather like the half stroke of a nearly crossed *t,* is the section belonging to Bruno, a professional comedian. In the summer he and the other two members of his troupe practise their act on a small stage in his yard, and I sit on my front steps to watch, not getting the jokes, which rely on wordplay or political satire, but applauding their hilarious slapstick routines. Bruno is a small, trim man whose mobile facial features can seem comic even in repose: just now, watching him walk to the mailbox, I find myself smiling, for he has the flat-footed gait of a clown.

More important, he has something to teach me about appearance and reality. At first, I found myself appalled by his disregard for what he terms middle-class values; the old cement-block outhouse in his unkempt front yard seemed so ugly, I kept waiting for him to "fix things up" and get rid of it, but it is apparent the outhouse is here to stay. If it's good enough weather for outdoor chores, he's off on his *vélo,* cycling for the entire day, coming back at nightfall exhausted and joyous. To Bruno, what matters is not how things look, but whether life is good.

The outhouse remains an eyesore but, as time passes, I am seeing the wisdom of his point of view. Bruno is not only a content man but a generous and kindly neighbour without whom life would be dull. He fires the ancient wood-burning oven attached to our barn, and we bake bread and pizza. He fixes my bicycle tires, offers advice when I am stymied by the linguistic convolutions of French bureaucracy, and he'll feed our cat, Ballou, if we're away. Last week he brought us a bag of *girolles,* wild yellow mushrooms that taste like the very first time you heard Chopin.

At the rear, there is an addition that would form the top of the *t*, home to a family whose big, rambling garden runs along the entire Mas on the side nearest the stream. Haddou is a friendly man in his late forties, but conversation with him is difficult because he is missing some teeth and, perhaps out of embarrassment, he bends his head and speaks rapidly. Malika, his plump, pretty wife, embraces me each time we meet, but is shy about speaking French, so we are limited mainly to smiles and gestures. They have five children—the younger ones, Leila and Hakim, still in grade school and the elder three trying to find work. Haddou and Malika are Moroccan, and they know even better than I what it is to live in a land where you are never completely accepted, although they've been here more than half their lives.

We do not talk of this so much as acknowledge it in sideways fashion, discussing the problems of getting jobs as I sit at their round table drinking sweet mint tea or strong black coffee, listening to the frustrations faced by the teenage girls, Sonya and Saphira, and their older brother, Hassan. I do what I can to help, driving them to interviews and typing their brief résumés, but in a region where unemployment is endemic and where there is underlying support and sympathy for Le Pen and his xenophobic National Front party, what colour your skin is and where your parents come from matter more than what your curriculum vitae looks like.

Haddou has worked twenty years in the vineyards of Béatrice, a middle-aged single woman with a boyish, bashful manner, who always wears a delicate gold chain and Huguenot cross even with her farm clothes. It is she who owns that section of Mas Blanc, and she allows Haddou to live there as part of his salary. On her farm, over the hill, Béatrice keeps goats and in good weather, if she is not occupied tending her vines, can be found striding out with her small herd and her dogs. Aided by her frail old father—in his nineties now, his help more token than real—she makes goats' cheese (called *pelardon*), which she sells from her home.

There, in the first room of the little cheese shed, sit snowy-white rounds of *pelardon,* so creamy and delicate that they are delicious eaten with fresh strawberries or figs. At the back of the shed are cheeses in various stages of maturity, becoming more dense and yellow with each week they spend on the airing rack. Béatrice's specialty is a very old cheese dried to half its original size, dark blue with mould and hard as rock, aged with herbs in a stoneware jar. For this, she gives me the following traditional Cévenol recipe: grate the cheese into a bowl and add the same amount of fresh butter and finely chopped walnuts. Mix well and serve on slices of warm baguette. Washed down with ice-cold rosé wine from the *Cave Coopérative*—the winery where, every September, she and Haddou take the grapes they've picked in the vineyard behind our house—this is sustenance of an elemental sort, tasting of this earth, this rain and sun, this air. This place where I live.

As I write this, intending to describe a middle-aged Canadian settling into the rhythms of rural France, it is obvious that I am seeking to convince myself, choosing words that will chase ambivalence into the shadows. A line floats into my head, so perfectly appropriate that it makes me laugh aloud: "If you can't be with the one you love, then love the one you're with." Easier said than done, of course. I know all about homesickness—sipping maple syrup from a spoon while listening to a tape cassette of loon calls, endlessly writing letters to friends asking for news, sifting through old photographs, weeping on the telephone. I've been there, that strange and dangerous place where longing can blind you to everything else. And so you learn to live with *mal de pays* as with a chronic illness or disability, you salt your days with *nostalgie*. Then finally you wake up and compare yourself to the millions of displaced people in the world who will never see their homes again, and you feel ashamed, and you stop.

You go for a walk in the hills and watch a hawk unwinding on an updraft. You know this hawk, he has a certain territory and he is part of the landscape you now know like the back of your hand. Or you put on gardening gloves and take your trowel and another bag of tulip bulbs and work at making a garden, while the falling leaves of the *micocoulier* land on your shoulders like rain. At night you fall into bed content that you are creating whatever it is that is *chez vous*.

The ghosts of the silkworms are as silent as they were in life, and you sleep without interruption, except for the hourly tolling of the bell at the *mairie* coming clear and sweet across the fields. It always rings the hour twice, as if to ensure that its message is heard: Listen, it says. Pay attention. This is where you are.

JONATHAN GARFINKEL

from

Ambivalence
Crossing the Israel/Palestine Divide

THEY SAY THE JEWS from Minsk, Belarus, came to Canada and built this shul in Kensington Market, 1930. Brick by brick, the design is identical to the synagogue they left behind to flame and smoke, blessed be its memory.

See the white chandelier hanging like a crown over the men in this room. And the silver Torah crowns that take in that light. And the paintings on the wall: to be strong like a lion, fast like a deer, words of encouragement in Hebrew. And more: paintings of trombones, clarinets and violins, sounds of my musical ancestors. *Praised be this klezmer, how I wish we could carry a tune.*

And the smell, wafting up from downstairs: Sarah's chicken soup, stale herring, the dust from fluorescent lights.

And the smell of men: sweet and rancid, sweat and mould, meat gone bad before the maggots.

Outside these thirty-foot-high wood doors linger the ghosts of Kensington: old Jewish, turn-of-the-nineteenth-century neighbourhood. Once there were synagogues on nearly every corner. On Chanukah, they say there wasn't a window or storefront on Augusta Avenue or Baldwin Street that didn't glow with festival candles. Gone are the kosher butchers, the Jewish tailors; gone to richer, suburban lives in Forest Hill, North York, Thornhill. Anywhere but this *shmutsik* ghetto that stinks of you-know-where, may those rotten shtetls only be remembered in Shalom Aleichem books. Now the windows of Kensington are sticky with sweet and sour pork, Café Kim cheap beer. And inside the Minsk, these fourteen men. Our lame out-of-time, out-of-tune prayer. Praying for the Sabbath Bride and a free meal, compliments of Perl's kosher foods.

Rabbi Spero is imported from Cleveland. He comes over to shake my hand. A smile on his face, a chuckle that says, "Good to see you, where the hell you been, you schmuck?" He wishes I were a better Jew. Who can blame him? I haven't been here in months. That's how it is with me, one month I believe, the next I don't. And yet in spite of my long absences the rabbi's black eyes are warm with forgiveness. His handshake is firm in a way that makes me feel solid, secure.

Spero's young for a rabbi, forty-two, has five kids and a beautiful wife we simply call *Rebbetzen*. His face as you'd expect: skin Elmer's Glue white and his beard thick from learning. What's surprising is the guy's in pretty good shape, has decent biceps. While two of his children hang on to his shoulders screaming for attention, he continues to pray. They're like monkeys, the two kids, climbing up his belly, his back, hanging from his neck. But the rabbi doesn't get upset or angry. Focused, he bends at the knees, bows his head and chants. How does he do it?

Sometimes I imagine the rabbi in his basement, shirtless but for his tallis, black moons of hair swirling his chest. Surrounded by candles he lies on the dank, cement floor and starts bench-pressing Torahs, five, six, seven, eight of them at once, precariously balanced one on top of the other.

"One more, Rebbetzen," he shouts to his wife. "Throw another Torah on top. This is how strong my faith is!"

I'M LOOKING FOR something to make me believe. It doesn't have to be rabbi-level conviction—half a Spero would do. It would be nice to stumble upon a burning bush, a parting of the sea. Even a neon sign that says, "This way to revelation, idiot." Of course, what I'd do with a miracle—if and when confronted by one—is a whole other matter.

I've witnessed one miracle in my life. It happened six years ago in Winnipeg with my Baba Jesse not long before she died. She was in her eighties and couldn't speak on account of a stroke that had frozen the right side of her face. Her smile was a half-smile. Half of her alive, the other half numb to the world.

It had been three years since Baba had uttered an intelligible word. I was visiting with Laura, my girlfriend at the time. We were hitchhiking across Canada that spring and we stopped in Winnipeg to spend some time with my grandparents. It was a warm spring day. Baba wanted to go outside, so I helped her struggle to the door with the walker. Laura was fixing lunch in the kitchen. In the hallway I could hear my grandfather's continuous scribble. Behind a pile of papers—pyramids of drafts, bills and documents—Zaida Ben worked at the dining-room table composing letters to Boris Yeltsin and Bill Clinton urging radical environmental reform. Earlier in the week he'd ordered vast quantities of canned tomato soup (the day Laura and I arrived we stacked 144 cans of the stuff next to the piano). An environmental chemist, he anticipated one global catastrophe after another; that week it was thermonuclear holocaust.

I helped Baba down the front four steps of the house to the walkway. She inched her way forward, feet stuttering on asphalt. Fifteen metres took five minutes. The lawns of Winnipeg's south end were smiling, winter over at last. While Baba worked with the walker, I read to her the day's news: market reports from Taiwan, financial goals in Australia, long-term predictions for Hong Kong. She loved when I read her the Business section, something I thought odd given her communist sympathies.

We stopped by the sidewalk to sit on lawn chairs. The sun felt good on the skin. Baba stared at me, and her gaze made me uncomfortable. She looked at me as though I were a foreign country. Tried to read me, a language she couldn't understand.

"Is she Jewish?" she asked.

"What?"

"Is she Jewish?" Baba repeated herself, as though to show this was no accident.

"Do you mean Laura?"

"IS. SHE. JEWISH?"

I saw two roads ahead of me.

One road was the truth: Laura was from an aristocratic family in equestrian country, New Jersey. Her ancestors came to America on the *Mayflower*. She celebrated Christmas, waxed nostalgic for Bing Crosby, used lard in her pies and bacon in her sandwiches.

The other road was the lie. I can't say I like lying too much. But I'm aware that lying is also a kind of longing. It's willing the right answer, wishing my grandmother a small measure of happiness in her final days. A gift.

I did my best to meet Baba Jesse's gaze. "Yes, she's Jewish."

"Good," she said, closing her eyes.

This was the last time my grandmother would ever speak.

THERE'S A WOMAN up in the balcony who looks a lot like my mother. I know my mother would never set foot in this synagogue unless there was a wedding or bris. She's uncomfortable with downtown Jews, the messiness of the Market, the lack of elegance in this eclectic hodge-podge of congregants. While I have nostalgia for all things Eastern European, my mother goes to the Narayever, the hippie shul a little farther north in The Annex. My mother has zero hippie in her, but the Narayever is modern, egalitarian and clean. Like her mother, Baba Jesse, she's irritated by the idea of women being confined to three narrow rows on the second-floor balcony. "Women closer to heaven, my foot," my mother would likely say. "Jonathan, this isn't the Dark Ages. Don't you think it's time for members of the female sex to be allowed to touch a Torah?"

Three years ago my mother returned from a vacation in Europe to find my father gone—packed up and moved out. After thirty-three years of marriage, three sons, weekly Shabbos dinners, kvetching, brises, brisket, bar mitzvahs, weddings, shivas, Seders, sukkahs, chametz, Hebrew, tears, latkes, guilt, the Marx Brothers, Baba's pickles, Zaida's mustard, it's no wonder I had dreams the basement in the house of my childhood had flooded. The news swamped the foundations: My father had abandoned ship.

I don't know if my parents were wildly in love when I was a child. By the end, they patiently endured each other. They managed to sweep every disagreeable sentence, emotion and argument under the rug. Everyone was happy, happy, happy. In the eyes of our neighbours and friends, we were perfect—my parents known as the Ward and June Cleaveritches of Forest Hill. We were Conservative with a dash of modern Orthodox. On Saturdays we went to a synagogue with separate seating for men and women, and we had two sets of dishes, milk and meat. My mother spent her days in the kitchen riffing on tradition. Her hand-made potato things tasted more *gnocchi* than *knish,* and her mandelbroit like the finest *cantucci* in Tuscany. Her gefilte fish was famous the street over, as was her cure-all chicken-carrot-ginger-mushroom soup (hers was a nouvelle-Yiddish cuisine, *herbes de Provence* meet the shit-streams of The Pale). My father went to work every day with a humble brown briefcase, drove a humble brown Ford, and attended to ballet dancers and *Playboy* centre-fold models with eating disorders at the Clarke Institute. Each morning he went to listen to the problems of the anorexic, the bulimic, the nearly dead.

After my father left my mother, the Jewishness in my family, as I knew it, came to an end. We tried to continue in splintered-off versions. A Passover Seder, the odd Friday-night dinner. But nothing was the same. Judaism is about ethics, Torah and prayer. But more than anything, it's family. And ever since mine has broken apart, I've been left wondering what remains of the religion I've inherited. This is partly why in the last three years I've started to go to shul again for the first time as an adult. I need to touch a fragment of my faith.

Four months after my parents' separation, my grandmother died. With her death in 2000, Baba's "Is she Jewish?" quotient appeared to be in grave danger. My brothers are now both engaged, to a Catholic and an agnostic. My father's living with a Presbyterian. My mother, who wouldn't let my ex-girlfriend Laura stay over in our house five years ago, is heading out on a date this week with a Presbyterian. Jewish Garfinkel blood is now on the endangered species list....

———————

WE SING THE ALEINU. I bend at my knees and bow my head, belt out the song by rote. I've sung it thousands of times in my life. It's as natural as breathing.

I'm thinking of you, Baba, the miracle of your speech. I'm wondering: Why does the communist who hates synagogue and rejects religion still care if my girlfriend is Jewish? What is this instinct that survives Marxism and the freezing of the left hemisphere of the brain?

Sometimes I imagine my Baba standing here with me in the synagogue. It sounds strange, especially given her secular leanings (and that she's of the female persuasion). But I would've wanted her to meet Judith.

"So you got rid of Laura and got a new girlfriend," Baba would say to me.

"Her name is Judith. And we've been together three years."

I'd point her out, sitting in the second row of the women's section in the balcony.

"Nice eyes. A real Jewess, that Yehudit. What she do for a living?"

"She's a theatre director."

"An artist? Not very secure, but nourishing nonetheless. You're going to have to be the man."

I wouldn't tell Baba that Judith and I have broken up two times already. Wouldn't tell her that our relationship is barely holding itself together, and when the weave is at its thinnest we seem to cling tighter to each other.

"So when's the wedding?" Baba Jesse would most certainly ask.

I TRY TO MAKE eyes at Judith. I want to catch her attention but she's engrossed in her siddur. I make a sour-cat face, cock my head to the side, but I know she won't look. Tonight I want something to overwhelm us. A prayer: *May the confusion of the heart scatter from its chambers.* For a moment it seems to work. Judith becomes beautiful again, the way I knew her when I first met her. Can you see her long black skirt, her river of black hair tied back in a ponytail, blue eyes at prayer?

In spite of our eternal road of bumpy patches, Friday is our night. We come to synagogue to feel clean again. Shabbat is the holiest day of the week for Jews—and lovers. For it is deemed sacred, a mitzvah, when a man and woman make love on this night. Life becomes simpler in the synagogue, connects us to the ancient.

IN THE BEGINNING Judith's hands were doves, two birds Noah sent into the world in search of land. To bring back an olive leaf, a resting place, a sign of peace.

When we fell in love Judith would place her head in my neck and coo-coo me with long fingers. She'd give her analysis of a Bruno Schulz short story while S-curving my back—delightful. She sang "Falling in Love Again" in a deep tenor's voice, read Heine and Goethe to me in German. Judith showed me how to read her palm, and we read each other's lives, the maps of ourselves, love, life, fate. I held her, kissed her thin aerodynamic ears (I often imagined her jumping out of an airplane and breaking all kinds of skydiving records). Once she pressed her hands against my ears saying, "Don't listen to the world outside. Go on, go in."

When Judith was my age she toured Europe as a street actor, studied theatre directing in Berlin. She's inspired me to write with passion, love with appetite, drink slivovitz straight from the freezer. And her dead Romanian father courses through her when she dances to gypsy music, late night over the wooden floors of the bakery we live above in Kensington Market.

I watch her read the English translation of prayers, following carefully with her index finger. She reads the words in her prayer book with the kind of awe someone has when first falling in love. Judith was not brought up with religion. Her mother, a Holocaust survivor, despised all things Jewish when Judith was a kid. It was only a few years before we met that Judith came to embrace her past. Now she wants to know more, learn the heritage she was refused.

She loves that I can speak Hebrew, is amazed by the fact I went to Bialik, a Labour Zionist day school in Toronto. From ages five to thirteen I studied everything that has been denied Judith: Jewish history and Israeli literature, Tanakh and Hebrew grammar. She constantly asks me questions. How can one be a Zionist but not be religious? Why do we face west when we sing the second-to-last stanza of Lecha Dodi? What is the Balfour Declaration? Why the shattered glass at a wedding?

We fell in love when I was twenty-six, lying on the purple dyed cotton of her Romanian grandmother's *plapuma*, sewn silver to reflect the light. We spent the first winter unemployed, reading to each other from a book whose name we did not know. *Madrigals*, we named it, an obscure surrealist novella by a writer whose name and title were torn off the cover (we found the book at a garage sale). Our voices became the words of that unknown author. She read me the story of the watchmaker who took his grandson to a beach in Tel Aviv. The grandson wanted to learn how to fly. The grandfather stared out at the horizon of sea, his grey eyes stained silver. Led by three balloons in his hand, the grandson suddenly left the earth and drifted over the Mediterranean.

"We create the reality we desire," announced the watchmaker, following the arc of his grandson's flight.

When I fell asleep I found myself flying too, so I wasn't sure if it was the book I was hearing or Judith I was following. I'd never dreamt of flight, not even as a child. But there I was, between waking and dreaming, the soft cadences of Judith's voice and the unknown passages of the book, soaring over a country I'd never been to, had only seen in films and textbooks.

That winter she proposed we travel. "We could go to Jerusalem." And the idea of the city glistened.

In the minds of lovers, boundaries break down, the walled-in thoughts seep under doors and a dream may be shared. The night she proposed the journey, we fell asleep reading *Madrigals* to each other, dreaming the same dream. The two of us, walking hand in hand, through the ancient walled city of David. Neither of us had ever been before.

WE'RE GETTING TOWARD the end of the service. The men are hungry, the smell of chicken almost overdone. Two women descend into the basement to make sure all is in order in the kitchen. Judith covers her mouth with her prayer book as though she were kissing its pages, looks at me from the corner of her eyes behind black-rimmed glasses. When I catch her, she turns away, pretends to concentrate on the book.

She's pissed at me. Four weeks ago I received a phone call from a theatre director in Israel who said that if I could come up with a good-enough proposal, he'd land me a playwright residency for a Tel Aviv theatre. *If* the proposal is good enough. The board wants something Jewish, Barak (the director) wants something with a broader universal appeal. "The catch," Barak explained to me over the telephone in his thick Israeli accent, "is to get it past the shit-for-brains board, while keeping me intrigued."

When I told Judith about the offer, she was thrilled, thinking we could fulfill the original dream. But she heard something wrong in my voice.

"Do you not want me to come with?" she asked.

I said nothing. Felt only confusion.

Aside from the fact I have yet to come up with a proposal Barak likes, there's another question that nags at me. Do I want to go to Israel? I've managed to avoid the place for thirty years and don't feel I've been lacking for it. I do not pine for Israel the way the rabbi longs for it as a place of study and spiritual revelation. Friends of mine have travelled there for free on "birthright" trips. Others have fought in the army, become Orthodox, thought they were messiahs. I have done nothing of the sort.

Bialik taught me the borders of Israel as understood by its former citizens—my teachers. For nine years I drew one map of the country after another each day in class: for Bible studies, geography, literature and history. I can draw the country by heart. As a child the maps I drew had borders that never varied—they were learned by rote as the teacher outlined the country on the blackboard, and we were expected to draw the same maps in our books. The eastern border was always the Jordan River.

I had dreams of these illustrations, my ballpoint pen tracing the lines, borders, cities, rivers, ink transforming itself magically into landscape. In my mind, I've already been to Israel.

Of course I knew I'd go to Israel at some point in my life. A Jew in the Diaspora grows up with this assumption: One must visit, *eventually*. Three years ago Judith proposed a new Jerusalem. It was a city different from the one I'd been taught as a child and this appealed to me—I could see Israel on my terms as an adult. But the promise of travel became the unwritten covenant of Judith and me: our destiny bound to Jerusalem. Whether or not we made it to Israel became the standard by which we measured our relationship's success. I certainly never intended it that way. I only wanted to visit the damn place.

Judith still talks about Israel as though it were some kind of holy mission, a life or death pilgrimage. She wants us to get married by the Kotel, the Western Wall in Jerusalem. Me? When she mentions the word *Israel,* I want to run, tear through a forest, bury my head in the ground. Forget the place even exists....

———•◦•———

I'M SIX YEARS OLD and I'm one of the chosen people. So my mother tells me.

MOTHER:	You've been chosen by God.
SHALOM:	What does God want me to do?
MOTHER:	He wants you to be a good Jew.
SHALOM:	Why does God care about me?
MOTHER:	This is the miracle of the nameless Almighty. He cares about little pishers like Shalom Garfinkel.
SHALOM:	Do you think God would mind if I'm a cosmonaut?
MOTHER:	It depends on whether you're a good Jew or not.
SHALOM:	Laika isn't a Jew.
MOTHER:	Who's Laika?
SHALOM:	Laika is a dog. The Russians sent her to outer space in her own private spaceship.
MOTHER:	You're not a dog, Shalom. Consider yourself lucky.
SHALOM:	I'm not lucky. Laika is still in outer space. I'm stuck here!
MOTHER:	Well you're going to an even more special place than Laika. Because you've been accepted. *Chosen.*

I eye my mother mistrustfully. Like God in the Torah, my mother has a very specific notion of what a special place is, one that likely differs from my notions of paradise. Heaven for me is to live in outer space like Laika the Moscavite Mutt who was sent up in the Sputnik II rocket. They say she never returned because the Russian engineers hadn't figured out a way to make spaceships come back to earth. I have my doubts. I think the Russian scientists actually had a way to get Laika to return, but she simply didn't want to. Laika *chose* to leave the orbit of this planet to seek better, sunnier destinations. "Hello, Laika!" I sometimes wave from my bedroom window. "Can you see me down here? How blue is the world? How blurry are the stars? And how is the orange Tang?"

I think about God, and I think about Laika. At least Laika has a name I can say. I even have a picture of her. That's more than I can say for the Nameless Whatever.

If I can't live in outer space, my second-best paradise would be to become the starting centre-fielder for the St. Louis Cardinals. I've never been to St. Louis, but my dad says it's got good stadium grass, and that's what's important. "You need good grass," he once explained, "for preservation of the knees, a true hop of the ball."

I look at my mother's sesame-brown eyes and curly brown hair. She may as well be God herself. After all, she's created the heavens and the earth, named all the plants and the animals. Now she's chosen where I'm to spend the next nine years of my life.

MOTHER: Bialik Hebrew Day School.
SHALOM: Is this where I'm going to study to be a
            cosmonaut?
MOTHER: You can be whatever you want, Shalom. As long
            as it's Jewish.

I cling to my mother's tough, fleshy palm. The sight of the school—its sallow brick and concrete, the parking lot they call a playground—burrows a hole in my stomach. This is not the Jewish space station I had imagined.

The building's only three storeys high but it's massive—like an entire country, foreign and hostile. The windows are narrow, long and filthy. Here, no one is allowed to watch things. "Thou shalt not lose thine eyes in worldly events!" say those windows.

Zionism, I think the building says.

I have no idea what the word means.

My mother taught me to ride a bicycle this past summer—guiding then pushing then letting go. I did not notice her absence as I careened south down Vesta Drive, rows of maple and pine flashing beside my eyes like the movie trailer of my life. Today I'm not letting go of her. There's no hope for speed, no death-defying balance to achieve. We walk toward the front doors of the school. Rain pitter-patters in small puddles beneath my rubber boots. The red and white flag of Canada and the blue and white flag of Israel stand wrapped together, soggy from the morning's rain.

Three times my mother tries to let go of my hand.

"You're strong," she says, "when you want to be."

I close my eyes and make two prayers.

1. May these hallways be decked with astrolabs and rare and exciting views of the cosmos.
2. If prayer #1 is beyond the means of the school, I'll settle for God instead.

(That is, if I can't meet Laika, I'd like to meet The Big Guy.)

I LET GO of my mother's hand.

Your mission, Shalom Garfinkel, should you choose to accept it, lies within these walls. I turn on my imaginary walkie-talkie and listen to its static. *Chhhh, Bialik,* I say to my right hand clenched in a fist. Nothing happens. *Bialik,* I utter to my thumb, pointing it like an antenna to the sky. The word is foreign but not alien. *Bialik,* I say, one more time. And a metal-framed glass door swings open....

———·•·———

THERE'S NO QUESTION Bialik was different from the world I saw around me as a kid. In Grade Three I was convinced my teachers were from another planet, their otherwise normal bodies taken over by strange, Hebrew-speaking beings. I mean, why else were they in Toronto, teaching me about a country godknowswhere?

That year I wrote a telegram to the powers that be and slipped it beneath the door of the principal's office:

Dear Dr Bialik [STOP] When the aliens recruited you from the outer orbits of Vulcanis why did they send you here to torment me [STOP] Sincerely Laika [STOP]

I DIDN'T KNOW ANY BETTER. Didn't know Bialik was a Labour Zionist school with roots in the Jewish National Workers Alliance, its birthplace somewhere between Czarist Russia and working class immigrant New York. At the age of eight, I couldn't comprehend the significance of these factions; the difference between secular and Orthodox lay in the road that separated Bialik from Etz Chayim, the all-girls *frum* school across the street. (Their otherness, their hidden playground. And they wore plaid skirts that made them oddly resemble the Catholic girls I fell in love with daily on the bus.)

What does it mean for a child to be sent to a Labour Zionist school? We were thrown into the waters of secular Jewish culture— Ben-Gurion and Singer, Shemer and Herzl, Amichai and Ahad Ha'am. We lived and breathed modern Hebrew, the almighty love of Israel. I became adept at the world of mixed messages. By night I lived in Forest Hill: Village of Jaguars, Ralph Lauren, the smooth skin of the pampered. In the days I went to a school that preached universal values of social justice and a commitment to class struggle in the name of the Jewish state. Is it any wonder I was confused?

DAVID LAYTON

Irving Layton, Leonard Cohen and Other Recurring Nightmares

THERE ARE TWO OBSERVATIONS I need to make about the week I spent in Los Angeles: first, it rained every day, and second, it was the Tibetan New Year. Neither event was related to the other, except that together they conspired to prevent me from achieving the purpose of my visit—interviewing my godfather, the poet-songwriter Leonard Cohen. I had some notion of doing an article on the performer's capacity for personal relationships, and I think Leonard knew I also wanted him to talk about my father, though I'd written him only that I wanted him to talk about himself.

"He is up in the mountain," was how my mother put it. I was staying at her house in West Hollywood. The mountain in question was Mount Baldy, one of the many snow-capped peaks that glitter in the California sun. I tried to locate it on a map, tracing the rumpled geographical folds northward towards Washington State and British Columbia. That's where I always imagined the Rocky Mountains to be, rising inland of the Pacific rain forest. Despite my many visits I always forget that pristine mountains hover within reach of the crowded Spanish bungalows and car-choked highways of Los Angeles.

It was around the second or third day into my visit that I first heard about the Tibetan New Year and the possible connection between this event and Leonard's absence. He was up on Mount Baldy, meditating. And the rain, it turned out, was keeping him there. The news was full of stories about swollen rivers, collapsing bridges and flooded highways. Leonard would not, could not, come back down.

That, at least, was the comfortable answer. Unfortunately, there was a more disturbing possibility—that Leonard was avoiding me. I wasn't here as his godson, to pay him a friendly visit, but as a journalist, to interview him, and it was conceivable that he'd had second thoughts about the whole idea, much as I was now having.

"He's an intensely private man," my mother said. This statement was meant to describe a general trait of Leonard's but it also encompassed his present absence from LA, which in turn hinted at another of the reasons I wished to interview him. I wanted his speaking voice on tape. Despite my childhood memories and more recent conversations with Leonard, I couldn't for the life of me remember more than three consecutive words he'd strung together. Stranger still, my mother had the same problem and she'd known Leonard since he was twenty. She could remember his then-plump face and awkward smile, and she could remember, in later years, the endless and constant conversations between my father and Leonard, but not a word or phrase in his own accents could she muster. Talking to Leonard was like listening to a melody that you couldn't capture the next day.

After eight days of watching the rain fall, of damp sheets and disturbed sleep, I decided to leave for Toronto. My mother, always anxious to dissipate family-induced anxiety, especially if it's being induced in her son, assured me that she would speak to Leonard when he got down from his mountain. I decided to leave it in her hands. When it came to either my godfather or my father, it was often smarter to leave it in her hands.

My father is the poet Irving Layton. He too is a performer although in his case he performs nonstop. His role is the potent genius. He truly believes that he belongs in the pantheon with Socrates and Homer and Dante and Shakespeare, and he never ceases to live up to his status. Besides me, Irving has an older son and daughter by his second wife, and a small daughter by his fourth. Up in the attic, my father enters the pantheon and out come poems about his wives. And his children. "Be gunners in the Israeli air force," his line goes in a poem titled *For My Sons, Max and David*. Or he stands on the podium and says, "This is for my son, David." People come up afterwards and say, "Your father must love you very much." But I am not—none of us is—as close to him as Leonard Cohen. My father, who first spotted him doing a reading in a Montréal coffee house, calls him the "golden boy."

They're not at all alike. Leonard requires himself to be considerate and polite in all encounters, even if he has to fake it. That doesn't keep him, too, from taking his private dramas and shaping them into poems and songs for public consumption. Long ago, there was Marianne, who wanted to marry him. He wrote her a song saying So Long. But Leonard's style is gentle, even patrician. My father's is not. Leonard's clothes always fitted beautifully, whereas my father dressed like a Romanian factory worker. "You see this shirt!" he'd say proudly, pinching the polyester cloth with his thumb and forefinger. "It cost me thirty dollars." My earliest recollection of Leonard was being driven around in his brand-new sports car. I must have been about six years old. The first car I remember my father driving was a Datsun with a roof so low that a permanent grease stain marked the spot over his head.

There were other differences, age one of them, since my father was two decades older than Leonard. Their backgrounds were another. My father had been born into terrible poverty, Leonard into the wealth and privilege of Westmount. But for all that they had one great thing in common—they were artists. And if my father's opinion was anything to go by they were much more—they were among the elect. Their poems and music would never die but would, like the severed head of Orpheus, sing for all eternity.

Leonard is also close to my mother. Not only was Leonard the first of his friends my father introduced to her, for months he was the only one. My mother, Aviva, is the third of Irving's five wives, though they never actually got married. They came close once. A few years before my birth my father announced one morning, a morning seemingly no different from any other, that he would marry Mother. They called Leonard and all three marched down to a jewellery shop in old Montréal where, incredibly, all Irving did was purchase a silver clasp for his previous wife and head out of the shop. My mother, the disinherited bride-to-be, stood over the glass counter and found herself unable to breathe.

Leonard, with that winsome smile of his, bought the ring my mother coveted, slipped it over her finger, and said, "Aviva, now you're married." During the twenty-five years that my mother spent with Irving, she never once took that ring off her finger. You can see from all this why the nature of the artist, and the nature of fame, and the effects of both on human relationships—on the possibility of intimacy—are subjects that interest me. And also why I can never get personal about my father without bringing in Leonard, or personal about my godfather without bringing in Irving.

IN OUR HOUSE the personal went something like this: I have homework and my mother pretends not to understand grade four math, this from a woman who has a Ph.D. in English literature. "Go ask your father." And up I'd go, to the attic, while my mother, safe in her kitchen, would glow with pride at her little, normal family. I'd knock and wait for the thunderclap. "What!" "I have some math homework," I'd say. Then Zeus would heave himself from his throne and admit me into his lair which stank of words and pipe tobacco. His forced benevolence would soon wear thin. "What's wrong with you, man?" His finger would jab at the open textbook.

What was wrong with me? It was a good question. I, the son of a great poet, would sit in the back of the classroom and be admonished for picking my nose. When not in class, I'd try to shove my hand between the legs of pink-cheeked girls. This last habit landed me a two-day suspension from school and a handsome accolade from my father. "That's my boy!" he'd shout. "Stick your hands up the dark mysteries of life." And then he'd thrust his own hand into the air and wiggle his fingers. "You see that?" he'd say to my mother. "He has the hands of an artist."

But now, as I tucked the unwieldy math book under my arm, and fled towards my mother's comforts, I knew that the approval had been withdrawn and forgotten.

"Did it go all right?" my mother would ask. I'd nod my head and tell her that everything was wonderful. "Dad really helped me," I'd say. But as she leaned over to kiss me, I could tell that she knew the truth.

When my father came down from Mount Olympus it was usually for food and an audience. Any audience would do. As I watched the mounds of meat and peas pass from the plate to his belly, my father would rail against the "Philistines" and "ass-lickers" who populated the literary landscape of Canada. If my mother came to the defence of any given writer, it would be dismissed with a wave of his hand and the words "literary tapeworm." Then my father would start to laugh, and he'd laugh until he choked.

The more excited my father became, the less food made it down his throat. It would come exploding out of his mouth, along with his invective, until at last the table would be littered with the organic matter that, in my young imagination, was the decayed remains of all those Philistines my father had chewed out.

He was different when we had real guests. Then my father would strain his head forward and listen. Carefully. And he'd wait until the conversation began to meander and then he'd mount a pointed interrogation. "What do you think the role of the artist is, exactly?" Then he'd fold his arms and wait again until it was time for him to become the Great Summarizer. He would gather in all the half-baked, drunken, confused, fragmented ideas that had eddied around him and begin to tell his audience what they had all been saying. It was a *tour de force*.

My father was eighty-one before I had an insight into his technique. We were sitting in an outdoor café, on a summer's evening in Toronto, when an attractive waitress came to our table.

"You're beautiful!" my father exclaimed. "Do you read books?"

The woman said she did.

"You like reading, then." My father had a way of making the obvious sound ominous. "What do you read?"

The waitress said something like "things," and became embarrassed.

"Have you studied?"

The waitress said she had received her bachelor's degree in English literature.

"English literature! Bravo. Do you read poetry? A.M. Klein, have you read him?"

The waitress looked increasingly uncomfortable as my father rattled off the names of several obscure Canadian poets.

"Irving Layton. Have you read Irving Layton?" Irving Layton asked.

To my extreme discomfort the waitress said she hadn't heard of him. I became nervous, but I didn't yet understand.

My father eyed her suspiciously, then said, "Leonard Cohen, have you heard of him?"

The waitress broke out into a radiant smile. "I love Leonard Cohen," she said.

"Good! Good! He's a wonderful writer." My father ordered another bottle of wine and we watched her walk away. I felt a slap on my arm. It was from my father.

"You see that, my boy, first you pull the rug from under them and then, when you give them a few crumbs, they think it's manna from heaven." My father sighed. "I'm too old for all this beauty."

AFTER I FAILED grade four, we packed our bags and, with no explanation offered, headed for Asia. At first I thought it was a summer vacation but after six months of travelling I became suspicious. Where the hell were we? A place called India, my mother would tell me. But I kept on asking. "Where are we?" India. The word held no meaning, explained nothing, couldn't possibly make me understand why we'd go off every night to a park in New Delhi and meet my "friend," the one whom I initially mistook for a dog. We'd call out his name and he'd come running towards us. On all fours. The crippled dog-boy, the one with the magnificent smile, the one we'd feed. Dog-boy and I would run towards the Red Fort and when I'd look back there would be my father, sitting on a bench, writing.

My father wouldn't hear of any "luxuries." This apparently included sheets for our beds, light bulbs and clean food. I became sick. Every half-hour what felt like a knife would rip through my belly. After several weeks, I was shitting on street corners. There would be my father, with an iron constitution, impatient with child and wife. He'd stride into the crowds, with a book in his armpit, and a sea of humanity would close behind him. In my pocket was a small note that became smudged with perspiration. It said: My name is David Layton. If I'm lost please take me to the Canadian Embassy at —. Attached to the note were a few rupees my mother had added.

Calcutta, Kuala Lumpur, Lahore, Jakarta. Names to be sick by. Names to fear. My father would be there one minute and disappear the next. When I was alone with my mother we would go to Western restaurants and gorge on fruits and vegetables.

We finally came to rest at some beach resort in some country that wasn't India. I spent an entire day building a giant castle with a moat and a pop-drink label for a flag. Towards the end of the day, some dark-skinned, menacing boys with rags for clothes came by and began to kick my walls down. They grabbed stones and swooped by, making artillery sounds as they released their ammunition. My father, sitting farther up the beach, merely watched. With a sense of resignation I walked over towards him as he cleared a space beside himself and patted the spot where I was to sit. Together we watched as a day's worth of labour was destroyed. The sun was setting in front of us and behind the boys who came, one by one, to kick my castle down.

"Look carefully, son, and learn. What you create men will come and destroy."

A year went by before we returned to where our "vacation" had begun: Greece. Our first port of call was Leonard Cohen's house on the island of Hydra. I'd been to Greece before, and had spent time in this very house. I felt safe, and desperately relieved to be back in a country whose name had a meaning that I could understand. Part of my relief was also attached to Leonard himself. He was like a calm sea where my father's boat could rest. With Leonard, my father ceased to be the Great Summarizer. He still made speeches, but he never prefaced those speeches with an interrogation.

As I played with my toys in Leonard's courtyard, I'd watch the two of them, their Greek sailors' hats perched rakishly on their heads, their drinks in hand, their bare chests exposed to the sun. I was just old enough to recognize a strange anomaly in the way they spoke to one another. If, as would sometimes happen, Leonard talked about his latest romantic failure my father would laugh and say, "Leonard, are you sure you're doing the wrong thing?" But right after that the conversation would switch to the third person, for Irving would then launch into a discussion about the poet. He'd speak about the poet as being conflicted. They'd examine the poet as archetype—albeit a vanishing one, along with the priest and the warrior—and about the poet as Lover. The poet, I'd hear my father say, "makes love to the world."

This last concept held a particular significance for me. Whenever my father roared this one out to my mother, I knew there was big trouble brewing. "Goddammit, woman, I'm a poet!" Which meant ipso facto that he was a Lover. This, my mother would point out, was precisely the issue: whose scent was on his shirt this time? My father would become infuriated. "I'm not a lover to a woman but a lover of Women," he'd say, as often as not launching into a speech about breasts as mounds of earth, vaginas as forests. He had no time for a petty mind, he'd say, meaning that he had no time for an unpoetical mind. I began at an early age to connect the word "lover" with my father's wrath.

Unlike my father, Leonard was a man who never seemed to raise his voice. He merely … disappeared. It was just off this very courtyard in Hydra, my father used to tell me, that Leonard had dropped himself and his typewriter into a pit and refused to come out. Marianne, who was living with him at the time, would implore him to come back inside but he continued to work on his second novel, *Beautiful Losers*. With tears in her eyes Marianne would drop food baskets into his hole. Leonard kept on writing until his fingers seized up. Now Marianne was gone.

For my father, this was as it should be. "Leonard happy?" I can hear him saying. "How can he be happy?" Leonard's destiny was to be more than a poet but a poet first. Let Leonard have everything, be anything: as a poet he wouldn't be able to enjoy it. My father always seemed quite delighted by Leonard's predicament, but his delight was never vindictive. Far from it—in my father's eyes it was the fulfillment of all that Leonard was fated to be.

Thus it only stood to reason that Leonard should lose his interest in sex at the very height of his fame. Women in elevators would throw themselves at him, would arrive at his hotel door with nothing on but a mink coat, but Leonard could give only an affirmative answer to my father's mirthful question, "Leonard, are you sure you're doing the wrong thing?"

It seems it was my father who, one evening in Montréal, hit on a ribald solution to Leonard's predicament. A little healthy competition between two great Lovers would spur Leonard's prick to life. Niema Ash, a woman who dressed only in purple, leapt in and offered to sit between the two men and, with their poetic members in her hand, stir the creative juices. "We need some inspiration," my father commanded. And so my mother, the erotic figurehead, balanced herself on the edge of the couch and thrust her bare breasts into the air.

Leonard won the competition.

It was my father's reported delight in his own defeat that gave me pause. For the first time, when Niema told me the story, it crossed my mind that for Irving to call Leonard "golden boy" was tantamount to calling him "golden son."

AFTER MARIANNE there had been Suzanne. Actually I remember Suzanne quite well because I had a crush on her. In our house we had a photo of Suzanne and Leonard taken outside in our front yard. If I looked carefully at the picture, and I did, I could see Leonard's fingers inching their way around the hem of her very short skirt. Leonard, no doubt, had the hands of an artist.

There is another memory I have of Suzanne. One day when we arrived at Leonard's house in Montréal, Suzanne was changing her son's diaper. While bare to the world the child began to pee. I was astonished at the power of his bladder. The yellow liquid shot out of his penis, made a magnificent arc over his head, and landed on Suzanne's cotton blouse. I followed the whole amazing performance with my eyes but, as I looked up at Suzanne's face, I saw what only could have been an expression of acute disgust. My mother hurried over to help her diaper the baby before her disgust turned to rage. As for my father and godfather, if memory serves me, they were huddled in a corner, talking in third-person pronouns.

But where was Suzanne now? Where were Leonard's children? Not here, in his house on Hydra. They had disappeared and while I missed Suzanne I was happy to have the kids out of the way. To my father, who constantly burdened himself with wife, children and mortgage, Leonard's recurrent solitude, even loneliness, must have seemed both appealing and exotic.

That was the autumn the Yom Kippur war broke out. Now the two of them, my father and godfather, would sit on Leonard's patio listening to the sombre voice of the BBC World Service, swivelling the aerial whenever the short-wave lost its focus. While I had only a vague notion of what was going on—"There were people hurting one another," was how my mother put it—I couldn't help but be impressed by how my father and Leonard discussed the war as if it were a personal matter. As in fact it was. The Israelis commandeered a Hercules transport plane to fly Leonard and his guitar to the front lines.

Not to be outdone, my father marched my mother and me down to the Israeli embassy in Athens and offered his services as a warrior and poet. They politely asked for a monetary donation.

This had less of an effect on my father than one might imagine. In his mind it was their loss, not his. The Israelis believed that they needed Leonard as much as my father believed that the Israelis needed him. It somehow amounted to the same thing. As famous men, as poets, no event, no matter how enormous, was outside their personal jurisdiction.

While they stretched out their arms to embrace the world, their wives, children and lovers kept slipping through the ever-widening circle.

IT WAS IN GREECE AGAIN, four years later, that my mother finally decided to get a "divorce." There was a new man in our life. He had eyes the colour of coal and a moustache whose ends he'd twirl with his fingers. I'd see him in the village, usually with my mother, sitting in a taverna. My mother introduced him as a "friend" and kept on using this euphemism for three entire months.

The village wrapped itself around the side of a hill and at its top, like a crown, stood the remains of a Byzantine fortress. Those who had money found homes in the lower part of the village, those who didn't found themselves in the shadow of the castle wall. The man with the moustache lived in the shadow. I don't think my mother ever looked better than that summer, what with having to run up the hill every night and run down the hill every morning, always remembering to stop at the bakery for the fresh bread and yogurt that her demanding family expected. That summer my father began to shuffle. He'd shuffle into the kitchen, where my mother would prepare breakfast, and then he'd shuffle back to his room. My mother wanted to pretend that what was happening wasn't really happening, so it was my father who told me, one morning when he'd shuffled into the kitchen and found no breakfast and no wife, only an empty space filled partly by a thirteen-year-old son, that things weren't going well between him and my mother. I had a towel slung over my shoulder and was anxious to meet Dania, the first love of my life, down at the beach. After what I thought an appropriate period of mourning I asked to be excused. As I skipped down the cobblestone streets, my father shuffled back into his room to contemplate his own demise.

My mother thought it right that my father and the man with the moustache, who I later found out was named Leon, have a "meeting." In full view of the artistic cabal that congregated every summer in the village, the two men made their way up the street, arm in arm, to an out-of-the-way taverna. Leon, who was expecting the full fury and pain of a man whose wife had been stolen and family destroyed, waited nervously for the explosion.

My father began to explain about the poet as a conflicted being.

"Poets," said my father, "don't make good husbands." Aviva needed to be set free. She needed a good man and Leon, my father implied, was a good man. Leon moved uneasily in his seat. He knew what he was being told: he might be good enough for Aviva, but he could never make love to Women.

My father moved from a treacherous benevolence—"Take her, she deserves better!"—to a rage that could not find a person but only a concept to attach itself to. "Be careful, Leon, women are castrating bitches. If they see one ounce, one OUNCE, of talent in you they'll rip your balls off."

That summer, my father was left with an audience of one. After the "meeting" he began to barge into my room where, with a fresh page of words in his hand, he'd sit beside my bed and carefully read me his newest poem.

Meanwhile, another picture of Suzanne and Leonard came to my attention. I stared at it for hours. There was Suzanne, looking beautiful and slightly cruel—exactly the same look of distaste on her face as when her son had pissed all over her. Only now the look had been transferred to Leonard.

For some reason it made me think of another story my father used to tell: about how Leonard once innocently tried to place a collect long-distance call through a Montréal operator "From Leonard Cohen to Suzanne, please." The operator was clearly stunned. Before she recovered Leonard asked her out on a date. Once lucky, he decided to try again, this time with another operator. Thinking that he was on to a good thing, he kept on with this game, until the night he found himself alone in a room dialling operator after operator, waiting for the breathless recognition he could move in on. It never came.

Now, in the picture, Suzanne was sitting in a beautiful restaurant with high-backed banquettes and long-stemmed glasses for the red wine. And there was Leonard, sitting beside her, looking miserable. "I've had," Leonard once told me, "that sense most of my life that it isn't working." In the picture, he was like a stain on the white tablecloth, a reminder that an accident had happened. Above the picture were the words "Death of a Lady's Man." It was the title of his new book and album.

Things, it occurred to me, were falling apart a bit for Leonard. Suzanne had left, and his own music was beginning to be defined as defining an era, something that should be played to remind you of what was and not what is. I hadn't yet learned that performers like Irving and Leonard have nine lives.

AT TWENTY-TWO I WAS living alone in a basement apartment in downtown Toronto. My mother and Leon were in Los Angeles. My godfather was just somewhere. Who knew with Leonard? It could have been LA, Paris, or Tahiti, and my father was in Montréal living with a twenty-eight-year-old woman named Anna. I'd see him on television talking about Love and Poetry and wonder if he'd actually been in town and not phoned. Sometimes, a friend would ring to tell me that he'd seen my father walking down the street. "Yes," I'd say, "he's in town for a few days." Which was in fact the case—I did, after all, read the newspaper.

Sometimes my father's face would slip through a crack in the door. He had once received, from an admirer, 1,000 envelopes with his face stamped onto them. His stern, unforgiving face, with hair tousled by the wind, would pop through my mail slot and out would fall a series of press clippings: "Irving Layton, Still Fighting Fire With Fire," "The Passion of Irving Layton." These headlines could denote either a speech made to the honourable members of the University of Chicago or a poetry reading given to the Housewives' Association of Mississauga. If there was a letter, it was always typewritten. "The battle has yet to be won," he'd write, and then, if I owed him fifty dollars, he'd speak of the moral imperative to pay back one's debts. And on the reverse side of the letter I could usually detect the carbon smudge left from the duplicate copy he'd made and then sent to the Irving Layton Collection at Concordia University.

It seemed a normal relationship with my father was impossible. Many years ago, when Leonard had given him two hits of acid, the books in my father's library had come out of their bookcase and bowed to one another. It was a ballet as Baudelaire stepped out and was introduced, by my father, to Ben Jonson and Edgar Allan Poe. "Leonard," he said, "I've been here many, many times." The place he was describing was the pantheon. He was there. With Socrates and Homer. He was breathing that air.

Leonard told me this story. He insisted that it was not something my father was putting on. "These," Leonard added, "are his concerns."

This was what I was afraid of.

Prominently displayed on my father's living-room table, whenever either of his sons came to visit, was an anthology of the writings of Freud. Irving's idea, his myth of fatherhood, was that we had come either to bless him or to kill him. His money was on kill. He was just letting us know. One time, I went there to face him down about it. I watched his fingers start their journey across the table and come to rest upon Freud's stern forehead in the cover photo.

"I hear you've been having some problems," he said.

"I need to talk to you," I answered.

He began to massage Freud's bald pate with a rhythmic drumming of his fingers.

I began to tell him that we needed to find some common ground. Perhaps, I suggested, if we told each other what we wanted and expected from each other, some kind of arrangement could be worked out. After sitting for fifteen minutes with arms folded, my father suddenly brought his open hand down on the table.

"What the hell are you talking about? 'Arrangements,' 'contracts.' Don't use these words with me. I'm very sorry for you, my son, but your father is not a lawyer, he's not a dentist. He's a poet! Men are vipers, villains, jackals, hyenas. If I've taught my children this one thing and this one thing only, then I have done my duty!"

My father leaned back in his chair. There was no point in trying to outperform the performer. I'd lose. But if I wasn't careful he'd start reading his poems to me.

I told him that for his sake I hoped he was one of the immortals but that I myself only wanted to be on some normal footing with my father. "And," I added, "I have another confession to make. I've never read any of your poems."

My father looked at me.

"You've never read any of my poems?"

"Not one."

He started to laugh. He laughed until he choked. "Bravo!" We spent the rest of the day smoking cigars and drinking port.

I MOVED OUT OF the basement and into a third-floor loft. I enrolled in university as a mature student and used the Christmas breaks to visit my mother and Leon in LA. If Leonard was in town, I'd go and see him for an hour or two and we'd talk about women, Greece and the mysteries of good coffee. I also started making the occasional trip to Montréal to see my father. I'd talk. He'd summarize. On one occasion I told him that a woman had left me. "Son," he said, "the worst thing you can find out about yourself is that you're replaceable." I never failed to come away feeling I'd been party to a historic event.

One day in Toronto I received a call from my half-brother's ex-girlfriend, now a well-known painter, who said that there was a book launch for my father's new "Selected, collected something or other. Would I like to come?" she asked. Hell, why not?

"My boy!" my father bellowed. "Look at you!" The reception was in full swing by the time I arrived. I grabbed a drink and began to talk to Anna, my father's new wife. While we talked, faces would push themselves into the conversation. "David? Is that you?" And I'd say, "Yes, it's me," and then they'd move on. But I'd been invited. Here was the intimate embrace: the invitation. My father, standing on the podium saying, "This is for my son, David."

Halfway through the evening, an awed silence descended. I turned around and saw him. It was Leonard Cohen, who had come from some corner of the globe to surprise my father.

"Leonard, my boy!" my father bellowed, "Look at you." I stood by the entrance, with a drink in my hand, and waited to say hello to my godfather, and thank you to my father. After thirty minutes the two, linked arm in arm, moved towards me, strode on past, and entered the hotel elevator where I watched them ascend to the heights.

THIS TIME I BOOKED my appointment with Leonard through his personal assistant. Leonard had a "window" on Saturday, in the late morning. That was three days away.

When I touched down at LAX there was only a thin strip of ozone where thick storm clouds had been on my last visit. I arrived at my mother's house on Friday evening and I thought about phoning Leonard. But then, why tempt fate? I waited until the hour of my appointment.

"Leonard?" The door to his house was slightly ajar. Before I'd even managed to pass the threshold, he was there, moving towards me, with that gorgeous smile of his. I couldn't help feeling that his presence was somehow attributable to my delicate magic. David Layton, the conjurer of shy spirits.

Leonard quickly deduced that we were short of certain materials. We jumped into his Nissan Pathfinder and headed for the liquor store. Leonard's clothes weren't as elegant as I remembered them; he wore a pair of grubby jeans. I noticed this fact as he moved down the liquor aisle. He spent an enormous amount of time looking at the tequila rack and peering into aromatic cigar boxes. He took the kind of time that indicates a man's occupation. No one who has spent a lifetime working nine to five would be able to develop such a luxurious spirit.

There was Leonard, searching for bottles in a deserted liquor store. With his ill-fitting pants and studious interest he reminded me of an aging professor searching for books in an obscure and neglected part of the library. The effect didn't make him appear old, just vulnerable.

Back at his house, Leonard offered me a ginseng-soaked cognac. He also placed a cup of coffee on the kitchen table and handed me a fat, lighted Dominican cigar. Before I'd taken my second puff, Lorca, his daughter with Suzanne, dropped by to see us. I've only known Lorca for a few years but even so I have a strange urge to treat her as my younger sister, which is no doubt partly attributable to my mother's desire to treat her like a long-lost daughter. But our links are tenuous and, as with all things in our family, ill defined.

Time passed. I placed my tape recorder on the table and tried to let it speak for me. I couldn't bring myself to ask Lorca to leave. We were the children of famous men and it was we who were always asked to leave.

Lorca, thankfully, saved me from my predicament by taking the initiative and leaving her father and me to conduct the interview. We were alone.

"I don't have much time," he said.

I pushed the record button.

"The relationship I had with Irving was not personal but it was intimate. We weren't friends in the sense that we knew or cared about each other's lives. We did know and care about each other's lives, but that wasn't what it was about. That's a personal relationship. This relationship was the poet talking to the poet about poetry. It was more intimate than a personal relationship could ever be. That kind of intimacy has sustained me my whole life and anything that is not that has always been troublesome."

On his table is a picture of Roshi, the spiritual leader of Leonard's retreat on Mount Baldy. He looks like an Oriental version of my father; the fleshy face, the truculent expression and, behind it all, the unmistakable hint of mischief. They have the faces of boxers, of men who know about getting in the ring and beating the immortal shit out of each other without hatred.

I couldn't help thinking the connection was more than a passing coincidence. Leonard invited the comparison. Leonard said, "When I study with Roshi, it's consciousness speaking to consciousness about consciousness." And anything else, I thought, is troublesome. A godson is trouble, children are trouble, and wives are the genesis of all trouble.

Speaking of consciousness, I was losing mine. The ginseng was hallucinogenic and the cigar smoke was making me exceptionally sick. "Leonard," I said, "I don't think I can drive home right now." "I know," Leonard answered. "The ginseng has been soaking in the cognac for six months. It's very potent." Leonard smiled. Then, just sitting across the table from me, he began to sing. All by itself Leonard's voice began to make my upper lip quiver. I cupped my hand over my mouth and when he had finished singing I excused myself and ran for the bathroom where, like some hormonally flushed teenager, I splashed cold water over my face.

When I returned to the kitchen Leonard was on his way out. He had to go, he said, but I could stay for as long as I liked.

He'd given me his intimate embrace: the performance. Now I was stoned and alone in his house. I looked for a picture of my father but couldn't find one. I started laughing, and once I started I couldn't stop. "Leonard!" I shouted. "Leonard, you bastard, you've done it again! You've disappeared."

MOIRA FARR

from

After Daniel

A Suicide Survivor's Tale

A CLOSED DOOR

WHEN I RECALL details of the day I found Daniel dead, as I have so many times in the five years since, I am tempted to detach myself, to watch the event unfold in my mind's eye without emotion, at the safe remove of time, in the light of selective memory, with the reputed benefit of hindsight and my capacity to fashion an interpretation that a reader might accept and understand. I can provide a version of events only. I am, after all, a flawed observer: biased, emotional, wounded, scarred, and at times still perplexed. There is so much I do not know, can never know. Daniel's suicide was a kind of ground zero in my life, and I must overcome the fear that if I poke around in the wreckage left in the wake of that devastation, I will find smouldering embers that still spark and burn. Yet this is something I must do, this clearing of dangerous debris, this making of a new, unobstructed pathway along which I may safely move forward.

To get to the centre of the experience, I have to start at its edges. What I see now is an emotionally stretched woman in her mid-thirties dancing as fast as she can around her boyfriend's depression. It's not as though depression itself is news to her. She's battled it herself and watched its insidious effects engulf others she's loved. She's no stranger to loss and grief, either, having survived a divorce and her mother's death from a stroke two years earlier. She has worked hard not to let her troubles swamp her entirely, and so far they haven't. She has seen enough human sadness and wasted spirit to know that not everyone lives happily ever after, and that she cannot simply expect it—happiness—to land in her lap, with no effort on her part.

But she doesn't always get it right. There's been therapy, enough to lay bare the obvious, all-too-common familial underpinnings of her own depression, and to show how this has—what else?—unconsciously predisposed her to choose similarly suffering souls as friends and lovers. Yes, she knows she's somehow programmed to be drawn to those who labour through difficult lives under the labels of "depressive," "addictive," "manic," and the like, to greater or lesser degrees. It's not hard to do anyway in creative circles, where artistic talent is often the saving grace of impoverished craziness—I use the term to encompass the spectrum, from garden-variety neurosis to more obvious manifestations of psychological pain and disorder.

And now there is Daniel, with whom she formed an intense and, for a time, happy relationship the previous year. They have reason to hope for good things, despite the difficulties Daniel is now having, emotionally and financially. She knows from hard experience that once depression has invaded and flourished, it takes time and care to prune it down from its threatening wildness to fit the garden of ordinary unhappiness. Still it can gain control in quick and frightening fashion, and it is almost impossible to ever weed out its deep roots entirely. She's kept it at bay for some time herself, and is determined to fight it off if it ever tries to take hold again.

Daniel too has been battling the infamous "black dogs" for years, with the aid of medications and regular visits to a psychiatrist he trusts. He talks openly about the help he gets and why he gets it. They have also talked about the shadow suicidal thoughts and feelings have cast on their lives in the past, and in Daniel's case, many years earlier, attempts. Their acceptance and compassion for each other are part of the strength of their relationship, or so it seems.

And though the depression may always be lurking, waiting for an opportunity to lunge, you would not know it, to view these two people pass the promising first months of their relationship. See them work, productively, at a variety of creative projects. Here they are striding up College Street, laughing and carrying on with friends. Here they are shopping and making meals together, collapsing on the living room floor at midnight during a heat wave, listening to each other's favourite music, discussing books, showing each other their work, sharing their most private dreams and desires. If there is an element of sadness in the mix, it isn't so hard to imagine, for those starting over with a new partner in their thirties are bound to feel the undertow of past failures. And that undertow is there all right. Along with the laughter and the light there are dark moments, when Daniel, recently separated, seems wracked by various guilts and regrets, and compelled to inform his new love, with extreme contrition, that he hasn't always behaved very nicely, especially back when he was a drunk. Sometimes, this need to confess and catalogue his sins strikes her as touching, incongruously innocent: "Listen," she wants to say, "if that's the extent of it ... there's worse than you in this world, and they're not half so sorry!" Often, it seems, Daniel walks in the shadow of his own self-condemnation, and expects others to be no more compassionate toward him than a Texas parole board. Though redemption has been staring him in the face for some time, it seems sometimes he cannot see it, or imagine that it is real.

Remarkably, Daniel actually said at the beginning of their happy times that there was one thing he could promise her he would never do, not so long as they were together, and that was to kill himself. It never occurred to her that he might break such a startling and candid promise, never occurred to her that he might have reason to. As far as she is concerned, she and Daniel are loyal allies in the war to survive the exigencies of a creative life in the hardbitten, downsized, fin-de-siécle world, with depressive illness thrown in as an added challenge, occasionally requiring the deployment of big emotional artillery. When it comes to these battles, she considers joint forces stronger than solitary troops.

After that declaration of Daniel's, suicide is not a part of their shared lexicon, not a spoken word that passes between them. But it seems in the end she didn't adequately perceive the degree to which her comrade had fallen and lost heart, or notice in time that his wounds had become life-threatening, that he'd decided to lie down and die, letting her run on—generously, he must have thought—sparing her the details of how badly off he really was. She always thought that one way or the other, they'd live to be hoary old veterans telling their war stories, stories Daniel had already begun to tell with such aching clarity in his poetry and fiction. The hope and optimism of their first summer together— how could she imagine it would be their last?—are a long way from the dead of winter to come.

NOW I SEE MYSELF in the early morning of that particular February day, walking down the two steep flights of stairs from Daniel's sprawling old apartment, with its rabbit's-warren layout and creaky hardwood floors, above a shoe store in a crumbling old brick building on College Street, in the middle of Toronto's now trendy "little Italy" neighbourhood. I set off to my small rented office farther east on College Street, where I do my work as a freelance magazine writer and editor. I am tired. I've been working hard, and Daniel has had the flu all week. With the physical symptoms of that to contend with on top of his other troubles, he is listless and sleeps fitfully, lying on the couch mostly, reading a little or watching TV. I feed him soup, keep him supplied with juice, throat lozenges, and Kleenex, cover him with blankets when they fall off while he dozes, run errands for both of us. Nurse Moira to the Rescue. Not a script I planned, or even knew I was following, but looking back, it appears I was quite a natural in my role among the ranks of failed saviours. As I now know, where there's a suicide, you'll often find us.

I see myself walking wearily up the street, wearing a black leather jacket, a black silk blouse, a black scarf splashed with a colourful floral pattern, the kind that hangs from racks by the dozens in the Latin American craft shops on Bloor Street between Bathurst and Spadina, and a pair of red denim jeans Daniel selected for me in a London boutique on my birthday the previous September. The colour red, a little alarming on a grey, sub-zero winter day in Toronto, is my one nod to Saint Valentine—I should mention shouldn't I, that it's Valentine's Day. This is something gossips would later make much of, attaching a bogus romance-tinged melodrama to Daniel's exit from life on that day; his actual death was the night before.

But the reality is less florid. True, Daniel's personal life was rather a mess; he was separated, not divorced, from his wife, and our relationship was suffering from his ambivalence about this. I'd distanced myself a bit, maintaining a separate place to live, though I ended up spending more nights than not with him. I rationalized this as easier on both of us while he went through the inevitable inner conflicts of unravelling a difficult attachment. But I don't believe that this ordinary, if trying, human dilemma was linked in Daniel's mind with the pseudo-event of Valentine's Day. I think his deepening despair had by mid-February entered a kind of terminal phase that would have rendered the date irrelevant.

Earlier in the month, Daniel had come quietly into the living room, where I sat reading and drinking tea, and stood looking down at me with his best rather bashful smile. "Um, happy Valentine's Day," he said and presented me with one of those lottery tickets that lie in trays at the corner store, this one covered in shiny silver, pink, and red hearts. I laughed and thanked him for such a sweet, goofy gesture. "You're early," I said. "Isn't it the fourth?" he asked, startled. Yes, I replied, but Valentine's Day is the fourteenth. "Oh," he said. "I always seem to get those days mixed up."

Oh well. Daniel sat down beside me, and laughing at ourselves, a pair of writers living on the financial edge, we scratched off the hearts with a penny to see if we had won anything. Yes, we had. Two bucks. Wow. We never did get around to buying another ticket, and I have never had the heart to do so since. The unredeemed ticket sits in a box at the back of my closet, among other random mementoes I cannot seem to part with, but don't like to think about....

I COULD NEVER HAVE imagined the turn my life was about to take, all the horrors that awaited. Now I flash back to the image of my oblivious, yet wary and anxious self walking back up the stairs in that dim hallway, my footfalls on the aluminum-trimmed linoleum steps echoing in my ears, the dry, acrid taste of fear gathering on my tongue. I reach Daniel's front door (a red door, as it happens, inviting the infamous coat of black), and turn the key in the lock, the words *he wouldn't* playing in my mind like a feverish mantra, their very presence unwelcome testimony that in some way, I actually think he would. I open the door with mustered determination, as though—I now tell myself wryly—a good attitude could have altered fate at that point. Christian miracles aside, I'm not one to believe that positive thinking can raise the dead.

But "dead" isn't what's on my mind in that moment. Now I tell myself everything is really okay, there is a rational and reasonable explanation for the morning's three unreturned phone calls. At worst Daniel is just in a deep sleep that has lasted into the early afternoon, after a restless night. I enter the apartment. The door to the living room is still closed, as it was more than twelve hours ago, when it seemed explainable. Daniel was sick, and the cat had disturbed him the night before, poking her paw in our faces and mewing to be fed at 5 A.M. He didn't want to keep me awake with his tossing and turning and coughing, so he told me he would sleep on the couch.

Yes, the closed door made sense then, but now my heart races and I somehow know I can no longer reasonably maintain the hope that everything is okay. I'm fending off the advent of deeper emotion by focusing on annoyance: *How dare you scare me this way? I will open the door, to hell with privacy, and say, "Daniel, what's going on?"* But when I turn the knob, the door won't budge. Locked. Another surge through my heart. I rattle the knob, pushing at the door and calling Daniel's name. Then I see the note. Tiny thing. A white piece of paper tacked on a white door. It says, in what is undeniably Daniel's hand, DO NOT COME IN. PLEASE CALL THE POLICE.

Later, I learned that the scant wording of this note supposedly echoed an event in a Martin Amis novel, but if Daniel had indeed intended to ornament the grim scene with a literary filigree, I'm afraid any such bookish allusion was lost on me then. Literarily speaking, the only thing I later at times wished was that I were possessed of the maniacally intrusive nature of one of Philip Roth's more memorable characters, namely Portnoy's mother, interminably haranguing her son every time he walks into the bathroom and shuts the door: "[Daniel], are you in pain? Do you want me to call the doctor? Are you in pain or aren't you? I want to know exactly where it hurts. Answer me." Yes, I have grimly thought to myself, if I were that kind of woman, perhaps I would have knocked sooner, knocked despite Daniel's telling me he needed an undisturbed night of sleep. I would have knocked and discovered the note much earlier, when there might have been time to save him, while he was still nodding into unconsciousness from the pills, before he had successfully affixed the plastic bags over his head and suffocated himself.

This is part of the futile and interminably self-punishing dialogue suicide survivors often have with themselves, the go-nowhere Dance of the Thousand If Onlys. For the other side of those musings is admitting that it is more likely (though not a certainty; I live with that painful truth) that Daniel was dead before I arrived back at the apartment the night before, after an evening's work toward a tight deadline at my office. The closed door did not signal danger to me then, and I did not knock or see the note. No, I was not a woman like Portnoy's mother. At that point in his life, Daniel was far more likely to choose the kind of woman who quietly respects privacy, who doesn't like to pry and prod, who would understand his needs, yadda, yadda, yadda, and who would consequently misread the final brick in a towering wall of despair as a perfectly understandable request for temporary sick leave. It has taken me years not to feel guilt about this; I do and always will feel regret. There is a profound and important difference.

In those awful first moments, however, I stand absorbing the note's message, stunned, my legs going weak. Now I am banging on the door, shoving myself against it, and shouting Daniel's name. When I stop for a moment to listen for an answer, a sound, anything, from the other side, there is only a terrible silence, settled and complete.

The mind's eye starts doing jump cuts here. I remember the next few hours only in a jerky, jumbled sequence. I know that once I had seen the note and it had registered that Daniel was not answering me, I ran to his office and dialed 911. Now I hear a strange sound issuing into the telephone receiver, a hysterical lady's voice, surely not mine, talking too rapidly of pills and a boyfriend and a locked door and *please send an ambulance now, right now.* Well, something like it, for I can't actually recall with any precision what I said.

Now, since I can do nothing about the locked door until help arrives, I am curiously driven to track through the apartment, roaming from room to room like some half-crazed zoo animal, with nothing to do but pace around the strange enclosure. What am I thinking? That Daniel is hiding under the discarded, claw-legged bathtub in a tiny back room used for storage? That he has somehow managed to squeeze himself in back of the refrigerator, or is planning to pop out from behind the bedroom door and say, "Fooled ya!"? I'm not thinking, just acting on dumb impulse. Yes, what I'd like is to make everything go back to "normal," anything, any explanation at all besides the one that is forcing its way into unwelcome being.

All I will let myself imagine in these moments is that Daniel has taken an overdose of medication, that he is unconscious, that as soon as the ambulance gets here, salvation and recovery will begin. That's it, an overdose, horrible enough, but right now, I am not thinking death, I will not allow death. "The heart did not believe," goes a line from Leonard Cohen's incantatory *Beautiful Losers,* and it is as accurate an expression of the human capacity to repel and deny loss as exists in the language. It's not so much a survival skill as it is an instinct, one that springs alert with particular strength in the face of abrupt, shocking death, wrapping us in a kind of protective psychological padding that dulls the impact of trauma.

So, no, I am still not thinking death, I am only thinking, and I believe saying aloud, things like *please hurry, please come, for Christ's sake get here, come now, please.* I don't know how long I wait, perhaps no more than five minutes, I don't think more than ten. Long enough to spin through the rooms, to shove myself against the door again, to shout Daniel's name and hear the awful silence, and finally, to fall to my knees on the patterned carpet in the hallway a few feet from the locked door, and the note that adorns it, feeling the word *NO* rising from my diaphragm, passing through my throat, and flinging itself hugely and forcefully from my mouth. As though *NO* could break down the door. As though *NO* could rip back time, sweep over the past, and reset its clockwork, so that it could resume ticking into the future minus this tragedy-in-progress. As though *NO* alone could go up against death itself and win.

Yet even though I am still fighting the possibility of death, a small part of me is getting the picture, and is now starting to bargain with God, or the gods, to think irrationally that perhaps a person can be a little bit dead, and can change his mind and crawl back to life, be scooped up and returned to the living, if he is not *too* dead, that is.

Finally, two bored-looking cops arrive, their black boots clumping up the stairs, the synthetic material of their massive blue winter coats incessantly swishing as they move. The older, bigger cop is dark-haired and blue-eyed; the other is blond and so young and fresh-looking that I almost want to apologize for exposing him to this.

I gesture to the door, and after they jiggle the knob and push against it themselves, they tell me to stand back, they're going to have to break it out of its frame. Shoulders to it, they heave their combined bulk just a couple of times, and I hear the oddly sickening sound of dry, old wood splintering, the wrenching give and groan of the heavy door falling inward and resting askew off its dislodged hinges.

Now that the door is open, the last thing I want to do, the last thing I am able to do, is enter that room. Shock has instilled in me a child's literal-mindedness: Daniel said in that note on the door not to come in, so I better not. Now that I am allowing for the possibility of death—death that can be bargained with, and reversed, mind you—I'm also starting to let myself form mental images of what scene might await. "He was capable of cruelty; he was meticulous, theatrical," writes Lynn Crosbie in her sad and beautiful poem for Daniel, "Geography." In it, she also writes of him as a "sweet friend," capable too of "rare, infectious bliss." But perhaps it is that cruel quality of Daniel's I recognize as I stand there, a quality that might have made him fashion some horrible tableau for the living to find. "An act like this is prepared within the silence of the heart, as is a great work of art," writes Camus of suicide in *The Myth of Sisyphus*. And what artful death, I could hardly have dared ask myself, had Daniel silently prepared?

It wasn't like that, in the end, but I suppose I had cause to fear Daniel's capacity for theatrics. He had told me of it himself and the memory of one such conversation stays with me. The previous summer, he and I had driven to Killarney to visit the family home of friends of mine, the prospect of "Jones camping" causing much hilarity in his circle. The general view was that the urban angst-man extraordinaire must be well and truly smitten to have agreed to let his Doc Martens tread on anything other than the concrete of a city sidewalk, to put himself beyond the orbit of the College Street *caffe latte,* even for a brief weekend. He did it happily, remarking on how strange it all was, how long it had been since he had placed himself in such a rugged environment, or done anything so outdoorsy as lounge on a wooden dock in a bathing suit, reading magazines. When he took a running dive and plunged into the cool lake, he popped up with a look of amazement on his face, and said, "I can't believe I did that. I don't know if I've ever done that," to the amusement of everyone else strewn lazily around the dock. It was like watching someone who usually lived within the squeeze of a vise-grip start to feel some loosening up, once again using muscles, emotional and physical, that have atrophied over a long time. Later, we spent an entertaining evening playing cards with my friend's good ol' boy brothers, who took to Daniel, even though it was obvious he aroused suspicions that he was a city guy of some airs and book learning. Besides, his drink of choice was Diet Pepsi, not Molson Ex. During a round of euchre, one brother turned to another and called him a "bohemian, bag-bitin' whore." Daniel and I exchanged looks and laughed till we nearly fell off our chairs. We swore later that we would race each other to immortalize this wondrous colloquialism in a book; I guess I win.

On the way back, we drove along roads that channel like arteries through Muskoka's masses of billion-year-old granite. Daniel and I talked, as lovers getting to know each other do, of who we'd been before we'd met, long before, back even to the primordial ooze of high school. Amid the shared stories of teenage ineptitude and heartache was Daniel's description of himself as a budding young high-school playwright. He admitted one of the reasons he liked to write his own plays was because he could give all the good roles to himself. "Like what?" I wanted to know. He thought about it, and replied casually, "Oh, well, God."

Something about the way the word "God" hung in the air between us—the big kahuna of theatrical roles, none better!— evoked such naive adolescent audacity, a troubled boy's yearning for mastery of his world. It was so astonishing that we both began to chuckle. I pulled the car into a picnic area along the side of the road so I wouldn't lose control of the car as I was convulsed with laughter. Eventually we composed ourselves, and resumed our drive through miles of blasted-out Precambrian rock, back into the city, with its altogether different terra firma.

Daniel told me other stories that revealed his flair for drama, his desire to be at the centre of his own scenes, but that story, and the moment of its telling, in which he revealed so completely the innocent and all-too-human underpinnings of his self-aggran- dizing tendencies, often comes back to haunt me. "I love you, Moira, and I'm sorry, even though you will not imagine it," he wrote in his suicide note, only two seasons after our intimacy was at its promising beginning. *Oh, but I do imagine it, Daniel,* I have responded many times in dialogues I can't help having with his absence. *Unfortunately, I imagine it all too well, have endured much time in which about all I could do was imagine it, and that is the problem with this suicide of yours, Daniel, you see, the very big, heart- breaking problem.*

SO, FOR REASONS I could not have articulated at the time, two images crowd my mind as I stand paralyzed in the hallway by the broken door, suspended between not knowing and knowing what Daniel has actually done. Neither of them makes sense, couldn't occur simultaneously, much less if my chief image of Daniel unconscious on the couch is closer to reality. What I see is Daniel hanging dramatically, accusingly, somewhere in the room, perhaps from one of the towering and crowded shelves that hold his thousands of beloved books, or from the ceiling in the middle of the room, though this could not be, logistically or physically. I also see Daniel blown utterly apart, my mind making a metaphor of my deepest fear, that Daniel is now fragmented beyond reconstruction, forever gone, and that he himself has somehow enacted the horrible, unconscionable dismemberment.

That's what I see, the messy, terrible aftermath of a furious and violent act. What I feel is his rage, a rage encompassing the whole imperfect universe, and the chaotic heap of self that he so desperately sought to escape, when it seemed to have slipped out of his control. Mostly, I think, it is rage saved up, gathering gale force over years and years, and then turned inward, transformed into self-loathing and suicidal depression. "I thought I was trying to change, but I was not," is about the kindest thing Daniel says about himself in his final note as he expresses the distorted notion that the only "right thing" for him to do is to remove himself from the planet entirely.

Young Cop and Older Cop do go into the room. I hear them murmuring, though I have no visual memory. Then, their boots clump to a standstill. A figure finally emerges from the room. Young Cop looks a little pasty as he looms before me. He is saying, "Why don't we go and sit down?" He is leading me away from the living room and into the kitchen. And I'm thinking, *Okay, so I don't have to go into that room, I don't ever have to see whatever sorry spectacle has unfolded there. I don't want to see Daniel in this undignified and horrible state of self-inflicted death. If he'd wanted me to see that, would he not have left the door unlocked? Would he have left the note explicitly warning whoever found it—and he had to know the person was going to be me—not to come in?*

I never do go into the room; I only catch a glimpse of Daniel's resting body as I leave the apartment, as the ambulance attendants and cops prepare to navigate the steep and narrow staircase with their grim cargo of a six-foot-one, 200-pound, thirty-four-year-old dead man. I feel no desire to behold this. The man I knew and loved is gone. Absurdly, I am not in a position to identify his body officially anyway, not being his "next of kin." That joyous job fell to his wife.

My memory of the last time I saw Daniel remains less violent, though it speaks of what was to come in a way I didn't understand at the time. The day had been good, companionable, quiet. Daniel stood in the hallway as I was preparing to leave for an evening of work at my office, saying he was not feeling well again. He went into the living room and lay down on the couch. Before I left, I sat down beside him as he faced inward, put my hand on his shoulder and asked if he was going to be okay. He nodded a little. Anything he needed while I was out? He shook his head. I kissed him on the cheek and said, "I'll see you later." As I recall, he did not respond. If the time he cites in his suicide note is correct, a little more than an hour after I left, he swallowed his overdose and began preparing to suffocate himself with plastic bags—a method that comes courtesy of the popular recipe book *Final Exit.* Dr. Sherwin Nuland describes the method in his illuminating study of modern death, *How We Die,* as about the most painless and humane way there is to go.

As we settle at the table and the young officer pulls out his notebook, I'm asking, in what must seem a spaced-out way, "Is he dead?" Somehow, he of the fresh face and stammering tongue manages not to answer that question directly. I am given a further reprieve from the truth, though of course, I know by now it is true, has to be. Why would everything be so very strange if Daniel were not dead?

I'm asked if I'd like a glass of water. Everything is happening very slowly now, as though we're immersed in something viscous, something jelling and holding us. Water? A glass of it? Are you going to get it for me? Why would you offer me a glass of water?

I strain to understand, as though grasping the precise meaning of this question might somehow explain what is going on in the other room.

More cops arrive, and ambulance attendants. Soon the apartment is crawling with large men murmuring in deep, urgent voices. In the end, it is a burly, deadpan, sandy-haired paramedic entering the kitchen wearing latex gloves who tells me that Daniel is dead. What he actually says is couched in some kind of official-speak about there appearing to be "no signs of life," that the coroner would have to confirm that and he'd be arriving shortly. Only at this point do I cry, though not yet in full-out sobs. I am after all a Wasp by training and upbringing. Loss of control will come later, alone.

For now, I sit like a good girl on my chair in the kitchen, feeling small and immobilized while the big men do their job. From where I sit, I see a blur of human traffic in the hallway, legs in dark pants, feet in boots, moving back and forth, clump, clump, clump. I fix on two objects on the carpet there. What are they, anyway? My jacket, curled and twisted in a heap, the arms inside out. I must have squirmed out of it and let it drop to the floor at some point. There's my scarf in a pile nearby too. I watch, numbly fascinated, as the succession of legs and feet step over these things, until one cop notices them and picks them up, straightening out the jacket and hanging it and the scarf on the back of a kitchen chair. It's the same officer who makes *shhhh* noises and rushes to close the kitchen door, seeing me put my hands over my ears as another cop in the hallway starts reading Daniel's suicide note out loud in a mocking tone to the assembled masses of post-mort officialdom. I sit, listening in speechless horror.

At some point, Young Cop escorts me to the phone in Daniel's office so that I may call a friend. But which friend? My mind is so addled, I cannot remember a single phone number. I sit for a while in this different chair, Daniel's chair, occasionally picking up the receiver and again, like a child imitating the movements of the adult world, press the numbered keys in what might be, but isn't, a familiar sequence. Young Cop hovers awkwardly behind me, asking if I have an address book and could he get it for me? Well, yes, I have one, but it's at my office, I explain.

It's mortifying. I finally remember that one of the women I share a house with, Jeannie, will be at the Ryerson School of Journalism today, and of all the numbers that dwell in my head, this institution's is the one I recall. An alarmed secretary—I guess I sound pretty bad—finds my friend and soon she is on her way over in a cab. The officers seem more able to talk with her than with me, for I recall bits of information being relayed to me through her as an intermediary. Older Cop—he who read Daniel's last written words out loud—enters the kitchen and, apparently trying to offer some condolences, stands beside me and says, "Ya know, Myra—is that how you pronounce your name?—if he was that far gone that he was capable of doing something like this, you're better off without him. With sick people like that, if it isn't this year, it's gonna be next, and there's really not much you can do about it."

So, Older Cop becomes the first in what was to be a long line of people to offer me pat truisms and pet theories about suicide, none of them useful to someone in the first stages of coming to terms with the actual suicide of a real human being she knew and loved. Yet training in handling suicides does exist for police officers; considering how woefully common it is for the police to deal with these situations—not least within their own ranks—it is difficult to understand why an officer at a downtown precinct of a metropolis with a population of millions would not know better. The last thing I hear, as I am being led down the stairs, I think by Jeannie and the one woman officer in the place, is Older Cop once again reading aloud from Daniel's note, and a snippet of the conversation of two other cops, who are standing in what had been the bedroom. "Great apartment, eh?" says one. "Yeah," replies the other. "Guy sure had a lot of books."

At my office a few blocks down the street, I compose myself and phone several people I think should know what has happened. I seem to need to say it to believe it. I transmit the information, I hear the stricken voices respond, I don't recall what was said to whom exactly. *I'm afraid I have bad news. Daniel killed himself, yes, that's right, yes, yes.* In the middle of my grim task, an editor calls from *Flare* magazine, which has just published a story of mine. A local radio station wants to interview me later in the week, and the editor reminds me that in such interviews I should use the name of the magazine as much as possible, as in, "Well, Bob, as I wrote in *Flare*...." "Okay, sure, no problem," I reply. "Happy Valentine's Day," she says with a small giggle as she signs off. "Same to you," I say as I hang up.

The woman officer knocks on the door. I gather some belongings, feeling dizzy, unreal. I follow her silently down the wide, sweeping staircase of this old building that was once an Orange Lodge in Toronto's good Protestant Irish days, one my paternal grandfather probably belonged to, and which by 1994 was housing an alternative cinema, as well as the offices of various writers and artists. Jeannie is in the front seat of the cruiser, holding my bug-eyed cat in her arms. The cat, as opposed to Daniel, had wedged herself under the old bathtub, and must have cowered there all afternoon.

I sit in the cruiser's back seat, shiny and worn from all the backsides that have graced it before mine, separated from those in the front by a wall of wire caging. I am surely one of the more docile passengers the car has transported. I stare through the window, up into the sky, beyond the tops of passing houses.

Is there something primal, universally human, in this intense urge to gaze toward the heavens after a death? The night my mother died, I sat outside in the October chill, compelled to watch the sky as dawn came, sure I saw her face in the wisps of cloud, moving slowly, grandly, through all the unique expressions of hers that are imprinted on my memory, passing overhead, dissolving, disappearing. Do we really imagine our loved ones have gone up there? Do we truly expect to see them waving goodbye to us, smiling, telling us they are going to be fine now? All I know is that I can't seem to stop myself staring up at the whitish-grey, late-afternoon sky, enlivened only by the stark contrast of dark, bare-branched trees, a matte winter canvas on which to rest my battered senses, as the cruiser ferries us home. No, no signs of Daniel up in that frozen, empty sky.

My other roommate, Grainne, has returned from work early, having heard the news from Jeannie. She is standing in the living room when we come through the door. Seeing the look of genuine pain on her face, I suddenly, momentarily, understand how this death is going to affect the people surrounding him, even those who are closer to me than to him; yes, suicide kills everyone, as the English essayist G. K. Chesterton astutely observed. Grainne rushes to put her arms around me. We stand together like that for a long time.

Later in the evening, several other close friends come to the house, and we sit in the living room for hours, long into the night, as the phone rings and I must speak again and again to the growing circle of people who now know of Daniel's death. We veer from deep and dreadful discussions of this thing that has happened, the reason that we're all gathered here so abruptly, and lighter conversation that keeps everyone connected to the world beyond this tragedy. I sit in my chair in the corner of the room, nursing an Irish whisky someone has thoughtfully placed in my hand as I return once again from the phone and listen dazed as the people around me engage in an exchange about canoeing. *Well,* I am thinking,

AFTER DANIEL 241

my head fuzzy from the combination of shock and alcohol, as I'm hit by a bizarre urge to laugh hysterically, *Daniel is dead, and what better time to plan next summer's excursion to Quetico Park?* It makes no sense, but nothing does. I can suggest no other subject that would be more suitable for a roomful of people who don't all know each other well, though they know me. Etiquette books say nothing about how to behave in the wake of a death by suicide, though Hallmark has recently designed a greeting card to send to someone grieving a suicide, with distinctly religious overtones. My friends' gentle, intermittent attempts that evening to socialize politely in the midst of accepting the enormity of the loss at hand were touchingly human. It won't be the last time that this sense of high absurdity will strike me in my struggle to accept Daniel's death and its many sad consequences.

BY TWO IN THE MORNING, everyone had either gone to bed or left, except the heroic Laima, whom I have known since I was a nervous nineteen-year-old at the University of Toronto. She had arrived earlier in the evening with her husband, Larry, both of them rather gussied up, which I didn't understand until later, when I remembered that it was Valentine's Day. My call had come just as they were heading out the door to enjoy a romantic dinner; instead of a relaxed, uninterrupted evening of candlelight and wine, they got suicide and canoeing in my living room. But I'm not aware of that right now, at 2 a.m. I say to Laima, "I just don't think I can go to bed. I don't think I can stand any darkness." She insists I lie down on the couch and at least rest. Hands folded in her lap, her dark skirt flared around her, like some nursing sister of mercy keeping vigil in the flickering candlelight at the bedside of a wounded soldier, my beloved friend says she will sit by me until I do fall asleep. Finally, after a fitful half hour or so, I pretend that I am taking the longer, deeper breaths of sleep, so that she can go home and get some herself. She tiptoes out and quietly shuts the front door. I reluctantly, painfully, drag myself upstairs to my own bed.

All through the night, Daniel is with me, trying to struggle back from death; or is it all me, still trying to rescue him? He hovers in the howling February night outside my window, tapping on the glass, a Heathcliff blown in from the moors. I pull him through and try to still his shivering, to warm his near-frozen limbs. He hangs in my closet, and just in time I cut the lethal knot. He falls to the floor, red-faced and coughing, living and breathing nonetheless. He calls to me from the bottom of a dark well, and somehow I find the strength to pull him up from the echoing depths. He is washed ashore on tumultuous, crashing waves, pulled back into the roaring black water by a taunting and relentless undertow; still, I grasp his hand and drag him to the safety of the windswept beach.

In all of these visions, I imagine someone who does not, who cannot, wish to die. It was a mistake, surely. Can't a person change his mind? Even when my thoughts aren't involuntarily racing to produce an image or metaphor to shoulder my pain and fear, I feel Daniel surrounding me—this was the man I'd slept with the night before last, the night before his last night alive, the man who held me in his arms and said, "I love you *so much*," in a tone that I will never forget, and that I now understand meant that he was saying goodbye to me. Lying there helplessly, I have what strikes me now as the most pitiable bout of magical thinking: *If Daniel were alive, he would be so sorry for the grief he has caused. He would wish he hadn't done this. He would want to take it all back.*

These strange feelings carry me through the night, and are the first in a long series of visions, dreams, and nightmares that I will have as I struggle to fill Daniel's absence with memories and fantasies of his presence. These images are not comforting: Daniel in prison, meeting me in the visitors' area, clearly having been beaten. There is no escape, and so little I can do for him: Daniel in some hellish psychiatric institution, where he has been lobotomized and fundamentally changed, no longer himself; Daniel kidnapped and brainwashed by evil forces, locked away in a strange house, where I can't find the way back out. Or, and this was a recurring and barely conscious hope that I admit with some embarrassment, Daniel is just away, gone to a far-off land; like some long-lost sailor in a classic folk tale he will one day appear on my doorstep, older and wiser, more weathered, altered, still recognizably himself; and filled with stories of pain and glory I am only too eager to hear, as we sip our tea, warm and safe, reunited by the fireside.

Yes, Daniel is many things in these visions, dreams, and nightmares, but the one thing he is not is dead. It will be four years before I have my one and only dream of Daniel in which he is not threatened or horribly changed or in some kind of danger. When I wake from it, I recognize that it was a dream in which Daniel at last appeared to me as he once was, not as I fear or wish he was, and that I had dreamed of him as I might have dreamed of anyone else in my life, without horror.

But it's only my waking, rational self that understands what his absence means in the beginning of this process of letting go. And on the night after his death, this rational self is utterly swept away by deep pain and emotion.

I couldn't have known, as I rose reluctantly to face the day that followed, that in this shattered state, I was about to embark on a long, arduous journey of mourning that I had no choice but to make.

The work of grief had only begun.

IAN BROWN

from

The Boy in the Moon
A Father's Search for His Disabled Son

FOR THE FIRST EIGHT YEARS of Walker's life, every night is the same. The same routine of tiny details, connected in precise order, each mundane, each crucial.

The routine makes the eight years seem long, almost endless, until I try to think about them afterwards, and then eight years evaporate to nothing, because nothing has changed.

Tonight I wake up in the dark to a steady, motorized noise. Something wrong with the water heater. *Nnngah.* Pause. *Nnngah.* *Nnngah.*

But it's not the water heater. It's my boy, Walker, grunting as he punches himself in the head, again and again.

He has done this since before he was two. He was born with an impossibly rare genetic mutation, cardiofaciocutaneous syndrome, a technical name for a mash of symptoms. He is globally delayed and can't speak, so I never know what's wrong. No one does. There are just over a hundred people with CFC around the world. The disorder turns up randomly, a misfire that has no certain cause or roots; doctors call it an orphan syndrome because it seems to come from nowhere.

I count the grunts as I pad my way into his room: one a second. To get him to stop hitting himself, I have to lure him back to sleep, which means taking him downstairs and making him a bottle and bringing him back into bed with me.

That sounds simple enough, doesn't it? But with Walker, everything is complicated. Because of his syndrome, he can't eat solid food by mouth, or swallow easily. Because he can't eat, he takes in formula through the night via a feeding system. The formula runs along a line from a feedbag and a pump on a metal IV stand, through a hole in Walker's sleeper and into a clever-looking permanent valve in his belly, sometimes known as a G-tube, or mickey. To take him out of bed and down to the kitchen to prepare the bottle that will ease him back to sleep, I have to disconnect the line from the mickey. To do this, I first have to turn off the pump (in the dark, so he doesn't wake up completely) and close the feed line. If I don't clamp the line, the sticky formula pours out onto the bed or the floor (the carpet in Walker's room is pale blue: there are patches that feel like the Gobi Desert under my feet, from all the times I have forgotten). To crimp the tube, I thumb a tiny red plastic roller down a slide. (It's my favourite part of the routine—one thing, at least, is easy, under my control.) I unzip his one-piece sleeper (Walker's small, and grows so slowly he wears the same sleepers for a year and a half at a time), reach inside to unlock the line from the mickey, pull the line out through the hole in his sleeper and hang it on the IV rack that holds the pump and feedbag. Close the mickey, rezip the sleeper. Then I reach in and lift all 45 pounds of Walker from the depths of the crib. He still sleeps in a crib. It's the only way we can keep him in bed at night. He can do a lot of damage on his own.

THIS ISN'T A list of complaints. There's no point to complaining. As the mother of another CFC child once told me, "You do what you have to do." If anything, that's the easy part. The hard part is trying to answer the questions Walker raises in my mind every time I pick him up. What is the value of a life like his—a life lived in the twilight, and often in pain? What is the cost of his life to those around him? "We spend a million dollars to save them," a doctor said to me not long ago. "But then when they're discharged, we ignore them." We were sitting in her office, and she was crying. When I asked her why, she said, "Because I see it all the time."

Sometimes watching Walker is like looking at the moon: you see the face of the man in the moon, yet you know there's actually no man there. But if Walker is so insubstantial, why does he feel so important? What is he trying to show me? All I really want to know is what goes on inside his off-shaped head, in his jumped-up heart. But every time I ask, he somehow persuades me to look into my own.

BUT THERE IS another complication here. Before I can slip downstairs with Walker for a bottle, the bloom of his diaper pillows up around me. He's not toilet-trained. Without a new diaper, he won't fall back to sleep and stop smacking his head and ears. And so we detour from the routine of the feeding tube to the routine of the diaper.

I spin 180 degrees to the battered changing table, wondering, as I do every time, how this will work when he's twenty and I'm sixty. The trick is to pin his arms to keep him from whacking himself. But how do you change a 45-pound boy's brimming diaper while immobilizing both his hands so he doesn't bang his head or (even worse) reach down to scratch his tiny, plum-like but suddenly liberated backside, thereby smearing excrement everywhere? While at the same time immobilizing his feet, because ditto? You can't let your attention wander for a second. All this is done in the dark as well.

But I have my routine. I hold his left hand with my left hand, and tuck his right hand out of commission under my left armpit. I've done it so many times, it's like walking. I keep his heels out of the disaster zone by using my right elbow to stop his knees from bending, and do all the actual nasty business with my right hand. My wife, Johanna, can't manage this alone any longer and sometimes calls me to help her. I am never charming when she does.

And the change itself: a task to be approached with all the delicacy of a munitions expert in a Bond movie defusing an atomic device. The unfolding and positioning of a new nappy; the signature feel of the scratchy Velcro tabs on the soft paper of the nappy, the disbelief that it will ever hold; the immense, surging relief of finally refastening it—we made it! The world is safe again! The reinsertion of his legs into the sleeper.

Now we're ready to head downstairs to make the bottle.

Three flights, taking it in the knees, looking out the landing windows as we go. He's stirring, so I describe the night to him in a low voice. There's no moon tonight and it's damp for November.

In the kitchen, I perform the bottle ritual. The weightless plastic bottle (the third model we tried before we found one that worked, big enough for his not-so-fine motor skills yet light enough for him to hold), the economy-sized vat of Enfamil (whose bulk alone is discouraging, it implies so much), the tricky one-handed titrating of tiny tablespoonfuls of Pablum and oatmeal (he aspirates thin fluids; it took us months to find these exact manageable proportions that produced the exact manageable consistency. I have a head full of these numbers: dosages, warm-up times, the frequency of his bowel movements / scratchings / cries / naps). The nightly pang about the fine film of Pablum dust everywhere: Will we ever again have anything like an ordered life? The second pang, of shame, for having such thoughts in the first place. The rummage in the ever-full blue and white dish drainer (we're always washing something, a pipette or a syringe or a bottle or a medicine measuring cup) for a nipple (but the right nipple, one whose hole I have enlarged into an X, to let the thickened liquid out) and a plastic nipple cap. Pull the nipple into the cap, the satisfying *pop* as it slips into place. The gonad-shrinking microwave.

Back up three flights. He's still trying to smash his head. Why does he do it? Because he wants to talk, but can't? Because—this is my latest theory—he can't do what he can see other people doing? I'm sure he's aware of his own difference.

Cart him into the bed in his older sister Hayley's room on the third floor where I have been sleeping, so I can be near him. Hayley, meanwhile, is downstairs with her mother in our bedroom so they can get some sleep. We take turns like this, reduced by the boy to bedroom Bedouins. Neither Johanna nor I has slept two full nights in a row in eight years. We both work during the day. After the first six months, I stopped noticing how tired I was: my days and nights simply became more elastic and similar.

Lay him down on the bed. Oh, fuck me dead—forgot the pump! Build a wall of pillows around him so he doesn't escape or fall off the bed while I nip back into the other room. Remember 4 cc's (or is it 6?) of chloral hydrate, prescribed for sleep and to calm his self-mutilation. (I tried a dose once: the kick of a double martini. William S. Burroughs was thrown out of school as a kid for experimenting with it.) Reprogram the pump, restart the familiar mild repetitive whine, his night pulse.

At last I sink into bed beside him and pull the wriggling boy close. He begins to hit his head again, and because we know of no acceptable way to restrain him mechanically, I hold down his small right hand with my large right one. This brings his left hand up to his other ear—"he's a genius for finding ways to hurt himself," his teacher told me the other day. I grab his left in my left, which I have threaded behind his head. He begins to kick himself in the crotch with his right heel, so hard it makes me wince. I run my big leg over his little leg, and lay my right hand (holding his right hand) on his left thigh, to keep it still. He's stronger than he looks. Under his birdy limbs, he's granite. He'll mash his ears to a pulp if no one stops him.

There is a chance, of course, that none of this will work. Every once in a while, the chloral hydrate rebounds and transforms him into a giggling drunk. It's not unusual to have to perform the entire routine again an hour later. When he has a cold (eight, ten times a year), he coughs himself awake every twenty minutes. Sometimes he cries for hours for no reason. There are nights when nothing works, and nights when he is up and at it, laughing and playing and crawling all over me. I don't mind those nights, tired as I am: his sight is poor, but in the dark we're equal, and I know this makes him happy. In the night, there can be stretches when he is no different from any normal lively boy. It makes me almost cry to tell you that.

Tonight is a lucky night: I can feel him slip off after ten minutes. He stops grunting, strokes his bottle, turns his back and jams his bony little ass into my hip, a sure sign. He falls asleep.

I hurry after him. For all this nightly nightmare—the years of desperate worry and illness and chronic sleep deprivation, the havoc he has caused in our lives, threatening our marriage and our finances and our sanity—I long for the moment when he lets his crazy formless body fall asleep against me. For a short while, I feel like a regular little boy's father. Sometimes I think this is his gift to me—parcelled out, to show me how rare and valuable it is. Walker, my teacher, my sweet, sweet, lost and broken boy.

IN THE EARLY YEARS, after Walker was first diagnosed with CFC syndrome at the age of seven months, the estimated number of people who suffered from the syndrome changed every time we visited the doctor. The medical profession—at least the handful of doctors who studied cardiofaciocutaneous syndrome, or knew what it was—was learning about the syndrome as we did. The name itself was nothing more than an amalgam of the syndrome's most prominent symptoms: cardio, for ever-present murmurs and malformations and enlargements of the heart; facio, for the facial dysmorphia that was its signal characteristic, a prominent brow and down-sloping eyes; cutaneous, for its many skin irregularities. The first time a geneticist ever described the syndrome to me, he told me there were eight other children in the world with CFC. Eight: it wasn't possible. Surely we had been blasted out to an unknown galaxy.

But within a year, after our doctors had begun to sweep the medical literature for references to CFC, I was informed there were 20 cases, because more had turned up in Italy. Then there were 40. (The speed with which the number changed made me sneer at the doctors: they were trained medical professionals, surely they ought to know more than we did.) More than 100 cases of CFC have been reported since the syndrome was first described publicly in three people in 1979; some estimates are as high as 300. Everything about the syndrome was a mystery, an unknown. It was 1986 before it had a name. Symptoms ranged wildly in severity and kind. (Some researchers believe there may be thousands of people with CFC, but with symptoms so mild the condition has never been noticed.) Some CFC children hit themselves, though most didn't. Some could speak or sign. All but a few were anywhere from mildly to severely retarded. Heart defects ranged from serious to unimportant. (Walker had a mild murmur.) Their skin was often sensitive to touch, to the point of agony. Like many CFC children, Walker couldn't chew or swallow easily; he couldn't speak; his vision and hearing were compromised (he had narrowed optic nerves, one more than the other, and skinny ear canals subject to incessant infection); he was thin and wobbly, "hypotonic" in the medical jargon.

Like virtually all CFC children, he had no eyebrows, sparse curly hair, a prominent brow, wide-set eyes, low-set ears and an often charming cocktail-party personality. The CFC features grew more noticeable, more "abnormal," as he grew older. I assumed my little boy was an average example of the condition. It turned out I was wrong. It turned out the average didn't exist—not here.

Nor did those conditions change. Today, at thirteen, mentally, developmentally—I'm terrified even to write these words—he's somewhere between one and three years old. Physically, he's better off than many CFC children (he doesn't have frequent seizures, doesn't have ulcerated intestines); cognitively, less so. He could live to middle age. Would that be good luck, or bad?

Minus a few new genetic details, this was and still is the sum total of what the medical profession knows about CFC. It isn't widely studied, as autism is. Most parents of CFC children know more about the affliction than their pediatricians. The CFC population isn't large and politically powerful like that of Down syndrome, which more than 350,000 people live with in North America, and which occurs once in every 800 births. CFC shows up no more often than once in every 300,000 births, and possibly as rarely as once in a million. The Office of Rare Diseases at the National Institutes of Health characterized CFC as "extremely rare," way out at the far, thin end of the statistical branch, alongside bizarre genetic anomalies such as Chédiak–Higashi syndrome, a bleeding disorder caused by platelet dysfunction and white cell abnormalities. There were only two hundred known cases of Chédiak–Higashi, in part because so few born with it ever survived.

Raising Walker was like raising a question mark. I often wanted to tell someone the story, what the adventure felt and smelled and sounded like, what I noticed when I wasn't running through darkness. But who could relate to such a human anomaly, to the rare and exotic corner of existence where we suddenly found ourselves? Eleven years would pass before I met anyone like him....

———•—

BUT LET ME ask you this: is what we've been through so different from what any parent goes through? Even if your child is as normal as a bright day, was our life so far from your own experience? More intensive, perhaps; more extreme more often, yes. But was it really different in kind?

We weren't disability masochists. I met those people too, the parents of disabled children who seemed to relish their hardship and the opportunity to make everyone else feel guilty and privileged. I disliked them, hated their sense of angry entitlement, their relentless self-pity masquerading as bravery and compassion, their inability to move on, to ask for help. They wanted the world to conform to their circumstances, whereas—as much as I could have put words to it—I simply wanted the rest of the world to admit (a minor request!) that our lives, Walker's and Hayley's and my wife's and mine, weren't any different from anyone else's, except in degree of concentration. I realize I was delusional. People often said, "How do you do it? How are you still capable of laughing, when you have a son like that?" And the answer was simple: it was harder than anyone imagined, but more satisfying and rewarding as well. What they didn't say was: why do you keep him at home with you? Wasn't there someplace where a child like Walker could be taken care of? Where two parents wouldn't carry the whole load, and could have a moment or two to work and live and remember who they were and who they could be?

I asked myself those questions too. I knew Walker would have to live in an assisted living environment eventually, but that was surely years away. I approached the subject casually, even at home. "We should put him on the waiting list for a long-term place," I'd say, off-handedly over breakfast. I tended to think about the problem in bed at night.

"Oh," Johanna invariably replied, "I'm not ready for that."

"No, no, not now," I would say. "Later."

Just as Walker turned two, he began to grab his ears and bite himself. He didn't stop for a year and a half. We thought he had a toothache, an earache. He did not. *Self-mutilating* appears for the first time in his medical chart in March 1999, shortly before his third birthday. He quickly graduated to punching himself in the head. He put his body behind the punches, the way a good boxer does. Hayley called it "bonking," so we did too.

The irony was that he had been making progress, of sorts: finer pincer movements with his fingers, a little eating. (He loved ice cream. If you could get him to swallow it, ice cream made him smile and scowl—from the cold—at the same time.) He could track objects and wave goodbye, and often babbled like a madman.

Then he flipped into blackness.

Was it self-hatred? I wondered about that. We enrolled him in a famous rehabilitation clinic, the Bloorview MacMillan Children's Centre (now Bloorview Kids Rehab) in north Toronto, where he was seen by a behavioural therapist. Everywhere else when people saw his bruises they wondered what we were doing to our child. *Cannot communicate,* Dr. Saunders noted.

Sometimes Walker was in agony as he smacked himself and

screamed with pain. At other times he seemed to do it more expressively, as a way to clear his head, or to let us know he would be saying something if he could talk. Sometimes—and this was unbearably sad—he laughed immediately afterwards. He couldn't tell us anything, and we had to imagine everything. More specialists crowded into our lives. Walker was diagnosed as functionally autistic—not clinically autistic, but he behaves as if he is—as well as having CFC. Dr. Saunders tried Prozac, Celexa, risperidone (an antipsychotic designed for schizophrenia, it has been known to allay obsessive-compulsive behaviour in children). Nothing worked. Once, in Pennsylvania, he bit his hand to the bone and, after an hour of surgery to repair the damage, spent a night in hospital. (The bill was $14,000.)

Dr. Saunders' notes began to track longer and longer stretches of horror. *"Bonking" ears x 2–3 days.* I remember that morning, especially the grief-stricken look on Walker's face as he bashed himself. He looked straight at me. He knew it was bad and wrong, he knew he was hurting himself, he wanted to stop it and couldn't—why couldn't I? His normally thin gruel of a wail became frightening and loud. From June 2001 to the spring of 2003, every entry in his medical records mentions his unhappiness, his irritability.

Did he know his window for learning was closing? Was his vision dimming? *72 hours aggressive behaviour. Unhappy crying x 5 days.* Even Dr. Saunders' handwriting became loose and scrawled, distracted by the chaos of those shrieking visits. *Screaming all day, needs to be held.*

I dreaded the doctor's waiting room, with its well-dressed mothers and well-behaved children. They were never anything but kind, but walking in with Walker yowling and banging his head, I felt like I'd barged into a church as a naked one-man band with a Roman candle up my ass and singing "Yes! We Have No Bananas."

Mother tearful, Dr. Saunders noted on December 29 of that awful year. *Urgent admission for respite.*

I remember that day too. We drove Walker home from the doctor, fed Walker, bathed Walker, soothed Walker, put Walker to bed. I heard his cries subside in stages. Normally Johanna was relieved when he dropped off to sleep, but that night she came downstairs from his bedroom sobbing, her arms wrapped around herself.

"He's gone away," she said. "My little boy has gone. Where has he gone?" She was inconsolable.

So perhaps you can understand why, the very next morning, I began to look in earnest for a way out. I didn't tell Johanna, but I had to find a place for Walker to live, somewhere outside our home. I didn't realize it would take seven years, that it would be the most painful thing I have ever done and that the pain would never go away.

The Authors

Marian Botsford Fraser is a freelance writer, broadcaster, and critic whose work has appeared in *Granta*, *The Walrus*, *The Globe and Mail*, and *Toronto Life*. She is the author of *Solitaire: The Intimate Lives of Single Women*, *Walking the Line: Travels Along the Canadian/American Border*, and *Requiem for My Brother*, which was nominated for the B.C. National Book Award for Canadian Non-Fiction and was the winner of the CBC's Northern Ontario Reads competition. She lives in Toronto, Ontario.

Dionne Brand grew up in Trinidad and moved to Canada as a young woman to attend the University of Toronto. Her published works include the poetry collection *Land to Light On*, winner of the Governor General's Award and the Trillium Award; the acclaimed novels *In Another Place, Not Here,* and *At the Full and Change of the Moon;* and the non-fiction books *Bread Out of Stone* and *A Map to the Door of No Return: Notes to Belonging.*

Ian Brown is an author and a feature writer for *The Globe and Mail* whose work has won a total of nine gold National Magazine and National Newspaper Awards. His memoir, *The Boy in the Moon: A Father's Search for His Disabled Son,* won the 2010 Charles Taylor Prize for Literary Non-Fiction, the Trillium Book Award, and the B.C. National Book Award for Canadian Non-Fiction.

Sharon Butala is an award-winning and bestselling author of both fiction and non-fiction. Her classic book *The Perfection of the Morning* was a #1 bestseller and a finalist for the Governor General's Award, and her short story collection *Fever* won the 1992 Authors' Award for Paperback Fiction. Butala is a recipient of both the Marian Engel Award and the Order of Canada.

Warren Cariou grew up on a farm in Saskatchewan and has worked as a construction worker, a technical writer, and a political aide. He holds a Ph.D. in English from the University of Toronto and now teaches Aboriginal Literature at the University of Manitoba. His first book, *The Exalted Company of Roadside Martyrs: Two Novellas,* garnered rave reviews, and his memoir, *Lake of the Prairies,* won the Drainie-Taylor Prize for Biography and was nominated for the Charles Taylor Prize.

Wayson Choy was raised in Vancouver, where he was cared for in a variety of Chinese households. His first novel, *The Jade Peony,* spent six months on *The Globe and Mail*'s national bestseller list, shared the Trillium Book Award in 1995, and won the 1996 City of Vancouver Book Award. *All That Matters,* a companion novel to *The Jade Peony,* won the Trillium Book Award in 2004 and was shortlisted for the 2005 Giller Prize. In 1999 Choy's first memoir, *Paper Shadows,* was a finalist for the Governor General's Award, the Charles Taylor Prize, and the Drainie-Taylor Prize for Biography.

Moira Farr is an award-winning writer and editor whose essays, reviews, and feature articles have appeared in numerous publications, including *The Globe and Mail,* the *National Post, Toronto Life, Chatelaine,* and several writing anthologies. Her first book, *After Daniel: A Suicide Survivor's Tale,* was shortlisted for a number of prestigious awards and was also the *Edmonton Journal's* top pick for non-fiction that year.

Jonathan Garfinkel is the author of the books *Glass Psalms* and *Ambivalence* and the plays *Walking to Russia, The Trials of John Demjanjuk: A Holocaust Cabaret,* and *House of Many Tongues.* His poetry and plays have been translated into Lithuanian, Swedish, Spanish, German, and Hebrew. Jonathan lives in Toronto.

Lorna Goodison was born in Jamaica. She is the author of numerous books of poetry and short stories, including *Travelling Mercies* and *Controlling the Silver,* and the memoir *From Harvey River: A Memoir of My Mother and Her People,* which was a finalist for the Charles Taylor Prize for Literary Non-Fiction and the Trillium Award, and won the B.C. National Book Award for Canadian Non-Fiction.

Ernest Hillen was born in Holland but moved, with his family, to Indonesia when he was three. During the Second World War he spent three and a half years in Japanese prison camps in Java. He immigrated to Canada in 1952. He has written for and edited major Canadian magazines including *Maclean's* and *Saturday Night.*

He is the author of *The Way of a Boy* and its sequel, *Small Mercies: A Boy after War*.

Isabel Huggan grew up in small-town Ontario, an experience that shaped her prize-winning first book, *The Elizabeth Stories*. In 1987 her husband's work took the family to Kenya and she has found herself living abroad ever since. Her travel memoir, *Belonging: Home Away from Home*, won the Charles Taylor Prize for Literary Non-Fiction in 2004. She still returns yearly to Canada from France.

Michael Ignatieff is a writer, historian, and politician. His many books include *Scar Tissue, Blood and Belonging, The Russian Album*, and *True Patriot Love*. Until 2000 he was a professor at the Kennedy School of Government, Harvard University. Since May 2009 he has been the official leader of the Liberal Party of Canada.

Wayne Johnston was born and raised in Goulds, Newfoundland. After a brief stint in pre-med, Wayne obtained a B.A. in English from Memorial University and an M.A. in Creative Writing from the University of New Brunswick. Among his works of fiction are *The Navigator of New York, The Colony of Unrequited Dreams*, and *The Custodian of Paradise*. He is also the author of the award-winning and bestselling memoir *Baltimore's Mansion*.

Thomas King was born in 1943 to a Cherokee father and a mother of Greek and German descent. He grew up in Northern California, received his Ph.D. in English Literature at the University of Utah, and worked for a number of years at the University of Minnesota as chair of their American Indian Studies program. He is the author of the acclaimed novels *Medicine River, Green Grass, Running Water*, and *Truth and Bright Water*. He has been nominated for the Governor General's Award and the Commonwealth Writers' Prize.

Janice Kulyk Keefer was born to Ukrainian immigrant parents in Toronto in 1952. She is widely admired for her novels, short story collections, poetry, and non-fiction, including *Thieves, Honey and Ashes, The Green Library* (nominated for a Governor General's Award), and *Under Eastern Eyes: A Critical Reading of Maritime Fiction* (also nominated for a Governor General's Award). She is a recipient of the Marian Engel Award, the Canadian Authors' Association Award for Poetry, and several National Magazine Awards.

David Layton is the son of Irving Layton and the godson of Leonard Cohen. He was born in Montreal in 1964 but has spent most of his life in Toronto and London, England. After travelling in Europe, Asia, and the Middle East, he earned a degree in philosophy at the University of Toronto. Among his many publishing credits are an acclaimed memoir, *Motion Sickness,* and the novel *The Bird Factory.*

David Macfarlane was born in Hamilton in 1952. He is the author of an acclaimed family memoir of Newfoundland, *The Danger Tree,* which won the Canadian Authors' Association Award for Non-Fiction in 1992, and the novel *Summer Gone,* which was shortlisted for the 1999 Giller Prize. He began his career as a writer and editor with *Weekend Magazine* and has since been published in *Saturday Night, Maclean's, Toronto Life,* and *The Globe and Mail,* among others.

Michael Ondaatje was born in Sri Lanka and came to Canada in 1962. He is the author of the internationally celebrated novels *In the Skin of a Lion, Anil's Ghost, Divisadero,* and *The English Patient,* which was awarded the 1992 Man Booker Prize and adapted into an Academy Award–winning film. His other books include *Running in the Family, Coming Through Slaughter, The Cinnamon Peeler,* and *Handwriting.*